Handbook to
SKIING THE ALPS

Edited by
CLAIRE WALTER
Freelance ski writer
and
Western Editor for Skiing magazine

Berlitz Guides
A division of Macmillan S.A.

How to use this guide

This Berlitz handbook is designed to help you choose a resort according to your requirements and, once you have made your choice, to take along with you for on-the-spot information and guidance. The guide covers five Alpine countries and 100 of Europe's top resorts, 70 in detail, with nuggets of information on a further 30 ''Best of the Rest''.

- For a general overview of European skiing, turn to the chapters Europe in Perspective, page 8, and Ski-Info Europe, page 311.

- A detailed explanation of how the resorts have been assessed can be found on page 7. The Resorts at a Glance, on pages 8 and 9, shows how the 70 major resorts included in the guide rate against each other.

- Each country has an introduction to its skiing, followed by the resort descriptions in alphabetical order. If two resorts are virtually inseparable in terms of information, they have been listed together as one resort.

- Every resort has a facts and figures section, with tourist office address, technical information such as number of lifts, ski runs, linked resorts, etc., and ski pass and ski school prices. The ratings here will help you determine whether a resort is suited to your particular needs.

- Each resort's facilities are described in detail under the heading The Resort, The Skiing, Après-Ski and Other Activities. Hotels, restaurants and nightspots have not been listed exhaustively, but certain ones picked out as an indication of what's on offer.

- Wherever possible, color maps of the ski runs have been included in the resort descriptions to give an idea of the extent of skiing available.

- Practical information relevant to an individual country, such as currency, customs regulations, health, etc., is contained in the blue pages at the end of the section on that country.

- Finally, the index at the back of the book will point you to all the major and secondary resort references in the guide.

Staff Editor: Christina Jackson
Assistant Editor: Alice Taucher
Design: Dominique Michellod
Layout: Max Thommen

Acknowledgments
The research and legwork undertaken by British authors Steve Pooley (for the Austrian resorts), Tessa Coker and Patrick Thorne (for the French resorts), Patrick Thorne (for the Italian resorts) and Alistair Scott (for the Swiss resorts) formed the basis of this handbook. The assistance and cooperation of Gerhard Markus and Elisabeth Karba of the Austrian National Tourist Office, Eve Peterson of the French Alps Commission, Hedy Wuerz of the German National Tourist Office, and Erika Faisst Lieben and Rachel Rohner of the Swiss National Tourist Office, and Franco Ferrara of the Italian Government Tourist Office in San Francisco were the key to speeding this project along. Gratitude is also extended to the representatives of all the local tourist offices for their cooperation, and for providing information, photos and maps of the ski runs, as well as to ADAC Verlag GmbH for allowing us access to the films of their piste maps.

Library of Congress Catalog Card No. 89-62737

CONTENTS

Europe in Perspective	5
How the Resorts Have Been Assessed	7
The Resorts at a Glance	8

Austria and its Skiing 13

Altenmarkt/Radstadt	19
Badgastein/Bad Hofgastein	22
Innsbruck/Igls	26
Ischgl	30
Kirchberg	33
Kitzbühel	35
Lech	41
Mayrhofen	44
Neustift/Stubai Valley	48
Obergurgl	51
Obertauern	55
Saalbach-Hinterglemm	57
St. Anton/St. Christoph	60
Schladming	65
Schruns/Montafon	68
Seefeld	72
Sölden	76
Söll	80
Zell am See/Kaprun	83
Zürs	86
Best of the Rest	90
Austria-Info	92

France and its Skiing 97

Alpe d'Huez	103
Les Arcs	106
Avoriaz	109
Chamonix	114
Courchevel	118
Les Deux Alpes	122
Flaine	126
Isola 2000	131
Megève	134
Les Menuires	137
Méribel	140
La Plagne	142
Tignes	145
Val d'Isère	149
Valmorel	153
Val Thorens	156
Best of the Rest	158
France-Info	160

Germany and its Skiing 165

Berchtesgaden	168
Garmisch-Partenkirchen	172
Oberstdorf	176
Reit im Winkl	180
Germany-Info	184

Italy and its Skiing	**187**
Bormio	195
Cervinia	198
Cortina d'Ampezzo	202
Courmayeur	206
Livigno	209
Madonna di Campiglio	212
Ortisei (St. Ulrich)	215
Sansicario	217
Selva (Wolkenstein)	220
Sestrière	224
La Thuile	226
Best of the Rest	230
Italy-Info	232

Switzerland and its Skiing	**237**
Adelboden	242
Andermatt	246
Arosa	249
Crans-Montana	252

Davos	255
Les Diablerets	259
Engelberg	262
Flims/Laax	265
Grindelwald	268
Gstaad	272
Klosters	275
Lenzerheide/Valbella	278
Mürren	281
Saas-Fee	283
St. Moritz	286
Verbier	291
Villars	295
Wengen	298
Zermatt	300
Best of the Rest	304
Switzerland-Info	306
Ski-Info Europe	**311**
Some Useful Expressions	**316**
Index	**319**

Although we make every effort to ensure the accuracy of all the information in this book, changes occur incessantly. We cannot therefore take responsibility for facts, addresses and circumstances in general that are constantly subject to alteration.

All ratings of resorts in this guide were made without bias, partiality or prejudice and reflect the author's own subjective opinion. The information on the facts and figures pages was supplied by the resorts themselves. Prices shown are the most up to date available from the resort at the time of going to press. They should, however, only be taken as an indication of what to expect.

Photo Credits

We'd like to express our thanks to the local Tourist Offices for illustrations:

p.: 12, 14, 15, 16, 17, 18, 23, 29, 38–39, 42–43, 50, 60–61, 64, 68–69, 75, 76–77, 88–89, 96, 113, 116–117, 119, 120–121, 124–125, 127, 130, 139, 141, 144, 159, 164, 166, 167, 168, 175, 182–183, 193, 197, 214, 216, 222, 223, 225, 239, 242, 244–245, 248, 250–251, 254, 264, 266, 269, 272–273, 276–277, 280, 282, 285, 293, 294, 299, 305. Other photographs were provided by Burton snowboards p. 237, Jürg Donatsch p. 13, 32, 34, 40, 56, 91, 158, 165, 219, 236, 261, Greg Evans p. 46–47, 54, 58, 82, 102, 105, 148, 157, 286–287, 303, Claude Huber p. 97, 99, 133, 155, 186, 187, 192, 194, 200, 201, 204, 205, 208, 227, 230, 231, 241, 258, Monique Jacot p. 136, Daniel Vittet p. 189.

Cover: Greg Evans
Cover photo: View of Matterhorn from Zermatt

EUROPE IN PERSPECTIVE

The Alps stretch across Europe from the fringes of the French Riviera, with the Mediterranean below, to eastern Italy and Yugoslavia not far from the Adriatic. They are home to people calling themselves Austrian, French, German, Italian, Swiss and Yugoslav—and draw skiers from the world over.

A ski vacation in the Alps is two vacations in one: a ski vacation and a trip to Europe. For some North Americans, skiing the Alps is a once-in-a-lifetime experience—a pilgrimage, like Mecca is to the Moslems. For others, it is the mountain range to which they return winter after winter—with the regularity of migrating swallows.

The skiing is neither better nor worse on one side of the Atlantic than the other. It is different. Skiing the Alps means getting into a cable car with a multi-national, multi-lingual group, rising swiftly above the timber line and disembarking in a wide, white world of endless snow and peaks that stretch to the horizon. There are no ski mountains as magnificent as the Alps, no on-mountain dining more civilized and no skiing more exciting.

There are beginner slopes as tame as tilted table tops, and there are radical chutes and near-vertical couloirs verging on the unskiable. There are busy slopes, crawling with legions of skiers, and there are isolated snowfields and lush powder pockets out of sight and earshot of anyone—or anything—else. Lunch, and perhaps a nap on a sun terrace, is a traditional ritual in the Alps—for these sun-kissed mountains are where Europeans flee from cities that are cold, rainy and gray all winter.

Some skiers are fiercely loyal to one country, one resort or even one hotel. Others like to shop around and find a variety of experiences. The resorts run the gamut from unspoiled villages that still wear the mantle of a simpler, more agrarian time to the most sophisticated international resorts, where it is possible to rub shoulders with the rich, the famous and the titled. By and large, there are basically four kinds of Alpine resorts—and they don't necessarily follow national boundaries.

"Tyrolean"-style resorts are found not only in that Austrian state, but in others such as Vorarlberg and Salzburg, too, as well as in the German Alps and Italy's Alto Adige (which was historically Austrian and is still a bilingual Italian-German area also known as the South Tyrol). These pretty towns filled with wood-trimmed chalets are blessed with that elusive quality Gemütlichkeit, which encompasses comfort, charm and warmth of hospitality. This type of resort caters largely to the intermediate level of skier. Kitzbühel, Saalbach-Hinterglemm, Schruns, St. Anton and Zürs are archetypal Tyrolean-style resorts in Austria. Oberstdorf and Reit im Winkl are their German cousins, while the Val Gardena resorts and, to some extent, Cortina d'Ampezzo in Italy are also representative of the style.

There are international-style resorts whose architecture is not so much a distinguishing feature as is the scope, variety and quality of the accommodations, skiing, non-skiing activities and après-ski. Switzerland dominates this category, with such cosmopolitan meccas as Arosa, Crans-Montana, Davos and St.Moritz, with no discernible or noteworthy building style, and Gstaad, Klosters, Saas-Fee, Wengen and, above all, Zermatt, which boast all the high standards—plus immense charm.

Two styles of French resort predominate, where the language, cuisine and ambience are Gallic. Traditional places which grew from historic town cores include Chamonix, Megève, Morzine and Val d'Isère in France and Les Diablerets in Switzerland. Courmayeur in Italy, just across the border from France, has a little of this flavor, too.

The built-for-skiing or "purpose-built" resorts of France, which have been developed since the 1960s, are known for ski-in, ski-out accommodations of sometimes futuristic design and huge lift networks. Avoriaz, Les Arcs, Courchevel, Flaine, Isola 2000, Les Menuires and Val Thorens fit this description. But the first of the breed, Sestrière and Cervinia, are much older and are in Italy, and France even developed Alpe d'Huez and Les Deux Alpes in the 40s. These older "new" resorts, however, lack the architectural harmony of the more recent ones, even if lately, there has been an effort to combine the warmth and charm of the old with the convenience of the new.

Any ski vacation has two main parts. One is the skiing itself, and the other is the totality of the resort experience, comprising accommodations, food, après-ski, non-ski sports and ambience. Your choice of resort will depend on your taste and pocketbook.

This handbook describes the best of them—the ones legitimately worth crossing an ocean for. Whichever you select, you will find the Alps are eminently seductive. The scenery, the villages, the food and the air of sophisticated international merriment send out a siren call which skiers heed—to return again and again.

HOW THE RESORTS HAVE BEEN ASSESSED

Different skiers have different requirements, and their choice of resorts is influenced by many factors. In addition to the resort descriptions and facts and figures sheets, we have assessed each resort in nine categories, rating each category from 1 to 10. Since we have included only the top resorts of the hundreds in the Alps, ratings below 5 are rare.

Skiing conditions refers to the range of skiing on offer, the quality and efficiency of the lift systems, how accessible they are and how well they interlink and whether lines are a problem. If the resort has access to the skiing of other resorts, the extent of the other resorts' skiing is also taken into account.

Snow conditions are governed by the height of the resort (low ones will generally have poorer snow cover at either end of the season) and its top station, whether the slopes are north- or south-facing, and whether there is snow-making. Due to climatic peculiarities, some low-lying resorts enjoy heavy snowfalls and a long season. Resorts with glacier skiing usually rate highly. Generally, however, even the best does not compare with snow in western North America.

The three headings **For Beginners, For Intermediates** and **For Advanced Skiers** refer to the skier's own ability, which is a major consideration when selecting a resort. Nothing is more frustrating than finding yourself out of depth if you are a less than expert skier on a very tough mountain or being obliged to trundle round easy slopes if you are looking for challenge. All resorts cater in some way for beginners; however, those that have attractive, snow-sure novice slopes or a particularly good ski school will rate more highly.

The **For Children** rating assesses a resort according to its facilities for the under-twelves, the provision or lack of kindergartens (for both skiers and non-skiers), proximity and difficulty of lifts, whether there are discounts for children in ski school and on the lift pass, and if the resort is, in general, a good place to take children. If a resort has special facilities for teenagers, it scores more highly. The profusion of infant-care nurseries that exists in North America has not yet spread across the Alps, children's classes are usually larger than in the U.S. and Canada, and ski schools taking children are fewer, too.

For many, **Après-Ski** is as important as skiing. The more lively the resort, the more it will score in this category, but you should also read the text carefully to be sure that the resort features the kind of après-ski you are looking for, whether loud and lively or quiet and congenial.

Non-skiers and the energetic also look to what else is on offer in a resort. **Other sports** covers all the non-ski activities available, and also includes cross-country skiing.

Value for Money does not necessarily mean low prices. The criterion here is whether the goods or services are worth the price put upon them. Some resorts are notoriously overpriced: the cost of the lift pass does not reflect the skiing available or the hotels and bars charge excessively. Other resorts may have similar prices, but you get much more for your money.

A number of Berlitz **Skiers** (from one to five) has been attributed to each resort, in the same way as hotels are given star ratings. These represent the authors' overall impressions and are mainly based on how extensive the skiing and ski facilities are, as well as how good the entire resort experience is likely to be.

THE RESORTS AT A GLANCE

	Altitude (feet)	Top Station (feet)	No. of lifts	Runs (miles)	Skier Rating	Skiing Conditions	Snow Conditions	For Beginners	For Intermediates	For Adv. Skiers	For Children	Après-Ski	Other Sports	Value for Money
AUSTRIA														
ALTENMARKT/RADSTADT	2,789	5,807	39	75	2	3	4	5	3	2	5	3	4	5
BADGASTEIN/BAD HOFGASTEIN	2,854	8,813	50	155	4	7	7	4	8	7	6	7	8	6
INNSBRUCK/IGLS	2,953	7,687	33	47	4	6	5	4	8	6	5	9	8	8
ISCHGL	4,592	9,397	35	93	4	8	8	5	9	8	4	8	7	7
KIRCHBERG	2,822	6,545	62	100	3	7	5	5	9	7	7	7	6	6
KITZBÜHEL	2,493	6,545	62	100	5	9	5	4	9	8	5	9	8	7
LECH	4,757	7,798	34	68	5	8	8	7	8	8	6	7	6	6
MAYRHOFEN	2,067	7,382	29	56	3	6	5	5	6	2	8	7	5	7
NEUSTIFT/STUBAI VALLEY	3,281	10,532	37	75	2	4	8	5	6	4	5	5	7	7
OBERGURGL	6,332	10,112	22	66	3	5	7	8	8	6	7	5	5	6
OBERTAUERN	5,709	7,710	25	75	3	8	8	6	8	6	6	5	5	6
SAALBACH-HINTERGLEMM	3,291	6,880	60	124	5	9	7	5	10	8	5	9	6	6
ST. ANTON/ST. CHRISTOPH	4,278	8,695	42	124	5	10	8	4	8	10	4	9	6	6
SCHLADMING	2,444	6,611	79	87	3	6	5	5	6	5	4	7	6	8
SCHRUNS/MONTAFON	2,297	7,828	73	128	3	6	6	6	7	5	6	7	7	8
SEEFELD	3,937	6,890	20	15	3	5	6	7	5	3	6	7	8	6
SÖLDEN	4,518	10,033	33	63	3	7	8	4	7	6	4	7	6	7
SÖLL	2,307	6,000	83	22	3	7	6	5	9	5	6	7	6	8
ZELL AM SEE/KAPRUN	2,460	9,938	52	81	3	7	7	5	8	4	5	6	7	6
ZÜRS	5,676	8,930	34	68	5	8	7	5	8	8	6	6	5	5
FRANCE														
ALPE D'HUEZ	6,103	10,991	81	137	4	9	8	9	9	8	7	6	5	6
LES ARCS	5,250	10,585	95	106	5	9	9	8	9	9	9	7	8	7
AVORIAZ	5,906	7,710	220	373	3	9	7	8	9	7	9	7	6	8
CHAMONIX	3,396	12,606	43	84	4	5	6	2	5	9	3	7	7	6
COURCHEVEL	4,265	8,983	200	310	5	9	8	7	9	98	9	8	7	
LES DEUX ALPES	5,414	11,707	63	122	4	8	6	5	8	6	7	4	6	4
FLAINE	5,250	8,203	84	161	3	7	7	8	8	6	9	3	4	8
ISOLA 2000	6,562	8,563	24	75	3	7	7	8	7	4	9	7	5	7
MEGÈVE	3,652	7,710	89	186	3	7	5	9	9	4	8	10	8	6
LES MENUIRES	5,955	9,351	200	310	4	9	8	8	9	9	8	6	5	7
MÉRIBEL	4,593	9,686	200	310	4	9	8	7	9	/	7	7	8	8
LA PLAGNE	4,101	10,663	100	124	4	9	8	9	9	7	7	2	4	7
TIGNES	5,086	11,352	110	186	4	10	10	3	10	9	8	4	7	8
VAL D'ISÈRE	6,070	11,648	110	186	5	10	10	7	9	10	6	7	7	8
VALMOREL	4,593	7,884	46	100	3	8	8	7	8	6	9	5	3	7
VAL THORENS	7,546	10,483	200	310	4	9	9	8	9	9	7	7	6	7

	Altitude (feet)	Top Station (feet)	No. of lifts	Runs (miles)	Skier Rating	Skiing Conditions	Snow Conditions	For Beginners	For Intermediates	For Adv. Skiers	For Children	Après-Ski	Other Sports	Value for Money
GERMANY														
BERCHTESGADEN	1,772	6,148	31	25	2	3	4	4	4	2	4	7	7	8
GARMISCH-PARTENKIRCHEN	2,362	9,731	55	72	3	5	6	4	6	5	3	9	9	6
OBERSTDORF	2,674	7,297	20	50	4	7	6	6	8	4	7	7	9	6
REIT IM WINKL	2,296	6,139	24	25	3	5	6	7	7	2	7	5	5	5
ITALY														
BORMIO	4,019	9,882	23	53	4	7	7	7	8	6	5	7	7	7
CERVINIA	6,726	11,457	36	65	3	7	9	6	8	6	5	7	6	5
CORTINA D'AMPEZZO	4,016	10,640	52	100	4	6	7	7	8	7	6	9	9	6
COURMAYEUR	4,016	11,385	32	62	4	6	8	6	9	7	5	8	3	6
LIVIGNO	5,958	9,138	28	53	2	4	7	7	5	4	5	8	2	6
MADONNA DI CAMPIGLIO	5,086	8,235	31	93	3	8	8	6	8	5	6	7	7	6
ORTISEI (ST. ULRICH)	4,055	8,262	85	109	2	5	7	7	6	5	6	7	5	5
SANSICARIO	5,627	8,842	100	186	3	7	7	6	7	6	7	6	5	6
SELVA (WOLKENSTEIN)	5,128	7,540	110	109	4	7	7	7	8	7	7	7	5	6
SESTRIÈRE	6,677	9,262	100	186	3	8	7	5	8	6	5	7	5	7
LA THUILE	4,728	8,668	30	84	3	7	8	7	8	8	5	5	5	6
SWITZERLAND														
ADELBODEN	4,593	7,645	44	74	2	4	6	6	6	4	6	6	7	7
ANDERMATT	4,738	9,722	13	34	3	5	7	6	4	7	5	3	5	7
AROSA	5,906	8,704	16	43	3	6	7	6	7	4	6	7	7	7
CRANS-MONTANA	4,922	9,843	34	77	4	8	5	6	8	6	7	7	7	6
DAVOS	5,118	9,331	55	171	5	9	7	5	9	8	5	9	9	7
LES DIABLERETS	3,937	9,745	39	56	3	6	6	5	6	5	5	5	5	7
ENGELBERG	3,445	9,909	24	32	3	5	6	5	6	6	6	7	7	7
FLIMS/LAAX	3,347	9,902	33	137	4	8	7	6	8	7	6	7	8	7
GRINDELWALD	3,445	8,098	41	93	3	6	5	6	8	7	6	7	8	7
GSTAAD	3,609	6,365	69	155	3	6	5	6	7	7	5	7	7	6
KLOSTERS	3,937	9,331	55	171	4	8	6	6	8	8	6	7	7	6
LENZERHEIDE-VALBELLA	4,922	9,400	38	93	2	6	5	6	7	5	5	5	7	6
MÜRREN	5,414	9,745	41	93	2	5	7	5	6	7	6	4	6	6
SAAS-FEE	5,906	11,484	26	50	4	7	8	6	8	7	7	8	8	7
ST. MORITZ	6,090	11,263	59	250	5	7	7	5	7	8	6	9	10	7
VERBIER	4,922	10,926	86	200	5	9	8	6	8	10	8	8	5	7
VILLARS	4,265	6,956	39	56	3	7	5	7	8	5	7	8	7	7
WENGEN	4,187	8,111	41	93	4	7	5	7	8	7	8	8	7	7
ZERMATT	5,315	12,533	37	93	5	9	8	5	8	9	6	9	8	7

THE ALPS

AUSTRIA AND ITS SKIING

For winter sports enthusiasts, Austria is synonymous with skiing. There are few of the high-altitude, purpose-built resorts to rival those in France but, instead, you'll find a charming welcome, traditional methods of ski instruction and an invariably high standard of accommodations.

The essence of Austria's skiing is not in the bald statistics poured out by the tourist office: 13,000 mi. (21,000 km.) of ski runs, 9,500 ski lifts of various types, 8,500 instructors... though these are certainly formidable. What draws visitors back year after year is the chance to enjoy first-rate skiing in an atmosphere of Gemütlichkeit—that elusive combination of cozy charm and friendliness that permeates many resorts. The world's image of the typical Austrian ski Dorf of stucco and wood chalets clustered round an onion-domed church is no fairytale creation. Most of them really are like that.

Vienna, Austria's capital, is on the country's eastern end, while the mountains are in the central and western portions. One common misconception is that Austria's skiing all takes place in the Tyrol, but from Vorarlberg to Styria, there are scores of resorts ranging from tiny ski villages with just a couple of modest hotels to internationally renowned centers such as St. Anton and Kitzbühel, which rank among the world's great winter sports destinations.

Vorarlberg is bordered by Switzerland, Liechtenstein, Italy and West Germany. Lech and Zürs, the most famous resorts in the state, are favored by European royalty, as well as stars of screen and sport. The Montafon Valley, popular with the neighboring Swiss for its reasonable prices and unstintingly high standards of comfort and efficiency, comprises five resorts all on the same lift pass. Schruns is the biggest of the Montafon villages. Ernest Hemingway spent some of his years in this enchanting hamlet.

The Arlberg lift network, straddling the border between

Vorarlberg and Tyrol, has its own regional lift pass good at Lech and Zürs, plus world-renowned St. Anton and its satellites St. Christoph and Stuben. St. Anton attracts a truly international clientele for peerless on-piste skiing and tough off-piste adventure.

Between the Arlberg and Innsbruck, seemingly every valley running north or south from the Inn Valley has its share of skiing. The Paznaun follows the Trisana rivers toward the Silvretta mountains. Ischgl is a smart and lively village whose skiing terrain overlaps that of Samnaun, a duty-free area over the Swiss border.

Continuing eastward, the Ötztal boasts two of Austria's most popular centers, Sölden and Obergurgl. To the north, there is a clutch of small resorts, notably Seefeld, a great cross-country mecca, which also has its share of downhill skiing.

Innsbruck, capital of the Tyrol, isn't exactly a ski resort in its own right but, with mountains rising sharply on all sides, it's a great base for visiting five ski areas covered by the city lift pass or even branching out farther afield to Seefeld or the Stubai Valley, which guarantees year-round skiing on its glacier.

East along the Inn Valley, Jenbach is at the junction of several valleys, notably the Zillertal, which contains no less than nine resorts including Zell am Ziller and Mayrhofen covered by the same lift pass, while the glacier at Hintertux is the site of summer training for the national ski teams of many countries. The Skigrossraum Wilder Kaiser-Brixental is the country's largest interlinked skiing network, fanning out from seven villages, including Söll, Ellmau and Westendorf.

The Kitzbühel Alps are named after one of Austria's great ski towns, and if it is true that Kitzbühel is the best known, attracting a cosmopolitan mix of guests, each of the clutch of resorts in the immediate vicinity provides a more relaxed approach. Kirchberg's skiing connects with Kitzbühel's Hahnenkamm area, scene of the most important downhill race on the World Cup calendar, and the circuit continues through a linked lift system to Jochberg and then on to Pass Thurn. On the other side of town is the Kitzbüheler Horn and beyond it, the separate resort of St. Johann in Tirol.

The state of Salzburg features many small resorts which linked together provide fast interconnecting networks for all abilities and ambitions. The biggest and best known is Saalbach-Hinterglemm, chosen as the site of the 1991 World Alpine Ski Championships. The circuit consists of 100 mi. (160 km.) of pistes, which can be skied in either direction with plenty of tough diversions en route.

Zell am See and Kaprun rather ambitiously style themselves as the Europa Sport Region. In addition to skiing, there are sporting opportunities aplenty, especially in summer when the lake is a kaleidoscope of color as windsurfers take to the water in the afternoons, having spent the morning skiing on the Kitzsteinhorn glacier above Kaprun.

The Gastein Valley is most famous for its spa facilities, and many visitors choose its major resorts, Badgastein and Bad Hofgastein, for their combination of skiing and taking the waters. The Tauern Alps, including Altenmarkt, Radstadt, Zauchensee, Obertauern and Filzmoos, offer everything a skier could want. It is possible to ski from one valley to the next and, if accompanied by a guide, to stay well away from the crowds. The Top-Tauern-Skischeck covers all of these resorts, as well as four over the border in Styria: Reiteralm, Rohrmoos, Haus and Schladming, the last-named a renowned World Cup center boasting the fastest downhill course on the circuit and the venue of the 1982 World Alpine Ski Championships.

Tourism is a major industry in Austria—and in the Austrian Alps. You will meet a cosmopolitan crowd, including British, Scandinavian and Dutch guests. English is widely spoken in ski schools, restaurants, hotels and shops. You will be treated with courtesy and charm by people who are adept at being good hosts to the international skiing and vacationing community.

Austria is particularly good for skiers of mixed ability, even non-skiers. If you are going for an all-round winter sports holiday, you'll find a whole range of après-ski and non-ski activities. Most resorts have cross-country skiing and walking trails, skating and curling rinks. Many have indoor swimming pools and tennis courts, while the better hotels have their own pool, sauna, steam room, solarium and massage facilities.

Many resorts organize a host of evening activities. A typical week's program will include tobogganing, a sleigh ride, an "Austrian evening" (which can vary from traditional entertainment to downright silly party games fueled by copious quantities of beer and Schnaps*) and a* fondue *supper.*

Excursions for non-skiers are usually available, the most popular being to two of Austria's most exquisite cities, Innsbruck and Salzburg, and over the Brenner Pass to the South Tyrol, the region that was ceded to Italy after World War I, but remains Austrian in language and culture. From some resorts, it is even possible to go to Venice for the day.

Robust fare is the mainstay of Austrian cooking. The specialties that have evolved over the centuries are the result of making tasty, filling meals from frugal resources for a people tackling the daily rigors of mountain life. For today's visitor, this means portions that are often too much to handle in two full meals a day. But nobody ever complains about being underfed.

Steamy mountain cabins where you can recuperate on a cold day with a bowl of Leberknödelsuppe *(soup with liver dumplings) or a glass of hot* Glühwein *are an essential part of skiing. On sunny days, relax with a cold beer and a plate of* Speck *(smoked bacon) and cheese. In the Tyrol,* Gröstl *is a hearty dish of beef or pork sautéed with sliced or diced potatoes, onions, caraway seeds and other spices and herbs.* Wiener schnitzel, *that Viennese classic of a large, thinly sliced cutlet of veal or pork, coated with egg and seasoned bread crumbs and crisply sautéed, is ubiquitous. If you want to lunch lightly, you can order a* Salat Teller, *but even that will come in Alp-like portions.*

Leave room for dessert! The national love of pastry is reflected in the variety on offer. The best-known chocolate cake is Sachertorte, *with a layer of apricot*

16

jam in the middle. Apfelstrudel, *thinly sliced apples with raisins and cinnamon rolled in an almost transparent flaky pastry, needs no introduction.* Kaiserschmarren, *a fluffy scrambled pancake with jam and sugar, is a Viennese specialty found all over Austria.*

To wash it all down you have a choice of white or red wines, from the South Tyrol or eastern Austria, or excellent local beers, especially Zillertaler. *The heart-warming regional firewater is, of course,* Schnaps.

With so much on offer, choosing a resort in Austria is not easy. But wherever you do go, you can be sure that from the grandest five-star hotel to the most modest Gasthof, *proprietors and staff alike will be unfailingly courteous and helpful.*

17

ALTENMARKT/RADSTADT

Access: *Nearest airports:* Munich (3 hrs.); Salzburg (45 mins.). *By road:* from Salzburg, A10 Autobahn, exit Altenmarkt/Radstadt/Zauchensee. *By rail:* station in Radstadt, bus to Altenmarkt.

Tourist Office: Fremdenverkehrs-verband, 5541 Altenmarkt, Austria. Tel. (06452) 74 61

Altitude: 2,789 ft. (850 m.).
Top: 5,807 ft. (1,770 m.)

Language: German

Runs: 75 mi. (120 km.) including Zauchensee-Kleinarl

Lifts: 39

Ski area: Kemathöhe

Ski schools: Schischule Radstadt, Schischule Altenmarkt und Zauchensee

Linked resorts: None

Season: December to April

Kindergarten: *Non-ski:* from 3 years. *With ski:* from 4 years

Prices: *Lift pass:* 6 days 1,205 S (children 740 S). *Ski school:* Group 1,020 S for 5 days; private 380 S per hour.

RATINGS

Skiing Conditions	3
Snow Conditions	4
For Beginners	5
For Intermediates	3
For Advanced Skiers	2
For Children	5
Après-Ski	3
Other Sports	4
Value for Money	5

THE RESORTS

Largely undiscovered by foreigners, Altenmarkt and Radstadt each have a small skiing area which combined provides a good variety of novice and easy-intermediate slopes. Either is an excellent base from which to explore the district which, straddling the border between Salzburgerland and Styria, has its own regional lift pass, the Top-Tauern-Skischeck covering 320 lifts. All the resorts covered by the pass make pleasant day-excursions, but you will need to make your own arrangements or get a rental car if you wish to travel easily from town to town.

Radstadt is the larger and therefore livelier of the two resorts, while Altenmarkt is prettier. If you are content to confine your activities to the immediate vicinity, the post bus runs an efficient service which takes you up the valley, past Altenmarkt's lifts, to Zauchensee and from there to Kleinarl via Flachauwinkl, where the *Autobahn* is crossed by the Winkl Express—a couple of open carriages hauled by a tractor disguised as a steam locomotive. A competent skier can make it to Kleinarl and back in a day, and most choose to take lunch at the café owned and run by Austria's great women's downhill champion, Annemarie Moser-Pröll.

THE SKIING

Altenmarkt and Radstadt form part of an ambitious ski region in the southern part of the state of Salzburg which practically invented the con-

cept of *Skischaukel* ("ski swing"), to make the most of a relatively limited terrain. The idea is to take a lift over the top of a hill, ski down the other side, and keep "swinging" back and forth, enjoying ever-changing views and the ego-pleasing notion of having skied a wide geographical area—even if very little of the terrain has been challenging.

From Altenmarkt it is possible to "swing" over the Kemathöhe to Radstadt and back. A short bus ride up the valley lies the hamlet of Zauchensee, which in turn offers skiing in two directions: over the Rauchkopf, where the terrain is developed on both sides of the upper slopes but does not yet extend down into the next valley, and over the Rosskopf to Flachauwinkl and thence via the Mooskopf to Kleinarl, the great Moser-Pröll's home town. From Flachauwinkl it is also possible to go back down the valley to Flachau, linked to Wagrain via the Griessenkareck *Skischaukel*, where there are many small, short lifts.

With the Kemathöhe top station at just 5,807 ft. (1,770 m.), Altenmarkt and Radstadt have a relatively short season, so it is best to check snow conditions if planning to visit before mid-January or after the middle of March.

There are a few off-*piste* opportu-

nities for experts, but the Altenmarkt-Radstadt area is best for easy cruising. Advanced skiers prefer Obertauern, also skiable on the regional pass.

APRÈS-SKI

Evening activities are low-key and informal, and neither town should be considered by anyone looking for glittering nightclubs with a black-tie crowd or celebrity-spotting. There are plenty of pleasant restaurants and a few lively, unpretentious discos (the Tauernstuben and Arche Noah) and *tanzcafés* ("dance cafés").

OTHER ACTIVITIES

The 31-mi. (50-km.) Tauernloipe network of cross-country trails links Altenmarkt and Radstadt with Eben, Wagrain and Flachau and is easily accessible from both towns, with several shorter trails nearby. There is a public swimming pool and another four pools in hotels, plus indoor tennis.

A tour of the Atomic ski factory in Altenmarkt can be arranged. The railway line runs north to Salzburg, for an elegant and sophisticated diversion from skiing, or eastward to Schladming and on to Graz.

BADGASTEIN/BAD HOFGASTEIN

Access: *Nearest airports:* Salzburg (1½ hrs.); Munich (3 hrs.). *By road:* from Salzburg, A10 Autobahn, exit Bischofshofen. *By rail*: station in Badgastein.

Tourist Office: Kurverwaltung, 5640 Badgastein, Austria.
Tel. (06434) 25 31-0

Altitude: 2,854 ft. (870 m.).
Top: 8,813 ft. (2,686 m.)

Language: German

Runs: 155 mi. (250 km.) in Gasteinertal

Lifts: 50 in Gasteinertal

Ski areas: Stubnerkogel, Schlossalm, Graukogel, Wengeralm

Ski schools: Schischule Badgastein, Schischule Bad Hofgastein

Linked resorts: None

Season: December to May

Kindergarten: *Non-ski*: from 3 years.
With ski: from 3 years

Prices: *Lift pass*: 6 days 1,450 S (children 870 S). *Ski school*: Group 1,150 S for 6 days; private 380 S per hour.

RATINGS

Skiing Conditions	7
Snow Conditions	7
For Beginners	4
For Intermediates	8
For Advanced Skiers	7
For Children	6
Après-Ski	7
Other Sports	8
Value for Money	6

THE RESORTS

The Gasteinertal's thermal springs have attracted tourists since the early part of the 19th century, when they were the meeting place of the crowned heads of central Europe, who congregated for the *Kur* and political debate. Today, visitors still flock here to benefit from the variety of treatments available, and tourism, apart from a little pastoral farming, is the only industry.

Badgastein is the best known of the quartet of the valley's resorts, which also includes Dorfgastein, Bad Hofgastein and Sportgastein (the last being no more than a ski area without accommodations).

Badgastein, a well-established spa town, is grander than most Austrian resorts, the architecture a departure from the Alpine stereotype of quaint chalets. Instead, grandiose hotels loom above the Ache River, and swimming in thermal baths or taking the *Kur* are more popular than disco dancing. The young set, therefore, tends to choose livelier places for a winter holiday, although the skiing above the valley is far from sedate.

Bad Hofgastein is a sturdily built town with an exquisite 16th-century church, excellent spa facilities, elegant hotels and restaurants as well as rambling, twisting alleys—a babbling brook completes the charming scene.

THE SKIING

The Gastein Superski lift pass, which covers Badgastein, Bad Hofgastein, Dorfgastein and Sportga-

stein, is good for 50 lifts and 155 mi. (250 km.) of well-maintained *pistes* and provides all grades of recreational skiers with plenty of variety and challenge. Far from resting on its considerable laurels, the region has made a huge investment in maintaining and developing the lift systems, notably the installation of the aerodynamically designed two-stage gondola from Badgastein to the Stubnerkogel at 7,369 ft. (2,246 m.). Its construction is such that there is minimal agitation in high winds. From the top there is a 7-mi. (11-km.) intermediate run to the Skizentrum Angertal, which is the connecting point between Badgastein and Bad Hofgastein.

The Hüttenkogel, at 7,318 ft. (2,231 m.), on the opposite side of the valley, is the start of the World Cup courses. The Kreuzkogel, accessible from Sportgastein, has a top station at 8,813 ft. (2,686 m.). On sunny days, there is glorious skiing above the tree line, with equally glorious views across, and down, the valley. If the weather closes in, the trees on the lower slopes aid visibility and give protection against bitter winds. The main part

APRÈS-SKI

of the skiing is on mountain pastures, which are almost entirely rock-free, so that skiing is possible with the lightest snow cover.

From Bad Hofgastein, a funicular railway connects with a chair lift and cable car to Schlossalm. The options are to swoop down to the valley along wide, open *pistes* which lead to tree-lined trails before arriving back at the bottom of the railway; or to take the Hamburger trail to the Weitmoser and Hohe Scharte lifts.

In Badgastein, the Metropolis and Mühlhäusl discos play throbbing music until the wee hours, but dancing to small bands in the Hotel Bellevue is more in keeping with Badgastein's image. Or you can join the high rollers in the casino; Badgastein optimistically styles itself as the "Monte Carlo of the Alps".

It is easy to imagine Bad Hofgastein and its neighbors as crammed

24

full of middle-aged people who, after a cursory examination of the slopes, indulge their rheumatic joints in the spa baths, but younger visitors looking for a lively time should not be discouraged, as there are plenty of nightclubs, bars and discos.

OTHER ACTIVITIES

Just about the full gamut of sporting activities is available: swimming in indoor and outdoor thermally heated pools, indoor tennis and horseback riding, squash, bowling, skating, curling, skibobbing, and walking along 22 mi. (35 km.) of cleared paths, plus some 50 mi. (80 km.) of cross-country trails around the valley.

In addition to taking the waters, you can visit the local history museum. For trips out of town, Badgastein is on the main railway line between Salzburg and Villach.

INNSBRUCK/IGLS

Access: *Nearest airports:* Innsbruck; Munich (2–2½ hrs.). *By road:* A12 Autobahn. *By rail:* station in Innsbruck.

Tourist Office: Fremdenverkehrsverband, 6021 Innsbruck, Austria. Tel. (05222) 59 85-0

Altitude: 2,953 ft. (900 m.). *Top:* 7,687 ft. (2,343 m.)

Language: German

Runs: 47 mi. (75 km.)

Lifts: 33

Ski areas: Hungerburg-Seegrube, Mutters-Muttereralm, Igls-Patscherkofel, Tulfes-Glungezer, Axamer Lizum

Ski schools: Schischule: Innsbruck; Renato Huemer (Igls); Erlacher (Patsch); Otto Peer (Mutters); Glungezer (Tulfes); Axamer Lizum

Linked resorts: None

Season: December to late March

Kindergarten: *Non-ski:* from 3 years. *With ski:* from 3 years

Prices: *Lift pass:* 6 days 1,060 S (children 800 S). *Ski school:* Group 200 S per day; private 2,000 S per day.

RATINGS

Skiing Conditions	6
Snow Conditions	5
For Beginners	4
For Intermediates	8
For Advanced Skiers	6
For Children	5
Après-Ski	9
Other Sports	8
Value for Money	8

THE RESORTS

Innsbruck is the single most popular Austrian ski destination for Americans. Plenty of accommodations, easy access, a wide variety of skiing, low prices and a taste of urban Europe combine to make Innsbruck so beloved.

Host to the Winter Olympics in 1964 and 1976, the capital of the Tyrol isn't really a ski resort in its own right. But it is a fascinating place to stay while sampling the five ski areas included on the city lift pass, none of them more than a half-hour ride on the free buses which disperse skiers to the mountains each morning. The city is perfect for an all-round winter holiday—soaring peaks gazing down on the elegant shopping arcades, museums and galleries, with all sorts of sporting activities close at hand.

The five ski areas covered by the Innsbruck lift pass are Hungerburg, Tulfes, Mutters, Igls and Axamer Lizum, the last-named constructed specifically for the 1964 Olympics. Tulfes and Mutters are both tiny Tyrolean hamlets, and Igls is a lovely village, much favored by British visitors who enjoy its traditional charms, and also the site of the Olympic bobsled and luge run. En route from the city, you pass the 90-m. ski jump, its top perched above a precipice. The view from the top: the Wilten cemetery! Hun-

gerburg is at the base of Seegrube/ Hafelekar, a steep skiing area high above Innsbruck, affording magnificent views.

Innsbruck is especially good for intermediate skiers who want to enjoy the variety of the five areas and all the other sports facilities close by. By contrast, Igls offers a traditional Austrian skiing holiday with all the delights of the city just 15 minutes down the mountain.

THE SKIING

Hungerburg is closest to Innsbruck (its funicular railway starts from just outside the city center) and has the toughest but most limited skiing. It's the locals' favorite, but south-facing slopes are quick to lose their snow, although the cover remains longer on the upper mountain called the

Hafelekar. Tulfes and Mutters have long, wide, easy trails cut through the conifers and informal and friendly mountain restaurants. They are perfect for a day's fast cruising and for beginners.

Igls shared the Alpine events in both Olympics with the Axamer Lizum and is on the itinerary of every self-respecting Austrian who wants to ski the Patscherkofel downhill course where the national hero, Franz Klammer, won his gold medal in 1976, one of sport's most thrilling moments. The run now has a new snowmaking installation over the entire course.

Instruction is available at each of the ski areas, and the Innsbruck ski school always has a platoon of instructors at the Landestheaterplatz, from which the free buses fan out to the various points each morning.

There is year-round skiing on the Stubai Glacier and excellent cross-country plus some downhill skiing at Seefeld, each about a 40-minute drive from the city.

APRÈS-SKI

Being a city of 120,000 inhabitants, Innsbruck is inevitably different from most other ski resorts. Immediately after skiing, the bars around Igls and Axamer Lizum, particularly, engender a typical Tyrolean atmosphere. In town, however, there is a more sophisticated environment, not hell-bent on supplying the needs of exuberant skiers. Ski clothing and loden coats mingle happily in the city's hostelries.

There are a few international hotels and many old inns—renovated to the highest of modern standards—which have bars, restaurants and nightclubs. The Schwarzer Adler houses a famed restaurant in typical, old Tyrolean rooms dating back 400 years. The Goldener Adler, in the Altstadt (the old, walled city), was founded in 1390, and its restaurants and bars are redolent of a bygone age. The atmosphere is sedate, charming and timeless as you are waited on by solicitous *Dirndl*-clad waitresses and waiters in breeches.

There are plenty of lively places, too, including discos and piano bars where local musicians play for beer-money, and it is usual to strike up conversation with the people at your table. A hokey Tyrolean evening at the Adambräu brewery is on many group agendas. Innsbruck's smart set congregates in the Club Filou, just inside the walls of the Altstadt.

OTHER ACTIVITIES

It is possible to take a ride on the Olympic bobsled run, a nerve-racking yet exhilarating descent. Innsbruck's hosting of the Olympic Games also produced an excellent ice stadium which is open to the public and has thrilling ice-hockey matches. There is little cross-country skiing in the city but plenty at Seefeld. That being said, it is commonplace to see local families out together on weekends skiing unmarked cross-country routes, enjoying the splendor of their mountains. There is a free winter hiking program, including bus transportation and guides, departing daily from the Landestheaterplatz.

Other activities include swimming, bowling, tennis, squash, horseback riding, and even hanggliding. Innsbruck is also a city for musical concerts, art exhibitions and other cultural offerings.

Innsbruck is the place that visitors to the rest of the Tyrol go to sightsee. A stroll through the sedate world of its Altstadt, now a pedestrian zone, will give you a glimpse into the

city's past, the 15th- and 16th-century houses ornamented with colorful Baroque façades. The city's most unusual monument, the Goldenes Dachl ("Little Golden Roof") was built for Emperor Maximilian I as a loggia or "royal box" from which to watch tournaments. To the east lies the cathedral, Dom zu St. Jakob, built in 1722, which stands in a tranquil square shaded by maples and copper beeches and surrounded by some of the town's oldest surviving houses. In contrast, you will see all the most modern sports installations designed for the 1964 and 1976 Olympics. Only 15 minutes away from Innsbruck, Hall in Tirol is a brooding, medieval town with twisting, cobbled streets.

Various tour companies organize excursions further afield to Ischgl, St. Anton, Hintertux, Kitzbühel and the Pitztal glacier for skiing, as well as trips to the Bavarian castles and Oberammergau, Zurich, the casino at Seefeld and even as far away as Vienna and Venice.

ISCHGL

Access: *Nearest airports:* Zurich (2 hrs.); Munich (2 hrs.). *By road:* A14 Autobahn to Bludenz, then via the Arlberg Tunnel and Landeck. *By rail:* to Landeck, then by bus.

Tourist Office: Fremdenverkehrsverband, 6561 Ischgl, Austria. Tel. (05444) 52 66/53 18

Altitude: 4,592 ft. (1,400 m.). *Top:* 9,397 ft. (2,864 m.)

Language: German

Runs: 93 mi. (150 km.)

Lifts: 35

Ski areas: Velilltal, Idalp, Alp Trida, Hölltal, Vesil

Ski school: Schischule Ischgl

Linked resort: Samnaun (Switzerland)

Season: December to early May

Kindergarten: *Non-ski:* from 2 years. *With ski:* from 4 years

Prices: *Lift pass:* 6 days 1,690 S (children 1,010 S). *Ski school:* Group 380 S per day; private 850 S for 2 hours.

RATINGS

Skiing Conditions	8
Snow Conditions	8
For Beginners	5
For Intermediates	9
For Advanced Skiers	8
For Children	4
Après-Ski	8
Other Sports	7
Value for Money	7

THE RESORT

Ischgl is the best known of the Paznaun Valley resorts and, as well as being available on the same regional pass as Tyrolean neighbors Galtür, Kappl and See, has direct links on skis with Samnaun, a duty-free village over the Swiss border. Ischgl attracts a mostly well-to-do crowd which doesn't mind paying quite high prices for an atmosphere of exclusivity without it being especially glamorous. The surrounding Silvretta range affords astonishing views, seemingly boundless skiing and an outstanding snow record.

Although much of the village is modern, it has charm and an interesting history—its first inhabitants trekked over from the Swiss Engadine, and the old Romansch language is reflected in the local Tyrolean patois of today.

A recently upgraded lift system, designed so that little walking is necessary, sometimes fails to cope with German weekend visitors, many of whom stay outside Ischgl and drive in daily. The other problem is that there is occasionally too much snow. When avalanche danger is high, the road up from Landeck, as well as some of the cross-country trails in the valley, may be closed. But Ischgl is popular with its regular visitors who feel that these are minor inconveniences when the variety of skiing, on and off-*piste*, and a good selection of hotels, cafés, discos and nightclubs are such that Ischgl ranks as one of Austria's top resorts.

THE SKIING

Ischgl has just about the full gamut of skiing, served by 35 lifts. Experts indulge in off-*piste* powder skiing, but otherwise there are few really demanding marked runs. More than 90 mi. (150 km.) of runs, untold acres of off-*piste* skiing and the cross-border adventure of skiing into Switzerland are included in an area that spreads over five major peaks and into six valleys.

Three gondolas leave the village from various points, two of them converging on the main Idalp dispersal point, which is also the ski-school meeting place, with additional facilities such as restaurants, an ice bar, shops and day nursery. To the north, a network of lifts serves the beginners' section, as well as the expert runs down from the Pardatsch-Grat, 8,609 ft. (2,624 m.), and the longer intermediate trail from Velillscharte, 8,386 ft. (2,556 m.).

In the opposite direction, the Hölltal and Vesil areas have a lot of challenging on-*piste* skiing and excursions through the trees to Bodenalp, 6,037 ft. (1,840 m.), or Paznauner Taya where there are several *Gasthöfe*, plus a splendid variety of off-*piste* options. (In view of the history of avalanches in the region, they should only be tried in the company of a guide or, at the very least, with official confirmation of their safety.)

Apart from skiing back to Ischgl, the alternatives from Idalp are to ski onto the Swiss side, either all the way down to Samnaun (walk or take the bus to the Ravaisch to return via cable car to Alp Trida) or concentrate on the Alp Trida section where there are more opportunities to sample off-*piste* skiing and a few mid-level *pistes*. Note that restaurants over the Swiss border are even more expensive than on the Austrian side.

Ischgl's main problem is staggering lift lines. You can avoid the rush by heading for the cable cars early. The local lift pass covers Ischgl and Samnaun, while the Silvretta ticket allows skiing at Galtür, Kappl and See, less than 20 minutes away by car or bus.

APRÈS-SKI

For early in the evening there are bars such as Café Christine, Taja and the Club Après for energetic drinking sessions and tea dances. Tyrolean evenings at the rather antiseptic Silvretta Centre are a little short on *Gemütlichkeit*. It is, however, a well-run setting for a variety of sporting pursuits and shows German-language films. Sleigh rides through the woods to Mathon engender a more typical Tyrolean feeling.

The three main nightclubs (Sälte Löbli at the Hotel Post, the Hotel Trofana's Tenne and the Madlein Wunderbar) have live bands, and the friendly Club Après disco keeps younger limbs and spirits happy until the early hours. The weekly ski-school presentation is eagerly awaited by participants.

OTHER ACTIVITIES

The Silvretta Centre is the place for swimming, sauna, steam room, massage and bowling. In addition, Ischgl has an ice rink for skating and curling. Ischgl's cross-country skiing amounts to about 6 mi. (10 km.); by either taking the bus or skiing all the way to Galtür, there is a further 28 mi. (45 km.)—with instruction available, if required.

Duty-free shopping in Samnaun is a chance to do something out of the ordinary. The old village of Mathon, a bus-ride away, has a charming folk museum.

KIRCHBERG

Access: *Nearest airport:* Munich (1 hr.). *By road:* A12 Autobahn, exit Wörgl-Ost. *By rail:* station in Kirchberg.

Tourist Office: Fremdenverkehrsverband, 6365 Kirchberg, Austria. Tel. (05357) 23 09

Altitude: 2,822 ft. (860 m.). *Top:* 6,545 ft. (1,995 m.)

Language: German

Runs: 25 mi. (40 km.); 100 mi. (160 km.) in Skigrossraum

Lifts: 16 (62 in Skigrossraum)

Ski areas: Gaisberg, Ehrenbachhöhe, Pengelstein

Ski school: Schischule Pepi Schöderböck

Linked resorts: Kitzbühel, Jochberg, Pass Thurn, Aschau

Season: December to April

Kindergarten: *Non-ski:* from 3 years. *With ski:* from 4 years

Prices: *Lift pass:* 6 days 1,450 S (children 725 S). *Ski school:* Group 1,050 S for 6 days; private 1,100 S for half-day.

RATINGS

Skiing Conditions	7
Snow Conditions	5
For Beginners	5
For Intermediates	9
For Advanced Skiers	7
For Children	7
Après-Ski	7
Other Sports	6
Value for Money	6

THE RESORT

Kirchberg shares much of Kitzbühel's skiing area but little else. Whereas Kitzbühel attracts an international set, Kirchberg has the atmosphere of a happy-go-lucky ski village where fur coats and evening gowns are positively pretentious. Kirchberg is known as the village "on the other side of the Hahnenkamm," and it is as sporty as befits a resort that abuts against the region's most demanding mountain.

There are a couple of first-grade hotels and plenty more modest places down to the most humble *Gasthof.* Several lively bars argue against Kirchberg's reputation for being a sleepy suburb of glitzy Kitzbühel, and Kirchberg fans quite rightly claim it offers the combination of top-quality skiing and energetic après-ski.

Kirchberg's main drawbacks are that most of the accommodations are a fair walk from the main lifts (a free bus, however, links hotels and lifts) and that its proximity to Kitzbühel is reflected in quite high prices, so that beginners or the impecunious might be happier elsewhere.

THE SKIING

Kirchberg is at the western end of Kitzbühel's Ski Safari which runs to Pass Thurn via Jochberg. It is a 23-mi. (37-km.) ski circus, fully connected (one way) although a bit of a walk is necessary in Jochberg.

Kirchberg's advantage over Kitzbühel as a base is that you can avoid the appalling lines for the Hahnenkamm cable car by taking a bus to

33

For map see pp. 36–37.

the Fleckalmbahn gondola or to Kirchberg's own lifts for easier access. The Kitzbüheler Horn, a separate area to the east of Kitzbühel, is also included on the lift pass as are the runs above Aurach from the Stuckkogel. As if all this weren't enough, Kirchberg has its own separate slopes on the Gaisberg. The runs are relatively short and easy, but also quite sheltered and less crowded. All in all, Kirchberg has access to a huge network which keeps experts and intermediates thoroughly entertained and, if unfit, exhausted.

APRÈS-SKI

Fondue nights, sleigh rides (with accordion music, yodeling and singing at the Achenstüberl) and the weekly ski-school presentation are the main features. There is also nightly bar hopping, discos, a few nightclubs and a couple of Tyrolean bars, making Kirchberg a merry place in the evening.

OTHER ACTIVITIES

Bowling evenings at the ancient Gasthof Unterm Rain are popular, with a variety of games and prizes— the latter, invariably, are shots of *Schnaps*. Kirchberg doesn't have its own toboggan run, but the one at Gasteig, near St. Johann, is convenient. The local skating and curling rinks are sometimes closed after a snowfall, but the weather won't affect swimming in the indoor pool at the sports center. The cross-country skiing opportunities are extensive, with trails reaching beyond Brixen to Westendorf.

There are organized excursions to Salzburg, Innsbruck, and to the wildlife park at Aurach, Berchtesgaden in Germany and Vipiteno in Italy.

34

KITZBÜHEL

Access: *Nearest airport:* Munich (1 hr.). *By road:* A12 Autobahn, exit Kufstein-Süd. *By rail:* station in Kitzbühel.

Tourist Office: Fremdenverkehrsverband, 6370 Kitzbühel, Austria. Tel. (05356) 22 72

Altitude: 2,493 ft. (760 m.).
Top: 6,545 ft. (1,995 m.)

Language: German

Runs: 100 mi. (160 km.) in Skigrossraum

Lifts: 62 in Skigrossraum

Ski areas: Hahnenkamm, Kitzbüheler Horn (including Ehrenbachhöhe, Pengelstein), Bichalm

Ski schools: Rote Teufel Schischule, two children's ski schools

Linked resorts: Pass Thurn, Jochberg, Kirchberg, Aschau

Season: December to end April

Kindergarten: *Non-ski:* 1–3 years. *With ski:* from 3 years

Prices: *Lift pass:* 6 days 1,450 S (children 725 S). *Ski school:* Group 950 S for 6 days; private 1,050 S for half-day.

RATINGS

Skiing Conditions	9
Snow Conditions	5
For Beginners	4
For Intermediates	9
For Advanced Skiers	8
For Children	5
Après-Ski	9
Other Sports	8
Value for Money	7

THE RESORT

In the same way that, say, New York, Paris and London are great cities, Kitzbühel is a great ski resort. To many of the old-money brigade it remains the *only* place to ski and it is the place to which those with social ambitions aspire. But for all the glamour, sophistication, entertainment and sheer wealth that attract visitors, there is a seedy side: it also draws a sizable young rowdy element with more money than drinking capacity.

But if the streets are sometimes noisy, a few of the bars highly boisterous, and the lines for the Hahnenkamm cable car tedious, Kitzbühel retains its unique status in the ski world due to several factors. First, the Hahnenkamm's great men's World Cup meet every January is rivaled only by Wengen's Lauberhorn for glamour and excitement in international racing. The attendant publicity assures Kitzbühel of world-wide recognition as a challenging skiing area.

Another factor, to the astonishment of many Americans who flock here like pilgrims, is that Kitzbühel is far removed from the picturebook ski *Dorf* depicted on chocolate boxes and calendars. Kitzbühel is a large, cosmopolitan town. Instead of sweet little chalets, there is a sturdy medieval center with large pastel-daubed buildings whose jagged rooftops resemble the nearby Wilder Kaiser mountains.

Conversation in après-ski bars and mountain restaurants is multilingual, for Kitzbühel attracts a truly international clientele. If the Amer-

Skigebiet Kitzbühel

THE SKIING

ican visitors who expect a romantic Tyrolean scenario are surprised initially, they quickly become entranced by Kitzbühel's skiing, shopping and sights.

Kitzbühel's long-established hotels, fine clothing shops and excellent restaurants make it a good choice for non-skiers. With a railway station in town, sightseeing jaunts to sophisticated cities such as Innsbruck, the Tyrolean capital, Salzburg, birthplace of Mozart, and farther afield are easy.

Kitzbühel can be credited with initiating the ski-circus concept. Today, 62 lifts in the Skigrossraum Kitzbühel are skiable on one pass, and the Ski Safari is the name of a skis-on circuit over more than 23 mi. (37 km.) of runs. Snow cover on the lower slopes can be uncertain at times, but essentially Kitzbühel's skiing remains exemplary.

For intermediates and all but the highest-level experts, Kitzbühel of-

fers skiing unsurpassed in Austria. Even if beginners and families with children might find somewhere smaller and cheaper more suitable, they couldn't be better provided for. The great Toni Sailer, whose trio of gold medals at the 1956 Olympics emphasized Kitzbühel's sizable credentials, runs a children's ski school. And beginners start their classes on the flat apron at the end of the formidable Streif downhill run on the Hahnenkamm.

With the Hahnenkamm cable car close to the middle of town, access to the slopes would be easier than in most Austrian resorts were it not for the fact that everyone wants to ride it in the morning. *Cognoscenti* take the free buses to the Fleckalmbahn gondola station or the Jochberg and Pass Thurn lifts, which are usually less crowded. The Fleckalmbahn rises to the Ehrenbachhöhe, the central part of Kitzbühel's lift system (which is also reached from Kirchberg, a smaller and less highly pressured village). Jochberg and

Pass Thurn at the far end of Kitzbühel's Ski Safari interconnect with
each other but only in one direction
with the rest of the system.

Good skiers flock to the Streif,
which demands a considerable
amount of skill and nerve (forget
that the great downhillers run it
around the two-minute mark). The
upper parts are steep, and even experts have to circumnavigate their
more nervous, less talented breth-
ren strewn about or tentatively side-
slipping down sections which World
Cup racers take in mid-air at 80
mph.

There is good skiing on-*piste* all
around the Hahnenkamm area, plus
some ungroomed slopes, notably
the Fleckhochalm run, which quickly become mogul infested. Beware
of taking what appear to be ski
routes. The map clearly shows con-
troled runs, which are well marked,
but there are dozens of occasions
when you will see tracks leading
down interesting-looking descents.
With a guide there is some spectacular off-*piste* skiing all over the
Hahnenkamm.

There is still more in the Jochberg
and Pass Thurn areas—each would
be a sizable resort in its own right if
there were more local accommodations—and the on-*piste* skiing is
generally easy. Again, with a guide,
there are scores of off-*piste* forays
through the trees, down steep gullies or on wide walls which require
a lot of walking and traversing. It's
worth the effort for the ultimate experience of skiing near-vertical
drops through pristine powder after
a fresh snowfall.

Two more separate sections
round out Kitzbühel's offerings. The
Bichlalm is a small area above Aurach (on the road between Kitzbühel
and Jochberg), and the Kitzbüheler
Horn, big in scale but disappointing
in scope for advanced skiers, is a

good choice for those wanting to avoid the Hahnenkamm's congestion. Since the slopes are south-facing, conditions are variable.

All over the mountains, there are restaurants and bars, some rustic, others modern self-service, and most of them expensive. If you can avoid the crowds, Kitzbühel offers some of the best skiing in Europe.

APRÈS-SKI

It's all there—except perhaps the steamy log-cabin charm of some of Kitzbühel's more typically Tyrolean counterparts.

Although there are a few bars at the bottom of the slopes conducive to taking a beer or *Jagertee* immediately after skiing, most people tend to head for town, where they can enjoy an outdoor drink amid a well-dressed, perfectly coiffed crowd, join a noisy "Happy Hour" or relax in the hotel bar.

Kitzbühel remains one of the Alps' great après-ski pastry headquarters. The Café Praxmair is a veritable institution; Café Kortschak and Konditorei Langer tend to get the overflow. Zur Tenne keeps the venerable practice of tea dancing alive, although little tea is consumed. The Londoner gets a young crowd, while the Landhäusl and the Stamperl draw people who persuade themselves that Tyrolean rusticity still exists in downtown Kitzbühel.

After dinner, the Glockenspiel and the Londoner begin with rock, while Take Five is Kitzbühel's wee-hours capital; Drop In, despite its casual name, is a pricey disco.

Kitzbühel boasts a casino, museums, fashion fairs and a series of concerts. Of the more traditional pursuits, there are sleigh rides past the Schwarzsee lake to Schloss Münichau, and medieval banquets, *fondue* suppers and Tyrolean evenings at the ancient Hotel Zur Tenne are popular.

The better hotels have top-quality health and sports facilities, as well as a choice of dining rooms and a nightclub. Kitzbühel's shops (where you can buy made-to-measure ski pants and custom-made Tyrolean hunting clothing, as well as the very best in ski and leisure wear) and a selection of bars, restaurants and discos offer a dazzling array from which to choose.

OTHER ACTIVITIES

The Kitzbühel lift pass allows entry to the Aquarena, equipped with a fitness center, swimming pool, sauna and solarium. Three indoor tennis courts, a squash court, artificial ice rink, indoor curling and a riding school mean that Kitzbühel has plenty to offer in addition to skiing. With 19 mi. (30 km.) of cross-country trails close at hand and, in the company of a free guide, a further 125 mi. (200 km.) in the region, the town can justifiably claim to be a true winter sports center.

LECH

🎿🎿🎿🎿🎿

Access: *Nearest airports:* Zurich (2½ hrs.); Munich (3 hrs.); Innsbruck (1½ hrs.) *By road:* A14 Autobahn to Bludenz, then via Langen. *By rail:* to Langen, then by bus.

Tourist Office: Verkehrsamt, 6764 Lech am Arlberg, Austria. Tel. (05583) 21 61-0

Altitude: 4,757 ft. (1,450 m.). *Top:* 7,798 ft. (2,377 m.)

Language: German

Runs: 68 mi. (110 km.) with Zürs; 124 mi. (200 km.) in Arlberg area

Lifts: 34 with Zürs 28

Ski areas: Kriegerhorn, Oberlech, Rüfikopf

Ski schools: Schischule Lech, Schischule Oberlech

Linked resorts: Zürs, Zug

Season: Late November to late April

Kindergarten: *Non-ski:* from 2½ years. *With ski:* from 2½ years

Prices: *Lift pass:* 6 days 1,420–1,620 S (children 810–920 S). *Ski school:* Group 1,080–1,180 S for 6 days; private 1,700 S per day.

RATINGS

Skiing Conditions	8
Snow Conditions	8
For Beginners	7
For Intermediates	8
For Advanced Skiers	8
For Children	6
Après-Ski	7
Other Sports	6
Value for Money	6

THE RESORT

If Walt Disney Productions wanted to create an instant traditional ski resort, they would model it on this perfect Vorarlberg village with a river running through the middle and sun-kissed slopes on both sides.

Lech owes its exclusive status to comparatively difficult access and high prices. Residents and visitors move with a self-confident, unhurried step, and while the most expensive, up-to-the-minute ski suits are in evidence on the slopes, fur coats are *de rigueur* for the daily promenade at tea time.

THE SKIING

Lech's skiing links with that of Zürs (3 mi. [5 km.] away by road), and the first impression is of perfectly manicured slopes designed to flatter the perfectly groomed, designer-clothed clientele. Closer inspection reveals much tougher work, especially off-*piste*, and the fact that many of the *glitterati* who assemble here each winter happen to be very good skiers.

A variety of lifts serve the fast, open trails down from the Kriegerhorn and around Oberlech, a satellite settlement perched above the valley. The difficult skiing is beyond, on ungroomed ski routes from the Zuger Hochlicht—Lech's highest point at 7,798 ft. (2,377 m.)—or down to Zug, a tiny hamlet.

A popular day trip is to ride the Rüfikopf cable car to Zürs's terrain, stop for lunch and then return via the Madloch in the afternoon. The

41

For map see pp. 86–87.

run back to Lech from Zürs merges into the one from Zug. The 12-mi. (20-km.) interlinked Lech-Zürs circuit is perfect for ambitious intermediates who will have to steel themselves for the occasional stern examination of technique. The other return from Zürs, from the top of the Rüfikopf cable car, is a steep and often ungroomed run. Skiing with a guide, especially after a snowfall, leads to the discovery of bowls and gullies of fresh powder.

Lech is at the far end of the Arlberg network of resorts which straddle the Tyrol-Vorarlberg border. The others included on the regional lift pass are St. Christoph, Stuben, Zürs and the most famous ski center in the region, St. Anton.

At lunchtime, the beautiful, or at least beautifully dressed, people congregate in Oberlech at the bar, under a huge red umbrella outside the Sporthotel Petersboden (which also has an indoor restaurant) or in the ancient dining room of the Goldener Berg. Apart from Oberlech's eateries, there isn't much alternative other than skiing back to town

or taking lunch at the Palmenalpe restaurant at the top of the chairlift from Zug.

APRÈS-SKI

Early evening activities can either take the form of shopping or sipping. Buys include top-quality sportswear, antiques and wood carvings. Skiers who still *must* have custom-made boots go to Strolz, the last such custom boot-maker. Many people simply wander the streets in the company of couples in matching furs (sometimes, it is rumored, the family canine will be similarly dressed!). Others prefer to take in the tea dance in the Tannbergerhof or pause for a hot chocolate or *Jagertee* (tea with rum) in the sumptuous lounge of the Gasthof Post, an Alpine institution constructed in sturdy chalet style and stuffed with antiques and famed for impeccable service, which appeals to royalty and jet-setters who choose it for their winter sojourn.

There is little hubbub in the streets later on, but inside the hotels, there are several good but pricey discos and nightclubs. A sleigh ride to the Rote Wand, a superb restaurant-cum-nightclub in outlying Zug, is a treat.

OTHER ACTIVITIES

There may be tobogganing evenings, as well as skating and curling at the small ice rink in the village center. The *Tenniszentrum* has four indoor courts and two squash courts, and there is a public swimming pool, as well as several pools in hotels. Cross-country skiers can take advantage of 14 mi. (22 km.) along the valley to Zug. Excursions to Innsbruck are possible by taking a bus to Langen and the train from there.

MAYRHOFEN

Access: *Nearest airports:* Munich (2½ hrs.); Salzburg (3 hrs.); Innsbruck (1 hr.). *By road:* A12 Autobahn, exit Wiesing/Zillertal. *By rail:* to Jenbach, then Zillertalbahn or bus.

Tourist Office: Fremdenverkehrsverband, 6290 Mayrhofen/Zillertal, Austria. Tel. (05285) 23 05

Altitude: 2,067 ft. (630 m.).
Top: 7,382 ft. (2,250 m.)

Language: German

Runs: 56 mi. (90 km.)

Lifts: 29

Ski areas: A-Horn, Penken, Horberg-Gerent

Ski school: Schischule Mayrhofen

Linked resort: Finkenberg

Season: Mid-December to mid-April

Kindergarten: *Non-ski:* 3–12 years. *With ski:* 4–14 years

Prices: *Lift pass:* 6 days Zillertal 1,050–1,280 S (children 770 S). *Ski school:* Group 790 S for 6 days; private 350 S per hour.

RATINGS

Skiing Conditions	6
Snow Conditions	5
For Beginners	5
For Intermediates	6
For Advanced Skiers	2
For Children	8
Après-Ski	7
Other Sports	5
Value for Money	7

THE RESORT

Mayrhofen could justifiably claim to be the cradle of British skiing, as its renowned ski school has taught the basics to innumerable children and adults over the last few decades. It is the largest of the Zillertal resorts, connects directly with Finkenberg and links by bus or train with Lanersbach, Hintertux (where there is year-round glacier skiing), Zell am Ziller and Fügen—all included on the regional lift pass.

Now quite a big town, it has lost much of the rustic character which first attracted skiers out for no-frills ski holidays with excellent instruction and a lively nightlife. It is, however, still a good place to learn to ski and to enjoy the discos and sleigh rides. Lying roughly at the mid-point of the valley's resorts, Mayrhofen is the best place from which to explore the Zillertal, as well as the Tuxertal beyond, giving better skiers a wide range of varied skiing.

THE SKIING

Novices start on the A-Horn just to the south of Mayrhofen. This small, confined ski area is also where the acclaimed children's ski school holds its classes. Waiting for the A-Horn cable car is still something of an ordeal, and although there is a trail all the way back home, it is for advanced intermediates. Beginners, therefore, have to queue again for the cable car back down at the end of the day.

45

On the other side of town, the Penken ski area has some more-demanding slopes. Such is the resort's popularity that the cable cars attract unwieldy lines each morning, a problem partially alleviated by the new lifts around Horberg, connecting with Penken. Below the Penken area, the slopes down to the beginning of the new Gerent gondola lift start gently enough, but become quite tricky lower down—beginners beware!

These inconveniences aside, Mayrhofen is always popular with the young set who benefit from painstaking instruction before graduating to uninhibited *piste*-bashing, and the glacier at Hintertux guarantees good snow, offset by occasional extreme cold, all winter.

A free bus service operates through town and serves the three lift base stations, and a six-day pass facilitates use of the train and bus services to neighboring ski resorts.

APRÈS-SKI

Taking tea at the imposing Hotel Elisabeth, near the railway station, is one of the more sedate events in merry Mayrhofen. Nightlife is generally informal and often quite boozy, either at discos (the Andreas Keller, Berghof and Schlüssel are among the liveliest). Tyrolean evenings, tobogganing, *fondue* nights and the weekly ski-school presentation ceremony are all enjoyed by Mayrhofen's predominantly youthful clientele. There are also a few friendly, downbeat bars and restaurants, and a movie theater, with films mainly in German.

OTHER ACTIVITIES

Many hotels have a pool and sauna. There is an indoor public swimming pool, ice-skating, curling on a nat-

ural rink, sleigh rides, horseback riding, indoor tennis, squash, bowling and para-gliding. A 13-mi. (21-km.) cross-country trail takes you around Mayrhofen, and there are 28 mi. (45 km.) of cleared paths for walking in the area. For children there are Punch and Judy shows.

Excursions are organized to Inns-

46

bruck, Kitzbühel and Salzburg, and Vipiteno and Cortina over the border in Italy. Mayrhofen is the terminus of the Zillertal railway, a one-hour ride through enthralling scenery. Shortly before arrival in Jenbach, crane your neck to see the chapel perched on the cliff to the left. Legend has it that if a girl visited to pray for a husband on three occasions and was still unheeded, she was required to throw herself to the valley floor. There are a lot of unlikely legends in this part of Austria! It is also ironic, since nowadays Mayrhofen and its Zillertal neighbors are renowned for providing a boy-meets-girl atmosphere.

NEUSTIFT/STUBAI VALLEY

Access: *Nearest airports:* Innsbruck
(½ hr.); Munich (3 hrs.). *By road:*
A13 Autobahn, exit Stubai. *By rail:* to
Innsbruck, then by bus.

Tourist Office: Fremdenverkehrs-
verband, 6167 Neustift im Stubaital,
Austria. Tel. (05226) 22 28

Altitude: 3,281 ft. (1,000 m.).
Top: 10,532 ft. (3,210 m.)

Language: German

Runs: 75 mi. (120 km.) in Stubaital

Lifts: 37 in Stubaital

Ski areas: Stubai Glacier, Serleslifte,
Schlick, Elfer

Ski schools: Schischule Stubaier
Gletscher, Schischule Neustift Hoch-
stubai

Linked resorts: None

Season: Mid-December to April; all
year round on glacier

Kindergarten: *Non-ski:* from 2 years.
With ski: from 3 years

Prices: *Lift pass:* 6 days Stubai Super
Ski Pass 1,450 S (50% reduction for
children). *Ski school:* Group 940 S
for 5 days; private 300 S per hour.

RATINGS

Skiing Conditions	4
Snow Conditions	8
For Beginners	5
For Intermediates	6
For Advanced Skiers	4
For Children	5
Après-Ski	5
Other Sports	7
Value for Money	7

THE RESORTS

Twenty minutes from the center of
Innsbruck, the Stubaital satisfies
everyone's ideal of the typical
Tyrolean valley: lovely, unspoiled
villages with onion-domed churches,
farmhouses perched precariously
above the valley close to high pastures.

Cozy cafés and old-fashioned hospitality make it the perfect antidote
to high-pressure, high-priced resorts. The villages, Neustift, Mieders, Fulpmes and Telfes, each have
good, but limited skiing close at
hand. The big attraction is on the
Stubai Glacier, at the head of the
valley, with skiing throughout the
year. In fact, the Stubai Glacier ranks
as the largest year-round ski area in
Europe. In winter it is snow-sure
and may even have great powder. In
summer, it's an especially memorable experience.

That's when the whole valley
takes on a new aspect. Sheep and
cattle graze by the roadside, fisher-
men angle for trout, hikers roam the
flower-speckled hillsides, even as
skiers head for the glacier, fairly
sure that they will spend the morning skiing under deep blue skies
until the early afternoon sun makes
the snow too slushy.

THE SKIING

Neustift and Mieders each have
limited local terrain. Neustift's
Elfer chair climbs 2,663 vertical ft.
(802 m.) to a mostly gentle high
snowfield. There are some challenging ungroomed options back to
town. Fulpmes and Telfes both have

small beginner slopes close to the village centers and share the Schlick 2000 Skizentrum, which may one day if Alpine politics allow— be connected with the Innsbruck Olympic ski venue, the famous Axamer Lizum. For the moment, it still offers limited terrain in a deep valley, plus the necessity of riding the lift back over the lower mountain.

It is the Stubai Glacier, however, which attracts most visitors to the valley. It guarantees excellent snow, and even at the end of May conditions are good down to the mid-

station. The top station is at over 10,500 ft. (3,200 m.), from which the views are magnificent. The upper slopes are gentle—perfect for beginners. Experts will find little challenge, unless they opt for race-training weeks in the summer.

APRÈS-SKI

There is a jolly, but plain, little bar at the bottom of the glacier gondola. Across the parking lot, the Alpen-sporthotel Mutterberg is almost a village in itself. Its facilities include

49

indoor pool, sauna, game room, bowling alley and nightclub. Further down the valley, each of the villages has several good bars and places for dancing. None of them are designed to appeal to jet-setters, but all are informal, friendly and less expensive than in better-known resorts. Neustift's Romanstube and Schihaserlkeller both combine good value, uninhibited dancing and a friendly clientele.

OTHER ACTIVITIES

Mieders and Telfes have cross-country tracks, and above Fulpmes and Neustift there are long, tree-lined toboggan runs. The sports center between Fulpmes and Telfes houses an indoor pool, tennis courts, sauna and Turkish baths. Most of the better hotels have good fitness rooms. In addition, you'll find skibobbing, skating, curling, bowling, hang-gliding, squash and horseback riding in one or other of the villages.

Innsbruck is just down the road, and one of the most interesting ways of visiting it is to take the streetcar from Telfes, which meanders its way through Mutters and Natters, before depositing its mixed cargo of skiers, shoppers and sightseers in Innsbruck.

OBERGURGL

Access: *Nearest airports:* Innsbruck
(1½ hrs.); Munich (3½ hrs.). *By road:*
A12 Autobahn, exit Ötztal, then via
Ötz. *By rail:* to Ötztal, then by bus.

Tourist Office: Fremdenverkehrs-
verband Gurgl, 6456 Obergurgl,
Austria. Tel. (05256) 258

Altitude: 6,332 ft. (1,930 m.).
Top: 10,112 ft. (3,082 m.)

Language: German

Runs: 66 mi. (107 km.)

Lifts: 22

Ski areas: Gaisberg-Hohe Mut, Festkogel, Wurmkogl

Ski schools: Schischule Obergurgl,
Schischule Hochgurgl

Linked resorts: None

Season: Mid-November to early
May

Kindergarten: *Non-ski:* from 3 years.
With ski: from 5 years

Prices: *Lift pass:* 6 days 1,590 S
(children 960 S). *Ski school:* Group
1,150 S for 6 days; private 350-450 S
per hour.

RATINGS

Skiing Conditions	5
Snow Conditions	7
For Beginners	8
For Intermediates	8
For Advanced Skiers	6
For Children	7
Après-Ski	5
Other Sports	5
Value for Money	6

THE RESORT

The Ötztal is a wild and isolated valley with soaring, craggy mountains
and small villages with hardy pop-
ulations. At the head of the valley,
with the Italian border in sight,
Obergurgl is remote, guaranteeing
its exclusiveness. It is a pretty village and tends to attract the same
clientele every year. The coziness of
Obergurgl's hotels and cafés contrasts with the wide-open spaces on
the mountain above.

Obergurgl is the largest of "the
Gurgls" and the middle one in altitude. Hochgurgl is a more modern
settlement high above the valley
and is, along with Untergurgl, available on the Obergurgl lift pass.
Sölden, a year-round resort with access to glacier skiing, is a 20-minute
car journey back down the valley,
and Vent, a climbing mecca and
home of Calgary double-medallist
Bernhard Gstrein, half an hour's
drive, but a separate pass is required for each.

Most visitors have their own cars,
convenient for being independent
of the free bus service to Untergurgl
or Hochgurgl and for venturing to
Vent or Sölden, but presenting diffi-
culties for parking in the twisting,
narrow streets.

Austria's highest parish, at 6,332 ft.
(1,930 m.), Obergurgl provides skiing right outside the village, reliable
snow and easy, conveniently situated
beginner slopes, which make it a
popular choice for families—some
children have inherited the Obergurgl bug from their great-grand-
fathers.

THE SKIING

The Gurgls are Austria's leading ski-in, ski-out resorts. Each village is tiny, and lifts are closeby. This is not a region of mega-cable cars or fancy lifts, but of good snow and excellent off-*piste* skiing.

Obergurgl's skiing is in two sections, Festkogel and Hohe Mut, which only connect one way, and Untergurgl and Hochgurgl constitute a completely separate ski area, linked to Obergurgl by bus.

All of the skiing is above the tree line, except the wide, twisting fast trail from Hochgurgl, 7,054 ft. (2,150 m.), down to Untergurgl, 5,883 ft. (1,793 m.). The ungroomed ski route from the Hohe Mut, 8,760 ft.

(2,670 m.), where there is a restaurant whose terrace affords views over the Rotmoos Glacier to the Italian border, is the only run down back to Obergurgl. It isn't too difficult if it hasn't been over-skied, but quickly becomes mogul-infested because it is narrow. Hochgurgl's short expert trail from the Wurmkogl and a couple more ski routes ending at the bottom of the Festkogellift offer additional challenge. There are, however, plenty of opportunities for good skiers if they take the fall line on some of the wider sections which are, in general, easy to intermediate slopes.

The tradition of high-mountain ski touring in the area still attracts adventurous skiers, and a choice of

interesting itineraries, some lasting several days, is suggested by the ski school.

Eight restaurants are strategically placed around the mountain, all of them at the top or bottom of lifts, and there are plenty more in the villages. The terrace of the Hotel Jenewein beside the Gaiserberg lift in Obergurgl provides one of the best lunch spots in the Alps. On sunny days, many skiers break for lunch never to return to the mountain!

Of the neighboring resorts, Sölden is much larger, with a wide-scope on- and off-*piste*. Good skiers should ski it for at least a day, even though it isn't covered by the same lift pass. Vent is tiny and worth a visit mainly for a change of scene.

APRÈS-SKI

Obergurgl offers both atmosphere and opportunities for dancing or listening to live music. Hochgurgl is much quieter (and more expensive), appealing to the crowd for whom skiing is more important than nightlife. Untergurgl is a tiny settlement whose guests usually drive or take the post bus to Obergurgl for an evening out.

Obergurgl's Josl, Gamper and Wiesental cafés are the usual meeting places at the end of the day, while the Edelweiss und Gurgl host both tea dances and the end-of-week ski school prize-giving. The Jenewein's disco and live bands at the Edelweiss are complemented

by "Fonduedunnit" nights at the Fender—diners at the *fondue* suppers enact a murder mystery!

OTHER ACTIVITIES

Some 8 mi. (13 km.) of cross-country trails, public swimming pools at the hotels Hochfirst and Mühle in Obergurgl, a rifle range, skating and curling rinks, and squash courts are among the non-skiing facilities.

Other than the Ötztaler bus service, which calls at all the valley's villages and has the occasional service to Innsbruck, there are few opportunities for exploring without a car.

OBERTAUERN

Access: *Nearest airports:* Munich (2½ hrs.); Salzburg (1½ hrs.). *By road:* A10 Autobahn, exit Eben. *By rail:* to Radstadt or Salzburg, then by bus.

Tourist Office: Verkehrsverein, 5562 Obertauern, Austria. Tel. (06456) 252

Altitude: 5,709 ft. (1,740 m.). *Top:* 7,710 ft. (2,350 m.)

Language: German

Runs: 75 mi. (120 km.)

Lifts: 25

Ski area: Obertauern-Nord, Obertauern-Süd

Ski school: Schischule Obertauern

Linked resorts: None

Season: December to April

Kindergarten: *Non-ski* from 3 years. *With ski:* from 3 years

Prices: *Lift pass:* 6 days 1,290 S (children 845 S). *Ski school:* Group 1,050–1,200 S for 6 days; private 380 S per hour.

RATINGS

Skiing Conditions	8
Snow Conditions	8
For Beginners	6
For Intermediates	8
For Advanced Skiers	6
For Children	6
Après-Ski	5
Other Sports	5
Value for Money	6

THE RESORT

Obertauern's wide main street is evidence that this was once an important staging post on the old pass through the Tauern Alps. Originally on the salt route between Salzburg and the south, today the town is bypassed by a modern *Autobahn.*

Anyone looking for a traditional Austrian ski village will be disappointed by the functional exterior. Once inside Obertauern's bars and hotels, however, there is true *Gemütlichkeit:* the discos exude a bop-'til-you-drop atmosphere, and the sports center recognizes the needs of guests who require a lot more than skiing for winter exercise.

THE SKIING

Quite simply, it is a bomber's paradise—unless there has been a heavy snowfall when waist-deep waves of powder snow form a sea of pleasure for off-*piste* aficionados. These extreme conditions are quite common, but Obertauern's recent reputation has been built on a 75-mi. (120-km.) circuit of groomed runs packed out of the endless ocean of white which can be skied at full-tilt in either direction. High-speed cruising is almost *de rigueur,* there is plenty to occupy most intermediates, and the beginner terrain is high and sunny.

Obertauern cannot claim a mind-boggling vertical, but because the resort itself is at the tree line, and since it is one of Austria's few ski-in, ski-out villages, the entire vertical is truly skied. The lift system has been designed so that there is no need to

For map see pp. 20–21.

remove your skis all day, apart from when climbing the steps to the cable car—the head of the ski school delights in demonstrating that even this is possible on skis, but he only does it on someone else's equipment! Better skiers can either enroll in the ski school for an off-*piste* tour with an instructor who does more guiding than teaching or, with a car, use the "Top-Tauern-Skischeck" at resorts down the valley.

APRÈS-SKI

The hard-working Oberhumer family rules the resort. One generation started the ski school, the current one continues it. They manage to combine ski instruction with playing Austrian music (much of which they have recorded) and running the Gasthof Taverne which attracts an early-evening throng for a sing-along to guitar and accordion accompaniment. Huge meat-dominated dinners fuel the disco dancing, which is unflagging until the early hours. Elsewhere, discos with live music include the Edelweiss and the Kupferstube in the International.

OTHER ACTIVITIES

The sports center has a swimming pool and indoor tennis courts. There is a 12-mi. (20-km.) cross-country skiing trail.

Salzburg is 37 mi. (60 km.) to the north. To the south, Villach is a great center for the pre-Lent *Fasching* carnival.

56

SAALBACH-HINTERGLEMM

Access: *Nearest airports:* Salzburg (1½ hrs.); Munich (3 hrs.). *By road:* A8 Autobahn, exit Salzburg, then via Lofer, Maishofen. *By rail:* to Zell am See, then by bus.

Tourist Office: Fremdenverkehrsverband, 5753 Saalbach/Hinterglemm, Austria. Tel. (06541) 72 72

Altitude: 3,291 ft. (1,003 m.). *Top:* 6,880 ft. (2,097 m.)

Language: German

Runs: 124 mi. (200 km.)

Lifts: 60

Ski areas: Schattberg Ost, Zwölferkogel, Kohlmais, Schönleiten, Hochalm, Reiterkogel/Hasenauer Köpfl, Bernkogel

Ski schools: Schischule: Saalbach; Hinterglemm; Mitterlengau; Schi- und Rennschule Hinterglemm

Linked resort: Leogang

Season: Late November to late April

Kindergarten: *Non-ski:* from 3 years. *With ski:* from 4 years

Prices: *Lift pass:* 6 days, 1,180–1,480 S (children 520–890 S). *Ski school:* Group 1,150 S for 6 days; private 1,800 S per day.

RATINGS

Skiing Conditions	9
Snow Conditions	7
For Beginners	5
For Intermediates	10
For Advanced Skiers	8
For Children	5
Après-Ski	9
Other Sports	6
Value for Money	6

THE RESORTS

We're going to be hearing a lot about Saalbach in the next few years. This picturesque village, together with its near-neighbor Hinterglemm, has been named the site of the 1991 World Alpine Ski Championships—the first time skiing's international governing body has awarded the competition to a candidate on the first ballot. It's a good choice. For these towns combine ineffable charm with excellent, accessible terrain. The ski circus is one of Austria's best, as the interlinks can be skied in either direction, the lifts are being steadily updated, and by the time the championships roll around, the already extensive snow-making installation will be even larger, covering all the racing trails. In addition, nightlife is excellent, appealing to well-heeled German and Dutch visitors who appreciate quality and sophistication and are willing to pay for it.

THE SKIING

The lift system allows over 120 mi. (200 km.) of skiing in either direction, making it easy to follow the sun around and providing fast on-*piste* skiing. There are also endless off-*piste* forays on both sides of the Glemm Valley. Leogang, a little village to the north of the Asitz summit, has its own ski area included on the Saalbach-Hinterglemm lift pass. Kaprun and Zell am See are both a short drive away, but require a separate lift pass.

The circuit can be entered from any of the base stations and done clockwise or counterclockwise. The Schattberg cable car—a 200-passenger behemoth, Austria's largest—starts from the middle of Saalbach and rises to 6,628 ft. (2,020 m.), the main starting point for the circuit to Hinterglemm or back to Saalbach via Jausern, with several choices for off-*piste* descents. Good skiers can take the Nord trail, an international competition course beneath the cable car, straight back to town.

A bit farther up the valley, accessed from two pairs of chairlifts out of Hinterglemm, is the Zwölferkogel, with medium-steep to quite steep runs back to town. By dropping off the Zwölfer's back, skiers reach the high, sunny and gentler slopes of the Seekar, the region's highest peak. Experts prefer the ungroomed ski route back down to Fassl, where they can cross the road to the lifts on the Spieleckkogel and excellent skiing terrain.

Most of the skiing on this side of the valley is of the novice to intermediate variety—and there's a lot of it. It is possible to cruise long runs from each summit to the base of the lifts of the adjacent mountain. The Spieleck complex, for instance, connects with the Reiterkogel/Hasenauer Köpfl network. This sector is also accessible directly from Hinterglemm by chairlift. From the Reiterkogel, skiers take a medium-challenging *piste* down to the Bernkogel summit. Its runs are on the gentle side, and its main lift is a triple chair rising from Saalbach. There is even a summit-to-base ungroomed ski route marked for intermediates. The next connection is to the Kohlmaiskopf/Bründlkopf system, which again provides skiing on the easy side.

Still farther down the valley is the Wildenkarkogel, more novice to intermediate *pistes* and a gondola ride from the map pinpoint called Vorderglemm. The Wildenkarkogel also accesses the lifts and runs of Leogang. Across the valley from the Wildenkarkogel gondola is a lift part way up the Jausernalm. Skiers descending from higher points are coming down from the Schattberg. The circuit has been completed.

APRÈS-SKI

Pulsating discos, crowded après-ski bars and one or two quiet cafés make for a lively atmosphere and an exciting time, day and night, without

the raucousness of a cheap'n'cheerful resort. Both villages have a lot to offer.

The Alpenhotel in Saalbach is almost a village in itself, with a quiet lounge overlooking the indoor pool, a merry bar, the rustic Kuhstall tavern featuring traditional music and the Arena, a full-scale nightclub with live band. Its restaurant is one of the best in town. There are plenty of other stylish cafés in town and some pleasant little bars.

OTHER ACTIVITIES

Many of the larger hotels have indoor pools. There are 12 mi. (20 km.) of cross-country skiing along the river bank in Saalbach and farther up the valley from Hinterglemm, which has an ice rink next to the *Tennishalle*. The Saalbach sports center has an indoor pool, tennis courts and bowling alley. Other activities include sleigh rides, tobogganing, and walking along 22 mi. (35 km.) of cleared paths.

The post bus runs to the head of the valley and on to Zell am See, a sizable ski resort in its own right and on the rail line from Innsbruck to Salzburg. This makes either close enough for shopping, sightseeing or just strolling through the ancient city centers.

ST. ANTON/ST. CHRISTOPH

Access: *Nearest airports:* Zurich (3½ hrs.); Innsbruck (1½ hrs.). *By road:* A14 Autobahn to Bludenz, then east through the Arlberg Tunnel. *By rail:* station in St. Anton.

Tourist Office: Fremdenverkehrs-verband, 6580 St. Anton am Arlberg, Austria. Tel. (05446) 22 69 0

Altitude: 4,278 ft. (1,304 m.).
Top: 8,695 ft. (2,650 m.)

Language: German

Runs: 124 mi. (200 km.) in Arlberg region

Lifts: 42 (77 in Arlberg region)

Ski areas: Gampen-Kapall, Galzig, Valluga, Rendl

Ski schools: Schischule Arlberg, Schischule Franz Klimmer

Linked resort: Stuben

Season: late November to late April

Kindergarten: *Non-ski:* 3–14 years. *With ski:* 5–14 years

Prices: *Lift pass:* 6 days 1,050–1,620 S (children 810–920 S). *Ski school:* Group 1,150 S for 6 days; private 1,700 S for 4 hours.

RATINGS

Skiing Conditions	10
Snow Conditions	8
For Beginners	4
For Intermediates	8
For Advanced Skiers	10
For Children	4
Après-Ski	9
Other Sports	6
Value for Money	6

THE RESORT

When hard-core skiers think Austria, St. Anton is the first resort that comes to mind. Since Hannes Schneider first gave lessons in 1907, the resort has been virtually synonymous with Austrian skiing. St. Anton has a vast lift and *piste* system, and boasts dizzying slopes, tre-

mendous off-*piste* skiing, a great array of accommodations (many recently renovated) and a vibrant après-ski scene populated by a largely young, international cast. The cosmopolitan cacophony of American, Japanese and Swedish voices is a testament to its worldwide appeal.

St. Christoph, atop the Arlberg Pass, with just a few hotels (notably the Hospiz), is a pristine and unique ski destination. In addition, such suburbs as St. Jakob and Nasserein offer budget lodging and proximity to St. Anton's splendor.

THE SKIING

Four main ski areas (three of them interlinked), an easy, direct connection on skis with Stuben, plus the proximity of Lech and Zürs, make St. Anton one of the truly great Alpine centers.

St. Anton's skiing takes place on two sides. South of town, linked by shuttle bus and accessed by gondola, is the Rendl, a broad, recently developed mountain with wide, mostly intermediate slopes. Two chairlifts were added in 1988, stretching the skiing to a 8,678-ft.

(2,645-m.) peak on the Riffel massif.

The skiing for which St. Anton is world renowned takes place on three interlinked areas north of town. The main access lifts start close to each other and fan out to different complexes above. The Kandaharbahn, a cog railway, and a series of parallel chairs climb to the Kapall summit, 7,631 ft. (2,326 m.), offering wide, open intermediate skiing. The Galzig cable car travels westward.

From the Galzig plateau, skiers funnel down to St. Christoph or continue up to the fabled Valluga, among the most challenging terrain not only of the Arlberg region but in all the Austrian Alps. The Vallugabahn from the Galzig or the newer Schindlergrat high-speed chair spill skiers onto the lower Valluga runs—sometimes in numbers too great for comfort. Access to the top of the Vallugagrat, 8,695 ft. (2,650 m.), is still limited by an old, low-capacity cable car. Just as well, for overloading the radical chutes of this awesome peak would be asking for trouble.

St. Anton is also well suited to speed-seeking intermediates who love to cruise the fast, groomed runs, of which there are dozens. One of the best is the freeway-like route from the Ulmerhütte to Rauz (and with a walk across the road, on to Stuben).

For the truly adventurous, strictly with a guide, it is possible to ski the "missing link" of the Arlberg region

from the Valluga peak down to Zürs, a half-day excursion which starts with the concentrated effort of edging along a ridge to start the descent down an icy wall, culminating in a narrow, rocky gully. Once the initial terrors are over, the pleasure is to be in high-altitude pastures, too high for animal tracks, before zipping into jet-set Zürs. Another, more expensive, treat is to go with a guide by helicopter, alighting on a cliff-top ledge beyond the Darmstädter Hütte, for another unbroken off-*piste* run back down.

If all this sounds too daunting to novices, it is true that St. Anton is a serious skier's town. Now that the ski school, whose reputation had been dented by accusations of arro-gance and over-sized classes, has renewed its traditional zeal in setting the highest standards, St. Anton is a good place to learn or, more particularly, improve. Children from 5 years can enroll in day-long classes which include games and lunch in the middle of the day and a race every Friday.

St. Anton being high on most skiers' list of resorts to visit, it is inevitable that there can be long lines for the main lifts each morning. Two ways of avoiding this congestion are to start the day on the less-crowded Rendl slopes or approach the main lift system from St. Christoph, ten minutes away by bus. The Vallugagrat cable car operates a reservation system, usually allowing time for a quick ski on the Osthang run prior to taking one's place.

For a resort of its size, there are few mountain restaurants. The self-service cafés at Gampen, Galzig and Rendl are all large and efficiently run, the last calling itself "Rendl Beach" for its large terrace, which takes on a Riviera-like atmosphere on sunny days. Many people ski back to St. Anton, St. Christoph or Stuben for lunch.

The Arlberg lift pass covers St. Anton and St. Christoph, plus Stuben, Lech, Zug and Zürs.

APRÈS-SKI

Après-ski starts early. One popular spot is the railway station bar where ski-bums from around the world congregate to discuss job prospects and swap tales of derring-do. Another is the Krazy Känguruh, scene of much Scandinavian merrymaking during "Happy Hour" between 3–4 p.m. in a noisy, verging on riotous, atmosphere. Be careful when skiing home late in the afternoon in this vicinity. While most young Swedes are good skiers, their equilibrium is quickly upset by a shot of *Schnaps* too many.

The famous tea dances in the Hotel Post aren't as sedate as they sound and, as the lifts close, the whole of St. Anton becomes a huge theater, every bar crowded with skiers chewing over the day's activities, forking into pastries, and sipping hot chocolate, *Glühwein* or beer.

Later on, most of the large hotels have discos or dancing to live bands. The Stänton in the Sporthotel is very popular with British visitors. There are restaurants to suit all pocketbooks. For a special dinner, take a taxi to St. Christoph and dine at the Hospiz, one of the great Alpine hotels.

OTHER ACTIVITIES

The sports center near the middle of town has indoor tennis and squash courts. Traditional winter pursuits such as skating, curling, tobogganing at the Rodelhütte, and sleigh rides are all available, as are swimming and bowling. There are 12 mi. (20 km.) of cleared walks and 25 mi. (40 km.) of cross-country skiing on the Rendl side of town, through the trees of the Ferwall Valley.

In town, there is a local history and ski museum, but the best sight of all is from the top of the Valluga cable car—mountains as far as the eye can see.

SCHLADMING

Access: *Nearest airports:* Salzburg (1½ hrs.); Munich (3 hrs.). *By road:* A10 Autobahn, exit Radstadt. *By rail:* station in Schladming.

Tourist Office: Verkehrsverein, 8970 Schladming, Austria. Tel. (03687) 22 2 68-0

Altitude: 2,444 ft. (745 m.). *Top:* 6,611 ft. (2,015 m.)

Language: German

Runs: 87 mi. (140 km.)

Lifts: 79

Ski areas: Planai, Hochwurzen, Reiteralm, Hauser Kaibling, Fageralm

Ski school: Schischule Keinprecht/Kahr-Schladming

Linked resorts: None

Season: Mid-November to late April.

Kindergarten: *Non-ski:* none. *With ski:* from 4 years

Prices: *Lift pass:* 6 days Dachstein-Tauern area 1,260–1,365 S (children 800–860 S). *Ski school:* Group 930 S for 5 days; private 1,450 S per day.

RATINGS

Skiing Conditions	6
Snow Conditions	5
For Beginners	5
For Intermediates	6
For Advanced Skiers	5
For Children	4
Après-Ski	7
Other Sports	6
Value for Money	8

THE RESORT

A bustling town which, with its neighbor Haus im Ennstal, hosted the 1982 World Alpine Championships, Schladming is the largest and best-known resort in Styria *(Steiermark)*. The town is dominated by the Protestant and Catholic churches

which stand defiantly against each other, producing a distinctive skyline. The old market center is pleasant and has a good range of shops. At night, Schladming is lively. It is an excellent choice for intermediate skiers who like to be fully occupied, get value for money and explore the other resorts on the Dachstein-Tauern lift pass.

THE SKIING

Several mid-level ski mountains along the south wall of the Enn Valley line up like soldiers. They have relatively low elevations, even at the summits, meaning that little of the terrain is above the tree line.

Only the fact that the runs mostly face north prevents frequent melt-offs.

It is technically feasible to connect some of these ski areas into one true ski circus (and some links are actually on the drawing board), but so far, the demand isn't there. From east to west, the five closest to Schladming, and skiable on the Dachstein-Tauern lift pass, are the Hauser Kaibling, accessible from Haus, the Planai, reachable from Schladming, Hochwurzen with access from Schladming or Rohrmoss, the Reiteralm above Pichl, and the Fageralm at Forstau.

The World Championship men's downhill course on the Planai is said

to be the fastest on the international circuit. When not groomed for racing, the top is easily negotiated by any competent skier, but the final section is treacherous, mogul-infested and steep. Otherwise, there is little really challenging on-*piste* skiing. Nearly all the marked trails are well maintained, with some lovely tree-lined runs for beginners. Hochwurzen is a gently sloped mountain with ample novice and intermediate terrain.

Better skiers try out the other areas available on the regional lift pass. Reiteralm, 6,103 ft. (1,860 m.), has wide, swooping *pistes*, mostly through the trees, marvelous views from the top and friendly mountain

restaurants. The Hauser Kaibling, 6,611 ft. (2,015 m.), has a range of runs, including some steep ones on top, and hosted the women's events in 1982. Both are reached by the local bus.

Having a car makes it easy to use the Top-Tauern-Skischeck, which includes the resorts in the immediate vicinity of Schladming, plus over a dozen or so in the states of Styria and Salzburg.

APRÈS-SKI

Nightlife in Schladming is good. There are fairly formal places at hotels like the Alte Post, where the options range from grand to folksy. More casual après-ski is found at jolly bars like the Talbachschenke, where multilingual sing-alongs are great fun in the cavernous tavern which also serves good, basic meals. There are also plenty of ordinary bars and several places with dancing.

OTHER ACTIVITIES

There is an excellent toboggan course on the Hauser Kaibling, including moonlight runs with *Glühwein* parties. The locals put into practice the philosophy of being close to nature by providing excellent networks of cross-country trails—15½ mi. (25 km.), and the lovely touring trails on the Dachstein plateau are across the valley. Curling and skating, swimming, tennis, squash and bowling are all available. There are 30 mi. (50 km.) of winter footpaths, sleigh rides and nature excursions to observe the local wildlife.

Graz, historic capital of Styria, is an easy day trip by car or train. A visit to Salzburg provides an eye-opening insight into one of Europe's loveliest cities.

SCHRUNS/MONTAFON

Access: *Nearest airport:* Zurich (2 hrs.). *By road:* A14 Autobahn to Bludenz. *By rail:* station in Schruns.

Tourist Office: Verkehrsverband Montafon, 6780 Schruns/Montafon, Austria. Tel. (05556) 22 53

Altitude: 2,297 ft. (700 m.).
Top: 7,828 ft. (2,386 m.)

Language: German

Runs: 128 mi. (206 km.) in Montafon Valley

Lifts: 73 in Montafon Valley

Ski areas: Hochjoch, Zamang, Silvretta Nova, Scharfberg, Golm

Ski schools: Schischule Schruns, plus seven others in Montafon

Linked resorts: None

Season: Mid-December to end April

Kindergarten: *Non-ski:* from 3 years. *With ski:* from 3 years

Prices: *Lift pass:* 6 days Montafon Valley 1,245–1,445 S (children 785–890 S). *Ski school:* Group 1,100 S for 5 days; private 400 S per hour.

RATINGS

Skiing Conditions	6
Snow Conditions	6
For Beginners	6
For Intermediates	7
For Advanced Skiers	5
For Children	6
Après-Ski	7
Other Sports	7
Value for Money	8

THE RESORTS

The Montafon ("Valley in the Mountains") has 12 villages with accommodations and five ski areas, only one of them good-sized, but when combined, they amount to a worthy ski region. Judicious use of the efficient post bus service means that it is possible to take full advantage of the lift pass and other amenities, although a car gives more flexibility.

Each of the five villages is different, and among them, they satisfy a variety of requirements. Gargellen, with a population of just 100, three four-star hotels and an international clientele, is the best choice for an elegant holiday. Caschurn and St. Gallenkirch share the Silvretta Nova, which has the biggest lift system and variety of runs for good skiers. Schruns is the liveliest, with good amenities, but is less atmospheric and has close-in ski terrain that is limited compared with the size of the town. Tschagguns, midway between Schruns and Gargellen in terms of style, was one of the Vorarlberg's original resorts and has most of its accommodations in *Gasthöfe* and private homes.

Living hard by the border with the Swiss canton of Graubünden, the Montafoners speak a local dialect tinged with traces of the old Romansch language. In fact, the first settlers arrived from Switzerland early in the 15th century and built a chapel in Gargellen in 1411. St. Gallenkirch's church was founded in 1254 by Celtic monks who established Christianity in the region. Pastoral farming and iron works were the Montafon's early industries, but today tourism is the lifeblood, and Montafon wood inlay is a thriving old craft.

It says a lot for the skiing and quality of accommodations in the Montafon that one of the biggest groups of visitors are the discerning Swiss, who enjoy lower prices than at home without stinting on quality.

THE SKIING

The Montafon-wide lift pass encourages visitors to sample all the ski areas—and most people do so. Gargellen has the smallest and easiest skiing terrain, but also offers splendid off-*piste* and touring opportunities, notably over the Swiss border to Klosters and back. Locals are keen to point out that the Prince of Wales has done it. Exposed at the top, 7,054 ft. (2,150 m.), and wooded lower down, the *piste* skiing is undemanding but pretty. It ends at the door of the Hotel Madrisa, a sophisticated pit stop at the end of the day.

St. Gallenkirch and Gaschurn have gondolas that share a top station and the most extensive and best skiing in the Montafon. St. Gallenkirch's skiing is below the Valiseraspitze, and Gaschurn is on the Silvretta Nova. Their lift systems meet on the Alpe Nova. Just about every type of skiing except long, difficult trails is found, but the off-*piste* sections are superb. A cable car from near the center of Schruns and one from just outside town serve the Hochjoch, a small area with easy to intermediate skiing. Tschagguns, host to several women's World Cup races, is north-facing and has a two-stage funicular railway plus a double chair and a high-speed quad to above the tree line. Staggering views and fast on-

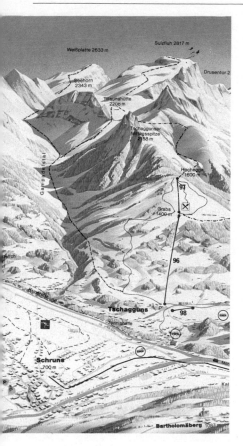

piste skiing are the name of the game here. The Montafon also offers para-skiing, heli-skiing beyond Parthenen at Bielerhöhe and ski-school tours to Klosters and Galtür.

A beautiful new mountain restaurant complex has been opened on the Silvretta Nova, with seven separate restaurants and a self-service cafeteria.

APRÈS-SKI

Each of the resorts has bars for a drink at the end of the day, but their nightlife in general does not appeal to a wild crowd. The high spots include the Chaverna disco in the Hotel Madrisa in Gargellen. The better hotels frequently have live music, with the occasional jazz combo as a supplement to the usual fare of standard international or Austrian regional music.

Schruns has a couple of lovely old coffee houses and several good hotel restaurants. The Altmontafon in Gaschurn specializes in Vorarlberg fruit and fish, and game dinners at the Heimspitze draw an eager crowd of diners from as far away as Bludenz.

OTHER ACTIVITIES

Schruns, Tschagguns and Gaschurn each have indoor tennis courts—the first two share artificial rinks for skating and curling, and there is a natural one in Gaschurn. The only swimming pool open to the public is in the Hotel Löwen (Schruns) and 13 others have pools for their guests, most with the usual health facilities such as sauna and massage. Ten hotels have bowling, and the Sporthotel Grandau in St. Gallenkirch features a squash court.

The best of the tobogganing is at Tschagguns—a 1½-mi. (3-km.) floodlit run between Latschau and Vandans, and the operators of the run from the Hotel Botle at Ziegerberg even issue helmets with lamps for evening descents.

The 68 mi. (110 km.) of cross-country Loipen provide treats such as the 9-mi. (15-km.) circuit on the frozen Silvretta lake at 6,562 ft. (2,000 m.) and the panoramic 7-mi. (11-km.) trail above Kristberg, beyond Silbertal.

The railway station in Schruns connects with Bludenz and Zurich, St. Anton and Innsbruck. By car, Feldkirch, Bregenz (where there is a casino), Liechtenstein, St. Anton, Lech and such Swiss resorts as Davos and Lenzerheide are easily accessible.

SEEFELD

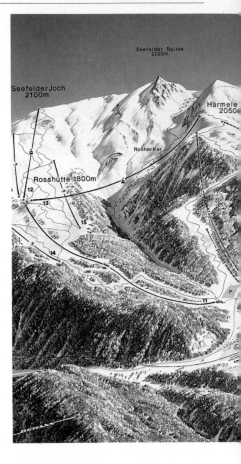

Access: *Nearest airports:* Innsbruck (½ hr.); Munich (1½ hrs.). *By road:* A12 Autobahn, exit Zirl-Ost. *By rail:* station in Seefeld.

Tourist Office: Fremdenverkehrs-verband, 6100 Seefeld, Austria. Tel. (05212) 23 13

Altitude: 3,937 ft. (1,200 m.). *Top:* 6,890 ft. (2,100 m.)

Language: German

Runs: 15½ mi. (25 km.)

Lifts: 20

Ski areas: Rosshütte, Gschwandt-kopf, Geigenbühel

Ski school: Schischule Seefeld

Linked resort: Reith

Season: December to late March

Kindergarten: *Non-ski:* from 4 years. *With ski:* from 4 years

Prices: *Lift pass:* 6 days 1,150–1,360 S (children 840–980 S). *Ski school:* Group 950 S for 6 days; private 300 S per hour.

RATINGS

Skiing Conditions	5
Snow Conditions	6
For Beginners	7
For Intermediates	5
For Advanced Skiers	3
For Children	6
Après-Ski	7
Other Sports	8
Value for Money	6

THE RESORT

The usual cliché is that Seefeld, set on a sunny plateau near Innsbruck, is a world-renowned cross-country center with a token amount of down-hill skiing. This does the resort an injustice, for Seefeld is one of the best places in Europe for an all-round winter sports vacation, especially for skiers who have turned from Alpine to cross-country and who value their creature comforts, who include beginners and children in their party, or who enjoy the après-ski and other sports facilities as much as skiing itself. German and Dutch guests strap both Alpine and

Nordic skis to their cars, pack swimsuits and walking boots to take full advantage of Seefeld's multifarious facilities, and take a jacket and tie or smart dress for eating in the better restaurants and visiting the casino.

A large, efficiently run village, Seefeld has dozens of hotels with sauna and other health facilities, public and private swimming pools, and a pedestrian zone with antique, clothing and souvenir shops. It is quite pricey. Nightlife is as sedate or lively (and late) as desired.

Seefeld is genuinely a resort for all tastes, with a long-standing reputation as a place to learn and develop ski technique. It is best known as the center for Nordic events at the 1964 and 1976 Olympics and it hosted the World Nordic Championships in 1985.

THE SKIING

There are three separate areas connected by a free bus service. Beginners start at the Geigenbühel slopes by the village center and quickly graduate to the Gschwandtkopf, with terrain for fast-learning beginners to moderate intermediates, and finally the Rosshütte.

The Gschwandtkopf, with a 984-ft. (300-m.) vertical, is as wide, sunny and altogether manageable a novice playground as one could wish. New skiers can remain on the wide, white swatch on the front of the mountain all day or can ski off the back to Seewaldalm on one side or Reith on the other.

More experienced skiers prefer the Härmelekopf/Seefelder Joch complex on the other side of town. A funicular railway climbs to the Rosshütte, 5,906 ft. (1,800 m.), the crossroads of most of the ski terrain. In a huge bowl around and above this mid-mountain restaurant are a number of easy to medium *pistes*. A cable car ferries better skiers to the Härmelekopf, 6,726 ft. (2,050 m.), with the one medium-steep groomed run or the more challenging ungroomed Reither Kar route back to the base. Experts may wish to climb another 500 vertical ft. (152 m.) around the back of the Härmelekopf's summit to ski the upper section of the Reither Kar, a popular option for guided groups of expert skiers. Currently, these slopes are never crowded because of the cable car's modest 25-person capacity, but that is slated to change since the Härmelekopf is targeted for Seefeld's next round of expansion, with two new lifts from the base.

The extremely small, modest and easy slopes of nearby Leutasch and Mösern are also skiable on the Seefeld lift pass.

APRÈS-SKI

Tea dances to the accompaniment of live bands in the hotels Kaltschmid (which claims to have the largest bar in Austria), Klosterbräu, Tyrol and igloo-shaped Siglu kick off the evening's entertainment in rollicking style.

The hotels have dancing to live bands after dinner, as do discos at the Post and Drop In, which are less expensive and cater to the younger crowd. The Britannia, which is much as you would expect, serves fish and chips. There is Tyrolean music with yodeling duets or a zither player in the Bräukeller in the Hotel Klosterbräu.

The shops in the pedestrian zone offer a higher standard of antiques and local crafts than is usually found in ski resorts. Seefeld's casino provides 200 Schillings of gambling chips in return for the 170-Schillings entry fee (jacket, tie and passport required).

Organized events such as *fondue* evenings and games nights are on the program. Seefeld sometimes seems awash with horse-drawn sleighs, not surprisingly, as the gently rolling surrounding countryside lends itself to leisurely exploration by day or night.

OTHER ACTIVITIES

The big activity in Seefeld is cross-country skiing on 124 mi. (200 km.) of mechanically prepared trails, with the full range between easy for beginners to tough for Olympians, all starting from the town's Sports and Congress Centre. Ample equipment-rental facilities and a well-respected ski school start new touring skiers off with the right stride.

Bowling, curling, skating, tennis, swimming and tobogganing are ingredients in Seefeld's mix of non-skiing activities.

As Seefeld is only 10 minutes from the Inn Valley, there is limitless opportunity for exploring the surrounding region by road—rental cars are available in the village. Seefeld is also on the railway line between Innsbruck and Garmisch-Partenkirchen in Bavaria, from which connections can be made to Munich.

SÖLDEN

Access: *Nearest airports:* Innsbruck (1 hr.); Munich (4 hrs.). *By road:* A14 Autobahn to Imst, then via Ötz. *By rail:* to Ötztal or Innsbruck, then by bus.

Tourist Office: Fremdenverkehrsverband Ötztal-Arena, 6450 Sölden, Austria. Tel. (05254) 22 12-3

Altitude: 4,518 ft. (1,377 m.)
Top: 10,033 ft. (3,058 m.)

Language: German

Runs: 63 mi. (101 km.)

Lifts: 23, plus 10 on glacier

Ski areas: Hochsölden, Gaislachkogl

Ski school: Schischule Sölden-Hochsölden

Linked resorts: None

Season: Mid-December to May, plus summer skiing

Kindergarten: *Non-ski:* 3–8 years. *With ski:* 3–8 years

Prices: *Lift pass:* 6 days 1,390–1,590 S (children 950 S). *Ski school:* Group 1,070 S for 6 days; private 350 S per day.

RATINGS

Skiing Conditions	7
Snow Conditions	8
For Beginners	4
For Intermediates	7
For Advanced Skiers	6
For Children	4
Après-Ski	7
Other Sports	6
Value for Money	7

THE RESORT

With the Gaislachkogl, 10,033 ft. (3,058 m.), flanked by two glaciers, Sölden is a year-round skiing center. If the town's first appearance is a little less than enchanting, its hotels, après-ski bars and nightclubs quickly persuade visitors that, in ad-

dition to being one of Austria's better skiing areas, Sölden is also one of the country's better all-round resorts. Hochsölden is perched above the Ötztal valley and consists of half-a-dozen ski-in, ski-out hotels and a couple of shops. It is the choice of serious skiers who would be content to enjoy a low-key atmosphere in the evening. But in fact Sölden is far from low-key and offers plenty of evening diversion. The clientele is international, and a high standard of accommodations and restaurants reflects the fact that most visitors are independent rather than package travelers.

The Ötztal runs from near Imst in

the Inn valley and peters out at Obergurgl (20 minutes' drive away from Sölden), for which a separate lift pass is required. Vent, a tiny ski and mountaineering village tucked in beneath the Wildspitze, 12,382 ft. (3,774 m.), also issues a separate pass.

THE SKIING

The skiing is in two sections which meet in the Rettenbach valley. The northern sector, with Hochsölden perched on one side of the terrain, offers long easy-to-intermediate runs from the Haimbachjoch, at 8,947 ft. (2,727 m.), and Rotkogl-hütte. Routes back to the valley can be crowded at the end of the day and are at their best during the first couple of hours in the morning when most other skiers are concentrating on the higher slopes. There is a large self-service restaurant, with waitress service upstairs, near the middle station, but the steamy Eugen's Obstlerhütte below Hochsölden has more *Gemütlichkeit* appeal.

The southern sector peaks on the small summit of the Gaislach-kogl, served by Austria's highest lift. The terrain is steeper than in the other complex and is reached by a new 24-person gondola. It has the exciting long, high-intermediate trail from the Gaislachkogl restaurant all the way to the valley, plus a sprinkling of expert runs, notably the steep Wilde Abfahrt ski route which starts from the same point.

Between the northern and southern sections is a summer toll road to the glaciers. The Rettenbach and Tiefenbach glaciers are on two sides of a steep ridge comprising Austria's largest glacier area for summer skiing.

Sölden's ski school has been the regular winner of the Austrian instructors' championships and employs a high-season staff of 200 (80% of them English-speaking).

APRÈS-SKI

In addition to the hotels and a couple of noisy but friendly outdoor bars in the main street, which quite literally do a roaring trade in the late afternoon, elegant cafés such as the Ca-

rola are the scene of quiet sipping of hot chocolate and civilized conversation. The evening atmosphere is carefree, whether in bars, discos or several nightclubs with live bands.

OTHER ACTIVITIES

The sports center features an indoor swimming pool (with a separate children's section), tennis courts, two large saunas, five solarium rooms, massage, table tennis, bowling and a rifle range.

There is limited cross-country skiing, but a popular evening diversion is to go by taxi to Zwieselstein for a bonfire party before taking the cross-country trail back again. Curling and skating on a natural rink are available.

Excursion possibilities are limited without a car, although the Ötztaler bus service runs to as far away as Innsbruck. Otherwise, the local buses run to Obergurgl, a pretty village with several restaurants with terraces overlooking the slopes.

79

SÖLL

Access: *Nearest airport:* Munich (1½ hrs.). *By road:* A12 Autobahn, exit Wörgl-Ost. *By rail:* to Kufstein, then by bus.

Tourist Office: Fremdenverkehrs-verband, 6306 Söll, Austria. Tel. (05333) 52 16

Altitude: 2,307 ft. (703 m.). *Top:* 6,000 ft. (1,829 m.)

Language: German

Runs: 22 mi. (35 km.); 130 mi. (210 km.) in Wilder Kaiser-Brixental

Lifts: 13 (86 in Wilder Kaiser-Brixental)

Ski area: Hohe Salve

Ski school: Schischule Söll Embacher

Linked resorts: Scheffau, Ellmau, Going, Itter, Hopfgarten, Brixen

Season: December to April

Kindergarten: *Non-ski:* none. *With ski:* 5–14 years

Prices: *Lift pass:* 6 days 1,040 S (children 580 S), Skigrossraum Wilder Kaiser-Brixental 1,180 S (children 665 S). *Ski school:* Group 950 S for 6 days; private 230 S per hour.

RATINGS

Skiing Conditions	7
Snow Conditions	6
For Beginners	5
For Intermediates	9
For Advanced Skiers	5
For Children	6
Après-Ski	7
Other Sports	6
Value for Money	8

THE RESORT

Söll is instant Tyrol. Pleasing to the eye, lively and welcoming, its attractiveness and competitive prices make it a favorite destination for young Britons seeking non-stop action, day and night. The village attracts a large number of young visitors from the singles fraternity. Value for money is Söll's stock in trade. If you are looking for a little more sophistication, choose one of Söll's neighbors, such as Scheffau or Ellmau which, along with Going, Itter, Hopfgarten and Brixen, share the Skigrossraum Wilder Kaiser-Brixental—the Tyrol's massive interlinked skiing area immediately to the west of Kitzbühel.

There are some top-quality hotels in Söll, too, notably the 13th-century Gasthof Post and its modern cousin next door, the Hotel Post, oases of civilized charm amid the merry bustle all around.

THE SKIING

Söll is a particular favorite for beginners or improving intermediates—the beginner slopes at the base do not require a lift pass. A sturdy intermediate can handle much of Söll's skiing and continue zig-zagging from mountain to mountain and town to town—a ski circus for almost all levels of ability. There are more than enough on-*piste* opportunities for good skiers.

Pretty Westendorf, whose lifts do not connect with the rest of the system, is included on the regional pass and is well worth a day's excursion (ski to Brixen and take the free bus). The pleasure for intermediates is to set off each day choosing Brixen or Hopfgarten as destinations via the Hohe Salve, 6,000 ft. (1,829 m.), where there is a little chapel, good self-service restaurant and, on sunny days, top-of-the-world views over the entire region including Westendorf below and Kitzbühel in the distance. There is a choice of descents to Itter, Scheffau, Ellmau and Going, all of which can also be reached by post bus or taxi.

There are two unavoidable bottlenecks around the Skigrossraum's "spaghetti junction" of lifts and pistes, but the whole area is an intermediate's dream. (A tip, if you want to get to Scheffau or Ellmau quickly, is to branch off to the Innerkert cable car rather than continuing up and over the Hohe Salve.) For fast skiing, there are some excellent routes. The mid-level run down to the bottom of Itter's new triple chair is usually uncrowded and a good intermediate feels like a champion downhill racer.

APRÈS-SKI

Every night is party night in Söll. There are surprisingly few bars for a resort with such an ebullient repu-

81

tation, but those which exist are boisterous and sometimes even rowdy. The traditional meeting place at the end of the day is the Post's ancient, cavernous tavern bar, while the Whiskymühle and the Hotel Tyrol's Dorfstadl discos throb on until the last customers flop into the streets. Tyrolean evenings feature *Lederhosen,* wood chopping, thigh slapping and all the attendant highjinks. *Fondue* nights and family evenings which include bowling are popular with groups.

OTHER ACTIVITIES

The illuminated toboggan run from Hochsöll to the base of the lift system is popular, as is the swimming pool. There is a natural ice rink, and sleigh rides around the village are possible.

The main excursions are to Berchtesgaden and Salzburg, the wildlife park at Aurach, Kufstein (with a stop at the Riedl glass factory), Innsbruck and Vipiteno (over the Italian border via the Brenner Pass).

ZELL AM SEE/KAPRUN

Access: *Nearest airports:* Salzburg (1 hr.); Munich (2½ hrs.). *By road:* A8 Autobahn, exit Siegsdorf. *By rail:* station in Zell am See, bus to Kaprun.

Tourist Office: Kurverwaltung, 5700 Zell am See, Austria. Tel. (06542) 26 00

Altitude: 2,460 ft. (750 m.) *Top:* 9,938 ft. (3,029 m.)

Language: German

Runs: 81 mi. (130 km.)

Lifts: 52

Ski areas: Maiskogel, Kitzsteinhorn, Schmittenhöhe, Zeller Berg, Sonnkogel, Areit, Sonnenalm

Ski schools: Schischule Kaprun, Schischule Zell am See, Schischule Zell am See/Schüttdorf, Schischule Stöphasius

Linked resort: Schüttdorf

Season: December to April; summer skiing

Kindergarten: *Non-ski:* from 3 years. *With ski:* from 4 years

Prices: *Lift pass:* 6 days 1,450 S (children 940 S). *Ski school:* Group 380 S per day; private 380 S per hour.

RATINGS

Skiing Conditions	7
Snow Conditions	7
For Beginners	5
For Intermediates	8
For Advanced Skiers	4
For Children	5
Après-Ski	6
Other Sports	7
Value for Money	6

THE RESORTS

These two Salzburg towns style themselves, rather grandly, as the Europa Sport Region. In fact, each is an excellent resort with different features, and they share a lift pass which encompasses the full gamut of skiing. Zell am See is a bustling little town and a popular summer destination, especially for water sports enthusiasts. Kaprun, a pretty, rambling village, is much quieter and in summertime attracts national teams and vacationers for skiing on the Kitzsteinhorn Glacier.

There is a full range of hotels, from Zell am See's renovated Grand Hotel on the lake (large bedroom suites, top-class service and indoor pool with adjacent health facilities) to Kaprun's Gasthof Mühle, whose kitchen specializes in regional dishes.

THE SKIING

Zell am See, with two World Cup downhill courses and stunning views over the frozen lake below, and Kaprun, a year-round ski area with guaranteed snow every day of the year on the glacier, combine to provide long tree-lined *pistes*, wide, open bowls, narrow gullies and gentle beginner slopes.

The region's claim of guaranteed snow means that while it is comforting to know that there will be skiing of some sort in even the worst winters, this is offset by the danger that if conditions are poor in nearby low-lying centers, everyone will flock to Kaprun with resultant overcrowding.

The two resorts just about provide the full range of on-*piste* skiing. The glacial terrain of Kaprun's upper area contrasts with Zell am See's tree-clad downhill trails. Zell am See has three cable cars serving the crescent-shaped Schmittenhöhe above town, and there is a new lift from Schüttdorf. In all, there is plenty of easy cruising, some diverting mogul fields and several long runs.

At Kaprun, a variety of lifts around the village lead to very pleasant easy slopes—low-lying, they may be closed in early and late season. The Kitzsteinhorn Gletscherbahn funicular railway departs from outside the village and rises through the mountain to the Alpincenter from which surface lifts and chairs disperse skiers around the glacier.

There is a cable car to the region's highest point. The open area below is ideal for perfecting technique or bombing furiously all day. In summer, it is a center for national teams' training camps, as well as for recreational skiers who relish the prospect of skiing under a deep, deep blue sky. The Kitzsteinhorn is also an excellent place for beginners to make their first runs in a clement climate—so different from icy *pistes* in February.

APRÈS-SKI

Kaprun is a dispersed village, without true *Gemütlichkeit* but with a certain charm. Since it lacks a real center, bar-hopping is difficult. The compensation is that it is friendly, and the nightspots are merry and informal. Several restaurants feature the regional specialty of meat and vegetables cooked in a huge frying pan over an open fire. Zell am See is much more lively, and if at first sight it seems far removed from the old-fashioned ski *Dorf,* the tradi-

tional pursuits such as tobogganing, sleigh rides, drinking in *Weinstuben* to the accompaniment of zither and accordion, Tyrolean evenings and tea dances are all available. A good number of informal bars and discos, reasonably priced, keep the action level high. Restaurants suit every pocketbook. There is plenty of shopping, and some of the hotels have top-rate health facilities.

OTHER ACTIVITIES

The Europa Sport Region has enormous possibilities for cross-country skiing: around Zell am See, with the frozen lake as the constant focal point. Kaprun hosts a marathon, which is an integral part of the annual cross-country skiing calendar. Skating, walking and ice-surfing on the lake are popular, and the leisure center at Kaprun is especially well appointed. Ice hockey and skating competitions are absorbing spectator sports. Indoor tennis, squash, rifle shooting, swimming and bowling are available, and when it is cold enough, there is curling. Horseback riding in an indoor ring, sleigh rides and tobogganing add to the general fun. There are a number of good shops.

ZÜRS

Access: *Nearest airports:* Innsbruck (1½ hrs.); Zurich (2½ hrs.). *By road:* A 14 Autobahn to Bludenz, then over Flexenpass. *By rail:* to Langen, then by bus.

Tourist Office: Fremdenverkehrs-amt, 6763 Zürs am Arlberg, Austria. Tel. (05583) 22 45

Altitude: 5,676 ft. (1,730 m.). *Top:* 8,930 ft. (2,722 m.)

Language: German

Runs: 68 mi. (110 km.) with Lech; 124 mi. (200 km.) on Arlberg pass

Lifts: 34 (77 in Arlberg region)

Ski areas: Trittkopf, Zürsersee, Muggengrat, Hexenboden

Ski school: Schischule Zürs

Linked resort: Lech

Season: Late November to late April

Kindergarten: *Non-ski:* 3–10 years. *With ski:* 3–12 years

Prices: *Lift pass:* 6 days Arlberg pass 1,420–1,620 S (children 810–920 S). *Ski school:* Group 1,280 S for 6 days; private 1,700 S per day.

RATINGS

Skiing Conditions	8
Snow Conditions	7
For Beginners	5
For Intermediates	8
For Advanced Skiers	8
For Children	6
Après-Ski	6
Other Sports	5
Value for Money	5

THE RESORT

Zürs is posh. Zürs attracts Europe's *glitterati.* Zürs is a bit precious. Zürs is also an excellent ski resort, 3 mi. (5 km.) from Lech and within a short drive or bus ride of St. Christoph, St. Anton and Stuben, all of them included on the Arlberg lift pass.

To many, this tiny settlement is at the heart of the most interesting and demanding skiing area of the Alps and, like Lech, it is a choice spot for Europe's royalty and jet-set community. Zürs looks like an ancient, rustic village, but closer inspection reveals that although there are a few old buildings, most are modern hotels constructed in traditional chalet style. All are beautifully furnished and boast opulent facilities. Most are appropriately expensive, and even the *Gasthöfe* are of the highest order.

With a limited number of guest beds, Zürs maintains its exclusive status, but if you are staying in any of

the neighboring Arlberg villages, be sure to visit it for the excellent skiing and special atmosphere.

THE SKIING

Just steps away from the hotels are lifts climbing two sides of the valley for skiing that is almost entirely above the tree line. On one side are the interlinked lifts on the Hexenboden, known for sunny lower slopes and a connection with Lech's Rüfikopf, and the Trittkopf, Zürs's highest peak, with steep upper runs. On the other side of Zürs is the Mug-

one mega-run, punctuated by broad lower snowfields, down to Zug and on to Lech.

Off-*piste*, too, there is enormous scope. The circuit of trails linking Lech and Zürs provides a lot of testing terrain. Farther afield, reached by car, taxi or the excellent post bus service, the three other resorts' mountains offer the full range of skiing experiences for the most demanding.

True experts, who must be accompanied by a guide, relish the off-*piste* return from the Valluga above St. Anton back to Zürs. For a more expensive thrill, there are helicopter stations outside Zürs along the Flexenpass and just outside St. Anton for powder skiing in otherwise inaccessible bowls and gullies.

APRÈS-SKI

Zürs has a very high proportion of visitors who return year after year, engendering the atmosphere of an exclusive club. The bars and nightclubs are sophisticated but certainly not stuffy, and several of the grander hotels have live bands each evening. There are also smaller places for a drink and romantic chat.

OTHER ACTIVITIES

Other than skiing itself, dressing up, in the most opulent ski and après-ski wear, is probably the most popular pastime, rivaled only by going to Lech to buy more. For those with a romantic turn of mind, moonlit sleigh rides are offered. Cross-country skiers have just 2½ mi. (4 km.) of trails in Zürs with 8 mi. (13 km.) more in Lech and Zug. Facilities in hotels include swimming, sauna, table-tennis, billiards, gym, bowling, indoor golf and tennis.

gengrat/Madloch area, accessed by a high-speed quad chair. The Muggengrat is exceptionally scenic, with medium-steep runs and bowls carved through dramatic rock formations, plus some demanding powder chutes skiable with an instructor. The Madloch is essentially

BEST OF THE REST

ALPBACH

The historic inn known as "Der Ja-kober" in this archetypically charming Tyrolean village served as the model for the base lodge at Stratton Mountain. It is fitting that this Austrian inn was the model for the centerpiece of what is Vermont's smartest ski area, for Alpbach draws the same kind of moneyed and discerning clientele. Recent and still-to-be-undertaken lift development promises to catapult this quaint village into international status in the next few years, but for the moment, the skiing remains predominantly fairly easy, though the living is very congenial.

BAD KLEINKIRCHHEIM

This small Carinthian hamlet in the Julian range of the Alps, close to the borders of Italy and Yugoslavia, is best known as the home town of Franz Klammer, acknowledged as Austria's greatest skiing hero. There are a few short mogul fields and an FIS-rated downhill course, but basically, the skiing is for novices and intermediates. Bad Kleinkirchheim, usually nicknamed BKK, and neighboring St. Oswald are low-key villages.

FIEBERBRUNN

This sprawling village prides itself on being in eastern Tyrol's *Schneewinkel* ("snow pocket"), regularly subject to heavier snowfalls than nearby Kitzbühel or St. Johann in Tirol. Although their elevation is not high, the north-facing slopes, mostly for novice and intermediate skiers, hold their cover well in April—and the ski school has an excellent reputation for its powder classes.

FILZMOOS

The Bischofsmütze, a twin-towered mountain which resembles a bishop's miter, gazes down on this picturesque village, whose gentle slopes are best suited to families and beginners. English-speakers abound, for Filzmoos attracts many British guests, and its popular Hotel Alpenkrone is run by the brother of British actress Susan Hampshire and his Austrian wife. There is skiing on three mountains—each limited but pleasant and all part of the Top-Tauern-Skischeck.

GALTÜR

This isolated hamlet at the end of the Paznaun Valley, close to the Tyrol's border with Vorarlberg and to Switzerland, is frill-free yet quite sophisticated. This remoteness in the awesomely beautiful Silvretta region translates into some delicious indigenous culinary specialties and a unique Romansch-tinged local dialect. Galtür was a favorite winter retreat of Ernest Hemingway, and today is popular with families who appreciate an excellent children's ski school, good snow and incredible charm.

ST. JOHANN IM PONGAU

While not the prettiest of towns, St. Johann im Pongau nonetheless offers excellent value in accommodations and extras, and provides access to the 3-Täler ("Three Val-

leys'') resorts, including Alpendorf, Wagrain and Flachau. None is a major-league, international resort, but together they offer an economical, very European skiing experience, especially popular with younger visitors who don't require super-steep slopes or a vast ski circus.

STUBEN

Stuben is the bargain resort in the Arlberg constellation. This historic village, nestled in a deep valley at the western portal to the Arlberg, offers budget lodging coupled with easy access to the glittering resorts and fabled skiing of the Arlberg region. Stuben's own mountain, the Albona, has a small cluster of runs in a high bowl, plus long roads back to the village. One breathtaking route, around the Maroisattel, requires a little walking uphill, but the powder is usually among the best in the region, and the experience of sweeping down into St. Christoph makes it all worthwhile.

91

AUSTRIA-INFO

ACCOMMODATIONS

The standard of accommodations in Austria is very high. The government's one-to five-star rating takes into consideration many factors, such as size and staffing, ratio of guest rooms to bathrooms, elevator and telephone services, and ratio of guest beds to seats in the restaurant. Five-star establishments meet the highest international standards. The least number of stars will be allotted to small, simple guesthouses with little public space, few amenities and probably some shared baths. All, however, are clean, comfortable and indicate value in their category.

Hotels. Most hotels fall in the three- to four-star category. English is spoken by all or most of the staff. The lower end of the scale usually designates small, family-run hotels known for hospitality and charm. The higher end designates larger, elegant, exquisitely appointed hotels that are fully staffed and usually equipped with such contemporary conveniences as an indoor swimming pool, whirlpool, sauna and solarium.

Austrian resort hotels offer half-board or MAP (Modified American Plan), which includes breakfast (increasingly, a lavish buffet) and a full dinner in the price of the room.

Gasthöfe. These small, family-run lodgings—often indicated by one or two stars—are casual and inexpensive. They are the equivalent of B&B (Bed and Breakfast) accommodations. Meal plans vary, and the family members may or may not speak English.

Chalets. Especially popular with British groups who find them congenial and economical, staffed chalet-style residences are rented out to groups of six or more. Some can be as elaborate as a hotel with their own bar and disco. Meal plans vary with the chalet arrangement.

Apartments. What Americans call rental condos, Austrians refer to as *Ferienwohnungen* ("vacation apartments"). They are available on a limited basis in some resorts, though they are generally neither favored nor encouraged by the locals, who find that apartment dwellers tend to become isolated from the community, compromising the congeniality on which Austria prides itself.

Room types. An *Einzelzimmer* is a room with one single bed, a *Doppelzimmer* has two single beds (placed right next to each other, but with separate sets of bedclothes). The American double, known in German-speaking countries as a "French bed", is only beginning to gain favor, and what Americans know as double-doubles, a pair of queens or kings are not found at all in Austria.

If a room is described as having a bath, it will have just that—a bathtub, usually with a hand shower. If the room is described as having a shower, it won't have a tub.

CUSTOMS/ENTRY REGULATIONS

Citizens of the United States, Australia, New Zealand and Canada require only a valid passport. No visa is necessary. Citizens of the United Kingdom need only show a British Visitor's identity card. A visa is required for South African nationals.

Currency restrictions. There is no limit on the amount of foreign or Austrian currency you may bring into Austria, but you may take out no more than 50,000 S in Austrian currency without special permission.

DRIVING

Rental cars. Rental cars are available at major airports and in cities such as Innsbruck and Salzburg. Some are affiliates of international chains. The minimum driving age in Austria is 18, but rental firms impose their own minimum of up to 25 years. An International Driver's License (available from your home automobile association) is required or a valid national license for Europeans. U.S. residents can obtain an official validation of a state license by the Austrian National Tourist Office in New York or Los Angeles, or from the Austrian Embassy.

Insurance. Foreign visitors driving a privately owned car must furnish proof of AS 8 million insurance against damage or injury. The AAA issues "unlimited accident policies" to upgrade coverage if required. Be aware that, under Austrian law, the person who causes damage or injury is liable for any balance unpaid by an insurance settlement to the extent of his or her personal property.

Speed limits. Where no specific speed limits are posted, they are 50 kph (31 mph) in town, 100 kph (62 mph) on secondary roads, and 130 kph (81 mph) on the *Autobahn*. In the state of Vorarlberg, the limit is 80 kph on secondary roads and 100 kph on the *Autobahn*. For vehicles towing trailers or with studded snow tires, speed limits are 80 kph on secondary roads and 100 kph on the *Autobahn*.

Driving regulations. Drive on the right, pass on the left. On an *Autobahn*, passing on the right is prohibited, and "keep right except to pass" is the rule. Drinking and driving is a serious offense in Austria; the permissible blood-alcohol level is 0.8 per mille. Seatbelts are obligatory. Children under 12 may not sit in the front seat.

Automobile Associations. The Öster-reichischer Automobil-, Motorrad- und Touring-Club (ÖAMTC) and Auto, Motor- und Radfahrerbund Österreichs (ARBÖ) offer 24-hour breakdown assistance on the *Autobahn* and other main roads.

Breakdowns. Austrian automobile clubs offer 24-hour breakdown service to all drivers on motorways and main roads. For the ÖAMTC call 120 and for the ARBÖ 123.

Road information. International pictograms are used for all road signs. Specific road condition and traffic information in English is available seven days a week from 6 a.m. to 10 p.m. from the ÖAMTC in Vienna; phone (0222) 72 9 97.

Mountain driving. In snow conditions, vehicles must be equipped with snow tires, studs or chains. Chains can be rented from the two Austrian automobile clubs. Trucks, buses and vehicles climbing uphill have priority on narrow roads.

ELECTRIC CURRENT

The current in Austria is 220 volts at 50 cycles AC. American small appliances and electrical gadgets require an adapter/converter, though many electric clocks, record players, and tape recorders will not work properly with such devices. Bathrooms in Austrian hotels are equipped with low-wattage outlets suitable only for razors; hairdryers and electric curlers, whether American models used with converters or European models, will not work from these outlets.

GETTING THERE

By air. Munich is the most convenient transatlantic gateway for all the Arlberg region—that is, most of the resorts in the Tyrol and all in the states of Salzburg and Styria. There are non-stop flights from New York, but flights from other North American cities require a transfer (or at least an immigration stop) in Frankfurt or Düsseldorf.

Zurich is the best gateway of all for the Arlberg region, as well as all the resorts in the state of Vorarlberg, Austria's westernmost. There are non-stop flights to Zurich from Atlanta, Boston, Chicago, Los Angeles, New York, and Montreal and one-stop service from Toronto.

Innsbruck, due to the requirements of inch-perfect descent through the spectacular mountains surrounding the city, is used only by small passenger aircraft. Salzburg is becoming increasingly popular among charter-flight operators, due to expansion, improved facilities and close proximity to resorts in Salzburgerland, Styria and eastern Tyrol. Salzburg and Innsbruck are both served by mainline railway stations. They are also close to a highway, making transfers by road very quick.

Some bargain packages fly skiers to gateways in northern Europe, but these normally require a change of planes or, more often, a long motorcoach ride to the mountains.

By rail. From Britain, rail is a viable alternative to traveling by air, especially if you are going to a resort either with or close to a railway station, as it can cut transfer times considerably. On arrival, there are buses that meet the train and transport you to the resort. The Arlberg Express will convey you direct from the Channel coast to Innsbruck, Salzburg or St. Anton. This is normally a daily service. For other destinations, a change is required en route.

For more information contact Austrian Federal Railways (*Österreichische Bundesbahnen—ÖBB*) or the Austrian National Tourist Office.

HEALTH

If you become ill or are injured, you will find that most resort doctors are reasonably multi-lingual and accustomed to arranging payment from patients from abroad. If there is a problem, your hotel can help straighten it out. Larger hospitals now accept credit cards, but you must pay your bill on the spot and submit the claim to your insurance company afterwards. For Britons, Austria has a reciprocal health agreement with the British National Health Service, but this is not recognized by all doctors or hospitals and you are well advised to take out additional health insurance.

On-*piste* accident victims are taken from the mountain by the ski patrol, who are paid professionals. In most cases, this evacuation is free, paid for either as part of your lift pass or by an automatic insurance policy extended to all resort guests. In a few cases, there may be a small surcharge for such services. Off-*piste* skiers who get lost and require search and rescue operations are charged per man-hour. In case of very serious injury, helicopter med-evac service is free.

HOLIDAYS AND SPECIAL EVENTS

Austrian holidays falling during the ski season are Christmas Day, St. Stephen's Day (Dec. 26), New Year's Day, Epiphany (Jan. 6) and Easter Monday.

Picturesque Christmas markets, featuring outdoor stands where regional delicacies, handmade ornaments, and other crafts may be bought, take place from December 1 through Christmas Eve in the heart of Innsbruck and Salzburg. Christmas is still primarily a religious and personal, rather than a social, holiday. New Year's Eve is for formal parties. During *Fasching*, the pre-Lenten carnival or Mardi Gras, hotels and restaurants are gaily decorated and everyone dresses up in Halloween-type costumes for rollicking masked parties.

Christmas, New Year and Easter are busy times on the slopes. Austrian schools usually have a mid-term break in early February, the dates varying from region to region, when resorts tend to be more crowded.

MAIL

Stamps may be purchased at post offices, at the hotel front desk, and at a *Trafik* which sells newspapers, magazines and postcards and other small items. In fact, many places that sell postcards also sell stamps for them.

Post offices are open Monday to Friday from 8 a.m. to noon and 2 to 5 or 6 p.m. Branches in railway stations may stay open round the clock, including Sundays and public holidays. In most resorts, post offices are also open on Saturday from 8 to 10 a.m.

MONEY MATTERS

Currency. The unit of currency is the Austrian *Schilling* (Abbreviated S, ÖS or AS), divided into 100 *Groschen*.

Coins: 10 and 50 Groschen and 1, 5, 10, 20, 25, 50 and 100 Schillings

Notes: 20, 50, 100, 500 and 1,000 Schillings.

Credit cards and traveler's checks. Major hotels and restaurants now accept credit cards, as do most shops. However, Austrian service stations do not accept U.S. credit cards, although those found also in America, such as Mobil, Shell or Texaco, take oil-company cards. Traveler's checks are always welcome.

Banks. Banks offer the most favorable exchange rate on traveler's checks and foreign currency. Banking hours are 8 a.m. to 12.30 p.m. and 1.30 to 3.30 p.m. on weekdays, until 5.30 p.m. on Thursdays. Exchange offices at airports and major city railway terminals are open seven days a week from 8 a.m. to 8 p.m. Major currencies can also be changed at the daily bank rate at all Austrian post offices, which have longer hours than banks (see MAIL above).

Value Added Tax. *Mehrwertsteuer* (Value Added Tax or sales tax) of 20% is imposed on all goods and services and is included in posted prices, sometimes abbreviated to M.W.S. For skis, skiwear, and other large purchases (1,000 S and over), it is worthwhile applying for a refund. Request and fill in a U-34 form from the store where you made your purchase and have the salesclerk stamp it properly. When you leave the country, the Austrian customs officer at the border or at the airport will validate the forms. (The

ÖAMTC has a quick-refund program as part of its service package.) Mail the original validated form(s) to the stores where you purchased the merchandise (or to a service office, if the store says it uses one) after your return home. You will receive a check, bank draft or international money order covering 16.66% of the purchase price by mail.

SKI SCHOOL

Austria, quite rightly, prides itself on its high standard of ski instruction, and if any credentials are needed, it seems that every ski school is headed by an Olympic, world or, at the least, national champion. Since Hannes Schneider started giving lessons in 1907 at St. Anton, Austria has defined techniques and, the claims of the *ski évolutif* or GLM philosophy notwithstanding, remains the most emulated method of teaching—its "feet together" style regarded as the classic way to ski. Instructors are required to undergo a thoroughly exhaustive regime of practice which includes teaching in foreign languages, notably English.

Most resorts have a ski kindergarten and classes are invariably fun. Adult classes are similarly high-spirited, and whilst infinite care in teaching skills is the main priority, it is usual for the instructor to take his class for a beer or *Schnaps* at the end of the day—he doesn't expect to pay, however! A week's course culminates in a race, with pins, medals or certificates to be won, followed by dancing and much merry-making.

Safety is a high priority. Good skiers may wish to join ski school, as the top class is usually competition standard, its participants intent on honing their technique to the highest level through an intensive course of backcountry touring, powder skiing, mogul work and slalom racing. Another reason for good skiers to join a class is to experience top-quality guiding of the region's skiing terrain with instruction thrown in.

TELEPHONE

The postal service also operates the telephone system. Hotels usually add astronomical surcharges onto phone calls, so these are to be avoided—especially for overseas calls. The most economical calls can be made from post offices or phone booths, which are found at railway stations, airports, outside post offices and in public places.

There are several types of pay phones in Austria, but general procedures apply. For local calls, insert several *Schillings* and dial. When the other party answers, the phone will automatically consume the money as long as you stay on the line, and there will be some kind of visual signal to indicate that your money is running out. Unused coins will be returned, but no change is made for time left when large-denomination coins are used.

It is also possible to purchase a 50- or 100-Schilling phone card at the post office, which is inserted into specially equipped public phones (a card is pictured on the phone booth). It is valid for multiple calls until the card's value is used up.

For calls back to the U.S., the best deal is AT&T's USADIRECT program. Insert a coin for local access. Then dial 022-903-011. You may have to wait for up to 30 seconds, but this number connects you directly to an AT&T operator, who will then place a credit card or collect call for you.

TOURIST INFORMATION OFFICES

The Austrian National Tourist Office (ANTO) can supply specific resort information, hotel price lists and other useful data. The main ANTO office is at 500 Fifth Avenue, New York, N.Y. 10110; tel. (212) 287 8742 (AUS-TRIA) for information services.

There are also branch offices in Chicago, Houston, Los Angeles and Toronto. All are open during normal business hours. During the ski season, 24-hour snow-condition reports are available from ANTO in New York, tel. (212) 944 6880, and Los Angeles.

In Britain ANTO has its office at 30 St. George Street, London W1R 0AL, tel (01) 629 0461.

Unless you are buying a ski package and don't have a specific hotel in mind in the resort you have chosen, local tourist offices can give you very specific and up-to-the-minute information on ski and lodgings, and even suggest a hotel and book your room.

FRANCE AND ITS SKIING

When Americans cross the Atlantic to ski, those who choose France tend to be skiers first and winter vacationers a distant second. The French have the loftiest peaks in the Alps, culminating with Mont Blanc, 15,781 ft. (4,810 m.), the highest in western Europe. The Mont Blanc massif actually sits where France, Italy and Switzerland meet, but Chamonix is the town most closely associated with it. Because of the resort and ski area elevations, which are high for the Alps, France normally gets the most and highest-quality snow, and as the range is at its most rugged here, the French resorts also have the steepest terrain. And they have discovered how to use it well.

The French invented the concept of ski-in, ski-out resorts. While most traditional ski villages nestle in low-lying valleys, the modern French resort, situated in a snow sure, high-altitude area, was designed to minimize fuss and maximize skiing. From your hotel or apartment, you can ski directly to one of many lifts fanning out to service a network of slopes for all abilities. And you can ski back to your door at the end of the day. You can see why these are sometimes referred to as "convenience resorts". Once experienced, many skiers won't accept less.

Of course, there are also many traditional resorts in France. Some are rural hamlets which have installed lifts and still have a rustic feel. Others have a long history of skiing and are frequented by film stars and royalty. Entertainment and general après-ski are usually livelier in long-established centers, which also tend to be more "French". Skiers may, however, have to walk to the lift in ski boots or wait for a bus which might be crowded, and snow conditions are less reliable at either end of the season.

It has to be said that there were some architectural mistakes in the fifties and sixties, resulting in resorts that are too sterile, but recent developments have seen a return to rustic edifices. Buildings are now restricted in height, and have sloping chalet-style roofs and wooden or natural stone façades. Valmorel is considered the prettiest "purpose-built" resort,

97

Belle Plagne is more tasteful than its satellite neighbors, and recent additions to existing villages reflect this trend. This engenders a cozier atmosphere, coupled with the advantage of skiing from and to your door.

France hosted the very first winter Olympics in Chamonix in 1924. Forty-four years after that, the Games were held in Grenoble, made most memorable by the triple gold-medal performance of favorite son Jean-Claude Killy. In the eighties, the ever-glamorous Killy devoted his energies to snaring the 1992 Games for France. He succeeded, and the Games will be headquartered in Albertville, with ski events scattered around the Tarentaise.

The investment of millions of francs for sports venues and support facilities will reap immeasurable benefits for skiers. The railways are upgrading (a station is being constructed at Lyon airport) and highway interchanges and bypasses are being improved. Most important, the antiquated, narrow road which serves the Tarentaise—the infamous N90 renowned as one of the most extended parking lots in the Alps (especially on Saturdays when the big "changeover" of vacationers arriving and leaving takes place)—is being widened from two to four lanes. These new works have been well thought out, for the French are conscious both of criticism which seems endemic to Olympic sites (at least before the Games) and of past mistakes.

France is the country where alternative snow sports took hold. This is where monoski took off a decade or so ago, followed by snowboards, not to mention parasailing and ski hang-gliding where people hurl themselves off peaks to float to earth suspended beneath a multi-colored parachute or delta wings. There is a whole sub-culture of bronzed youth dressed up like birds of paradise.

An offshoot is the creation of alternative ski schools. In addition to the Ecole du Ski Français (ESF), which offers traditional teaching methods (although increasingly more mono and off-piste instruction), new ones have emerged. The Ski Ecole Internationale, as the name implies, usually has instructors proficient in foreign languages and caters for adventure, as well as traditional instruction, in smaller groups than the ESF. There are other splinter groups (usually ESF-trained) set up with specific aims, such as off-piste tours.

France is also the country of the ultra-modern lift. The usual Alpine high-capacity cable car is now supplemented by a futuristic assortment of high-speed chairlifts, gondolas and télécabines, which are a hybrid of gondola (a rapid-fire succession of separate cars) and tram (skiers, up to 20 per car, ride standing).

Surface lifts, even the fast-paced Pomas for which the country was famous, are giving way to the most modern, most inventive aerial lifts—and even traditional Europeans are glad to be able to ride in comfort.

The newest development in France, pioneered in Switzerland and Austria, is the underground funicular railway. Val d'Isère was the first French resort to install one. Les Deux Alpes quickly followed, providing an alternative route to the high-glacier skiing which will be operational whatever the windspeed. Not to be outdone, Tignes now plans to replace the two-stage gondola (which often had long lines) to the Grande Motte Glacier.

Probably the greatest attractions of France are the huge ski areas created by linking dozens of lifts at several resorts into one mega-ski area with miles of skiing all covered by one lift pass. France does this better than anywhere else. The 3 Vallées ("Three Valleys" comprising Méribel, Courchevel, Val Thorens and Les Menuires) and the Tignes/Val d'Isère complex, known as Espace Killy, are the most extensive. There is a rumor that by the 1992 Olympics all the Tarentaise resorts will be lift-linked, which will join the above-mentioned ski areas via La Plagne and Les Arcs.

The Portes du Soleil region comprises eight French resorts (including Avoriaz and Morzine) and seven Swiss resorts and claims to be the largest international ski area in the world, encompassing 12 valleys and 50 peaks. Farther south, there is the Milky Way complex where Montgenèvre is linked to a string of Italian ski stations. Another Franco-Italian area, which should be operational by 1991, is the Croix du Sud linking Valloire/Valmeinier with Orelle, Valfréjus and from there Bardonecchia.

The Mont Blanc area, though not ski-linked, also offers a regional lift pass, with free buses between the 12 resorts, including Chamonix, Argentière, Megève, St-Gervais and Les Contamines. On the same pass, you can also ski one day in Courmayeur in Italy (through the Mont Blanc Tunnel). Another big unlinked region which allows skiing in participating resorts is La Grand Galaxie comprising Les Deux Alpes, Alpe d'Huez,

Serre Chevalier, Puy-St-Vincent, Bardonecchia and the Milky Way.

In some cases, traditional villages are linked into the extremities of a purpose-built resort. Examples are the Grand Massif around Flaine (Samoëns, Morillon and Les Carroz), La Plagne (Champagny and Montchavin) and Avoriaz (Morzine).

France's major ski resorts are in the southeast, close to the borders of Italy and Switzerland. The old duchy of Savoy has been split up into the modern départements of Haute-Savoie (north) and Savoie (south). Proudly independent from France until as recently as 1860, the local folk have a strong regional accent and a naturally friendly character. The Haute-Savoie runs, very loosely, either side of the Autoroute Blanche between Geneva and the Mont Blanc Tunnel to Italy. Exits to ski resorts are all along the throughway. The area is bordered by Lake Geneva (Lac Léman) and Switzerland on one side, Savoie and Italy on the other. All the Mont Blanc, Portes du Soleil and Grand Massif resorts are in this region, as are La Clusaz and Le Grand-Bornand.

Savoie's main ski areas are the Tarentaise (3 Vallées and Valmorel), Haute Tarentaise (La Plagne, Les Arcs, Val d'Isère and Tignes), and further south the Haute Maurienne (Valloire, Valfréjus and Val-Cenis).

Going south, the département of Isère, of which Grenoble is a part, comprises the Oisans region, including Les Deux Alpes and Alpe d'Huez in the Grande Galaxie complex. Hautes Alpes contains the remaining Grande Galaxie resorts of Serre Chevalier and Montgenèvre, which links into resorts over the border in Italy, as well as Les Orres and Risoul.

Finally, Isola 2000 is in the département of the Alpes Maritimes, north of Nice. The mountains here are less rugged and are sometimes called Alpilles ("Little Alps").

The sports club is a staple of French resorts, offering both sports facilities and ticketing services. Make it an early stop in your visit. Purpose-built resorts run nurseries for toddlers and even tiny babies, offer "snow-gardens" for pre-schoolers and have wonderful, separate learn-to-ski areas with giant models of cartoon characters. Older children can play and wander safely after skiing, since many of these resorts are traffic-free. Accommodations tend more toward apartments with no meal service but with cooking facilities, so families on a tight budget can keep costs to a minimum. However, compared to the luxurious, spacious condominiums at U.S. resorts, the French variety tend to be tiny and modestly furnished.

Whether you opt for a purpose-built resort or a traditional village, there will be that unmistakable air of romance, with enough Latin influence to make it noticeably different from home. In France you feel abroad. But, brush up on your French. Most international resorts have some English-speaking personnel and ski instructors, but a knowledge of French will always come in handy and be appreciated.

At the very least, bone up on your culinary French. Mountain areas are famous for cheese dishes such as unctuous fondue savoyarde (melted Beaufort cheese, white wine and kirsch into which you dip pieces of bread) and hearty croûte au fromage (a glorified Welsh rarebit), also known as croûte du skieur. Local mountain cheeses include Tomme, Chèvre and Reblochon.

Variations on the fondue theme involve dipping cubes of meat in boiling oil (bourguignonne) or bouillon (Chinoise) and then in a selection of mayonnaise-based sauces. Other meat dishes will be accompanied by French fries (pommes frites) or the classic gratin dauphinois, thin slices of potato baked in cream. More extravagant items include crayfish gratin (gratin d'écrevisses) and potted duck (confit de canard).

In the southern Alps, garlic and herbs of Provence will be in evidence, as well as dishes with an Italian flavor, such as soupe au pistou (vegetable soup with basil), or pissaladière (the Niçois version of pizza).

Most well-known French wines are available, but you can also sample local vintages. In Savoie, look for the appelations contrôlées: Vin-de-Savoie (red, rosé and white) or Roussette-de-Savoie (white). Further south try l'Hermitage or the popular Clairette de Die, while Provence is famous for its Châteauneuf-du-Pape. Marc du Pays, the local firewater, would strip the bottoms from your skis; Genepi is a soothing sweet liqueur with a distinctive herb flavor.

Most skiers are content to ski all day, every day, but some might like to take a day off and do some sightseeing in the immediate area. Purpose-built resorts are usually up tortuous mountain roads, so excursions down the valley are less feasible, although there may be a cable car and there are usually bus services to other villages close by and to the nearest railway station and airport.

Most resorts offer non-ski activities and other sports to keep energetic or non-skiing members of the group amused. But when it comes down to it, you chose France because you want to ski. Make the most of the experience.

ALPE D'HUEZ

Access: *Nearest airports:* Grenoble (1½ hrs.); Geneva (2 hrs.). *By road:* A48 Autoroute to Grenoble, then via Vizille and Le Bourg-d'Oisans. *By rail:* to Grenoble (TGV), then by bus.

Tourist Office: Office du Tourisme, 38750 Alpe d'Huez, France. Tel. 76 80 35 41

Altitude: 6,103 ft. (1,860 m.). *Top:* 10,991 ft. (3,350 m.)

Language: French

Runs: 137 mi. (220 km.)

Lifts: 81 with linked resorts

Ski areas: Signal, Pic Blanc, Signal de l'Homme

Ski schools: Ecole du Ski Français, Ski Ecole Internationale

Linked resorts: Auris-en-Oisans, Villard-Reculas, Vanjany

Season: Early December to early May, plus summer skiing

Kindergarten: *Non-ski*: from 2 years. *With ski*: from 3 years

Prices: *Lift pass*: 6 days 700 F (children 574 F). *Ski school*: Group 72 F for half-day (children 55 F); private 120 F per hour.

RATINGS

Skiing Conditions	9
Snow Conditions	8
For Beginners	9
For Intermediates	9
For Advanced Skiers	8
For Children	7
Après-Ski	6
Other Sports	5
Value for Money	6

THE RESORT

Alpe d'Huez grew up in the fifties and sixties as one of the first resorts with doorstep skiing convenience. A lift links upper and lower parts of the village during the day. It is very "French" and as yet relatively undiscovered by other nationalities. The architecture is essentially unattractive apartment blocks, with some modern, sloping-roofed chalets dotted across the mountainside.

THE SKIING

This is a place for serious skiers, be they enthusiastic beginners, smitten intermediates or ardent experts. The morning walk to a lift is a maximum of five minutes, and a profusion of lifts and *pistes* ensure minimal lines by European standards. Lovely, sunny beginner slopes grace the bowl around the resort. The higher you climb the harder it gets, culminating in high-altitude demanding runs from the Pic Blanc, 10,991 ft. (3,350 m.).

A daunting 10-mile (16-km.) run drops from the summit over the Sarenne Glacier to the village, offering upper-mountain steeps and thigh-frying length—the longest inbounds expert run in the Alps.

Otherwise, the Pic Blanc terrain is tiered like a wedding cake. There are three major lift levels and many smaller ones serving three levels of slopes. The lower eight-seat gondola from the base accesses mostly novice terrain. The mid-mountain cable car serves intermediate turf, while the top cable car leads to the summit and its demanding slopes.

Easier terrain is found on either side of the village on two smaller mountains, the Signal and the Signal de l'Homme. Skiers can drop off the backs of these peaks to the villages of Villard-Reculas and Auris-en-Oisans deep in the valley and even be ferried back up to Alpe d'Huez by helicopter. The network is still expanding, with plans to install some new lifts. A new cable car system has opened skiing from neighboring Vaujany.

High altitude ensures that there is good snow cover from December to April, and there is summer skiing up on the glacier. Off-*piste* is extensive, but there are no trees, so it is pretty grim when the weather closes in.

Alpe d'Huez is part of the Grande Galaxie, which entitles lift-pass holders to ski one day at Les Deux Alpes (helicopter link), Serre Chevalier, Puy-St-Vincent, Bardonecchia (Italy) or any of the southern Milky Way resorts (huge area spanning France and Italy).

APRÈS-SKI

If partying is part and parcel of your skiing vacation, Alpe d'Huez ranks reasonably high for a new resort. There are plenty of bars and discos, but apart from weekends and public holidays when there is an influx of French, the nightlife can be on the quiet side. Apartment-dwellers like to eat at the many excellent restaurants, especially down the narrow backstreets of the older part of the village.

Le Saint Huron is famous for seafood. The fashionable Igloo nightclub also has a piano bar serving cocktails, and if you get hungry after a night on the town, there are restaurants still serving in the small hours. Prices tend to be high in the smarter nightspots.

OTHER ACTIVITIES

In addition to long, open cross-country trails, there is an excellent outdoor heated swimming pool and an artificial ice rink for hockey, curling (through the Sports Club) or just skating around. Both facilities are free with your lift pass. The intrepid can shoot off the slopes on a hangglider. The indoor sports center offers a choice of squash, tennis and even golf. You can hire a car and learn advanced driving skills on ice. The Community Heritage Museum has exhibits of local culture and history.

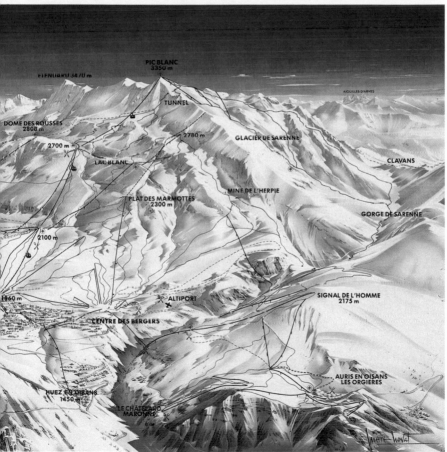

LES ARCS

Access: *Nearest airport:* Geneva (2 hrs.). *By road:* A41 or A43 Autoroutes to Chambéry, then via Albertville and Bourg-St-Maurice. *By rail:* to Bourg-St-Maurice (TGV from Paris), then by funicular.

Tourist Office: Office du Tourisme, 73700 Les Arcs, France.
Tel. 79 07 48 00

Altitude: 5,250–6,562 ft. (1,600–2,000 m.). *Top:* 10,585 ft. (3,226 m.)

Language: French

Runs: 106 mi. (170 km.)

Lifts: 95

Ski areas: Les Deux Têtes, Arpette, Col des Frettes, Aiguille Rouge, Grand Renard

Ski school: Ecole du Ski Français

Linked resorts: Peisey-Nancroix, Villaroger

Season: Mid-December to late April

Kindergarten: *Non-ski:* from 4 months. *With ski:* from 4 years

Prices: *Lift pass:* 6 days 730 F (children under 7 free). *Ski school:* Group 450–570 F for 6 half-days; private 150 F per hour.

RATINGS

Skiing Conditions	9
Snow Conditions	9
For Beginners	8
For Intermediates	9
For Advanced Skiers	9
For Children	9
Après-Ski	7
Other Sports	8
Value for Money	7

THE RESORT

Les Arcs is made up of three hypermodern resorts, known by their heights in meters—1600, 1800 and 2000 respectively. They are all compact, isolated developments, attractively designed. Les Arcs is one of France's most international resorts, with as many foreign visitors as French; it is the only resort to have offices of its own in London, Frankfurt and Amsterdam.

The arrangement of each complex is intelligent, using natural

windbreaks and providing covered walkways. It's all the brainchild of the late Robert Blanc, who introduced the graduated ski-length method of teaching for beginners *(ski évolutif)* here, and promoted the "ski to your door" ideal. Les Arcs remains a pioneer in the latest snow sports—offering the most up-to-date in monoski, snowboarding, speed skiing, parasailing and others. Avid ski-film-watchers will recognize Les Arcs from the fantastic "Apocalypse Snow" series—and thrill at the opportunity to tackle the mountains with some of the stars. When speed skiing is introduced at the 1992 Olympics, Arc 2000 will be the venue.

THE SKIING

Les Arcs is one of the most stunning ski areas in the Alps. Even without wide-ranging interlinks with other destinations, this three-tiered resort provides all the variation and vertical of a major ski circus. For variety, there are hidden powder pockets, steep headwalls, grandiose bowls, mild meadows and even stands of glades. For vertical, nothing approaches the fabled super-steep run from the top of the Aiguille Rouge to the village of Villaroger—7,006 vertical ft. (2,136 m.) of steady challenge.

A new cable car connects the Bourg-St-Maurice railway station directly with Arc 1600 in just seven minutes, but other than that, all of the uphill transportation is via chair or surface lift. No matter at which level a skier stays, there are runs and lifts right outside the door. It is also easy to connect all the villages on skis or by lift, and half-a-dozen runs around Arcs 1600 and 1800 are now lit for night-skiing.

Arc 1600 has a few beginner and novice slopes right next to the village, plus some nice intermediate runs through the trees. A handful of steeper runs are found off Les Deux Têtes, 7,546 ft. (2,300 m.). Arc 1800 has the lion's share of the easier skiing on the lower portions of Arpette, 7,872 ft. (2,400 m.), and Col du Grand Renard, 8,038 ft. (2,450 m.). A long ridge, including a mid-point peak called Col des Frettes, enfolds this massive sector. On the upper face of the ridge is some high-intermediate terrain. Behind it is a vast, isolated bowl which gives Les Arcs its reputation as a true ski mecca.

This awesome terrain, most efficiently reached from Arc 2000, is one humongous bowl enfolded by the Aiguille Rouge and other peaks that soar 10,000 ft. (3,000 m.) and higher. There is one low-intermediate run for the curious venturing up from below, but essentially, this vast expanse is for advanced and expert skiers. Here are the toughest *pistes*, the most vertical headwalls, the most radical chutes, the most heart-stopping cornices and even the world's fastest super-groomed, ultra-steep speed-skiing course.

When you consider there are no linked resorts other than this trio, plus two tiny villages in the valley, the 106 mi. (170 km.) of *piste* are especially impressive. Add to this the unlimited and regularly patroled off-*piste*, and you begin to build up the picture of a top-class resort.

The ski pass now covers Les Arcs, Villaroger (reached from Arc 2000), Peisey/Nancroix (interlinked with Arc 1800) and the Bourg-St-Maurice cable car. The Carte Blanche is a good deal for skiers who would like to sample Les Arcs' varied offerings.

APRÈS-SKI

Most of the nightlife is in Arc 1800. In Arcs 1600 and 2000, it could perhaps be described as more "mature"— it's certainly quieter. There's a movie theater in each resort and Radio Les Arcs broadcasts to all apartments, with programs and snow reports in several languages.

Organized events during the winter season have previously included Antiques Week with local curios, Wine Week (Win your weight in wine...), Nouvelle Cuisine Week, Barman's Fortnight (for lovers of strange concoctions), Bridge Week and Jazz Week.

OTHER ACTIVITIES

A wide variety of snow sports includes everything from heli-skiing (on the other side of the Italian border) to dream skiing (with a personal hi-fi). In Arc 1600 there's a swimming pool from April, aerobics, ice rink, parascending, archery and hang-gliding; in Arc 1800: squash courts, ice rink, sauna and gym (Hôtel du Golf); in Arc 2000: fencing, karate, aerobics and an ice rink with broom hockey.

AVORIAZ

Access: *Nearest airport:* Geneva
(1½ hrs.). *By road:* A40 Autoroute,
exit Cluses, then via Les Gets. *By
rail:* to Geneva or Thonon-les-Bains,
then by bus.

Tourist Office: Office du Tourisme,
74110 Avoriaz, France.
Tel. 50 74-02 11

Altitude: 5,906 ft. (1,800 m.).
Top: 7,710 ft. (2,350 m.)

Language: French

Runs: 373 mi. (600 km.) in Portes du
Soleil

Lifts: 37 (220 in Portes du Soleil)

Ski areas: Chavanette, Les Hauts
Forts, Col de la Joux Verte

Ski school: Ecole du Ski Français

Linked resorts: Morzine, Champéry, Morgins and other Portes du Soleil resorts

Season: December to April

Kindergarten: *Non-ski:* 2 months–
5 years. *With ski:* 3–16 years

Prices: *Lift pass:* 6 days Portes du
Soleil 714 F (children 478 F). *Ski
school:* Group 58–91 F for half-day
(children 46–68 F); private 135 F per
hour.

RATINGS

Skiing Conditions	9
Snow Conditions	7
For Beginners	8
For Intermediates	9
For Advanced Skiers	7
For Children	9
Après-Ski	7
Other Sports	6
Value for Money	8

THE RESORT

Avoriaz is refreshingly different.
The architecture is unique to the
Alps: tall, multi-faceted wood-clad
buildings appear as futuristic now
as they did two decades ago. Building began in the late 1960s and will
be finished in three apartment
blocks' time. Although the wood is
showing its age on the older buildings, the architecture seems to
match the mountainscape better
than less adventurous designs in
other new resorts. There are no real
roads or cars, just snow-covered
paths for pedestrians, horse-drawn
sleighs and hand-towed utility
sleds.

THE SKIING

If there is a center to the giant Portes
du Soleil ski region, this is it. The
area brought together under this
name cannot really be called a "circuit", since the 12 or so resorts participating are not easily connected.
Rather, they form an erratic zig-zag
along the Franco-Swiss border, but
Avoriaz is as well linked as any to
the rest of the Portes du Soleil resorts.

Located high above the old town
of Morzine, Avoriaz sits on a sunny,
slightly canted plateau with skiing
on both sides. Lifts and runs are
within an easy walk of all accommodations, and it is simple to move
among the sectors. On the plateau
itself, just above the village, is ample beginner terrain. Les Hauts
Forts, a sizable bowl comprising the
main ski area, has steepish runs on
top, some good skiing among the

trees near the bottom and lots of medium-level open-slope skiing in between. Good skiers take the partially moguled run down to Les Prodains, half-way to Morzine and the valley floor.

There is more wide, open intermediate skiing between Pas de Chavanette and Col du Fornet on the other side of Avoriaz. Col de la Joux Verte is essentially a long, totally skiable north-south ridge between Chavanette and the headwall above Morzine. Chavanette is also the access point to Switzerland—Les Crosets at mid-mountain and the villages of Champéry and Morgins below. The Swiss Wall, which tends to bump up, takes up the first thousand vertical feet. Below is Les Crosets, with broad snowfields and also the destination of skiers coming from the lower Swiss villages.

Most of the skiing on the French side of the Portes du Soleil (certainly the most interesting parts) requires crossing Morzine. It is necessary to ride or ski down, cross the village and take lifts up to the Pointe de Nyon, 6,624 ft. (2,019 m.), or Le Ranfolly, above the village of Les Gets.

Children are well cared for in the Village des Enfants, "Children's Village", run by former French ladies' ski champion Annie Famose, who teaches children to ski through playing games.

APRÈS-SKI

Avoriaz is made up almost exclusively of apartment blocks filled with British skiers until February, when the French school holidays begin. Thus the predominating après-ski accent changes with the time of season. Generally, this is an unpretentious resort which nevertheless does not prevent prices being some of the highest in the region.

Snow paths between buildings might be excellent for skiing, but necessitate much staggering about at night. Most people choose not to stray far, rarely a problem, since there are plenty of bars and reasonably good restaurants. Later in the evening, discotheques draw the night crowd. The most expensive, Le Roc Club, is, as the name suggests, cut out of the rock wall. Swedes flock to Le Manhattan, which is larger and offers better value. Alternatives include the movie theaters, with the much-publicized Fantasy Film Festival in January. There's a good range of shops. Horse-drawn sleighs jangle around the resort.

OTHER ACTIVITIES

In the last week of the season, a special snow sports festival highlights snowboarding, monoski, speed skiing, parascending and ski hanggliding. Most are available during the rest of the season, too. There is a good range of cross-country runs, totaling 25 mi. (40 km.), mainly above the tree line. The open-air swimming pool maintains a constant 28°C. There's also a fitness center with dance and aerobics.

CHAMONIX

Access: *Nearest airport:* Geneva (1½ hrs.). *By road:* A40 Autoroute, exit Le Fayet. *By rail:* station in Chamonix (TGV to St-Gervais).

Tourist Office: Office du Tourisme, Place de l'Eglise, 74400 Chamonix, France. Tel. 50 53 00 24

Altitude: 3,396 ft. (1,035 m.). *Top:* 12,606 ft. (3,842 m.)

Language: French

Runs: 84 mi. (136 km.)

Lifts: 43

Ski areas: Le Brévent, La Flégère, Aiguille du Midi

Ski school: Ecole du Ski Français

Linked resorts: None

Season: Mid-December to mid-April

Kindergarten: *Non-Ski:* 3 months–10 years. *With ski:* 2½–14 years

Prices: *Lift pass:* 6 days 730 F (children 600 F). *Ski school:* Group 500 F for 6 days; private 140 F per hour.

RATINGS

Skiing Conditions	5
Snow Conditions	6
For Beginners	2
For Intermediates	5
For Advanced Skiers	9
For Children	3
Après-Ski	7
Other Sports	7
Value for Money	6

THE RESORT

Chamonix is a busy town just off the main route to Italy. Surrounded by dramatic mountains and dominated by Mont Blanc, it has attracted climbers for over a hundred years. Parts of old Chamonix are picturesque, but new developments alongside mar the effect. The character of the place, however, has not been lost, and visitors range from real mountaineers and hard-core skiers to less

114

active people who simply want to check out this famous spot.

Seduced by its long-standing reputation as a ski resort and by lots of economy hotels and sparkling nightlife, American skiers have long flocked to Chamonix. The town remains a fascinating destination, but evaluated purely as a ski resort, it is doubtless overrated. There are six separate ski areas—some limited in size, some awkward to get to, many suffering impossible lines at the

main access lifts and most of them geared to advanced skiers. In terms of sheer quality skiing, old Chamonix has been eclipsed by newer French resorts. In terms of charm and convenience, some of the smaller towns have done better in maintaining a true Savoyard ambiance.

Close by and linked by bus are Les Houches, Argentière and Le Tour. These are quieter, more traditional villages in which to stay if nightlife is not high on the priority list.

THE SKIING

The skiing around Chamonix consists of several unlinked areas of which only one, Le Brévent, is accessible from the town center. Ski buses run until 7 p.m. to La Flégère, Les Houches, Argentière and Le Tour. Normally you would decide which area to ski and stay there for the day.

It takes a degree of fitness just to get to Le Brévent on foot, since the access lift (a relatively new six-place gondola) is up a steep hill. Once at the Planpraz, skiers have a choice of continuing up to Le Brévent, 8,285 ft. (2,525 m.), or to a top station part way up the Aiguille de Charnalon, 7,488 ft. (2,282 m.).

There are not a lot of options, but most of the terrain is demanding. A recently installed double chair on Col Cornu opens the possibility of a ski link with La Flégère. This massif offers similar skiing to Le Brévent's—somewhat limited in scope though slightly less demanding in skill.

Apart from the skiing on Les Grands Montets above Argentière, with its challenging runs and extensive off-*piste* possibilities, each area is limited. Although the resort is not a spot recommended for beginners, there are some novice runs in all sectors, mostly closer to the valley, with the accompanying risk of lack of snow. Le Tour is probably the best bet for beginners. The other

areas are essentially intermediate.

Anyone who visits Chamonix solely for skiing on-*piste* will be in for a disappointment. A large proportion of the people who gravitate here are good skiers looking for off-*piste* adventure surrounded by breathtaking scenery. The most famous off-*piste* run is the Vallée Blanche. People come from resorts all around to take the cable car to the Aiguille du Midi, 12,606 ft. (3,842 m.). A qualified mountain guide is essential for this late-season ritual, for much of this 12-mi. (20-km.) route is on a glacier riddled with crevasses (the "Mer de Glace"). Otherwise, it is not a difficult run at all, but long and steady, which leaves you free to enjoy the scenic experience.

The Mont Blanc Ski Pass is good at any of 13 resorts in the region, including bus transport between them. The Chamonix area is in the process of updating its lift system to increase capacity and reduce lines—and perhaps polish up its tarnished reputation.

APRÈS-SKI

This lively town has something to offer everyone. There are plenty of bars and restaurants, some serving excellent French cuisine. Savoyard specialties should be tried, but international fare is also available. Choucas, Jean's Bar, the Edward Wymper Pub and The National are popular with English-speaking visitors. There are a few discos (Le Pélé is among the liveliest) and a casino. Those staying in the outlying villages will need to go to Chamonix for a night out (taxi service, however, can be spasmodic).

OTHER ACTIVITIES

There is good cross-country skiing for all levels from Chamonix all the way to Argentière, and at Les Houches. In 1924, the town hosted the first winter Olympics—and the tradition of multiple action and spectator events remains strong. There is a car rally on ice every January, plus jumping meets, skating, hockey and other events.

Chamonix also has an indoor swimming pool with a separate learning pool, an indoor Olympic-sized ice rink (with adjacent bar/restaurant) and an outdoor rink with a speed skating area. The sports center offers indoor tennis, squash, dance, gymnastics, table tennis and judo. Many of the hotels have their own pools/sauna. For those with a cultural turn of mind, there is a library and an Alpine museum.

COURCHEVEL

🎿🎿🎿🎿🎿

Access: *Nearest airport:* Geneva (3 hrs.). *By road:* A41 or A43 Autoroutes to Chambéry, then via Albertville and Moûtiers. *By rail:* to Moûtiers (TGV), then by bus.

Tourist Office: Office du Tourisme, 73120 Courchevel, France.
Tel. 79 08 00 29

Altitude: 4,265–6,070 ft. (1,300–1,850 m.). *Top:* 8,983 ft. (2,738 m.)

Language: French

Runs: 112 mi. (180 km.); 310 mi. (500 km.) in 3 Vallées

Lifts: 67 (200 in 3 Vallées)

Ski areas: La Loze, Le Biollay, La Saulire

Ski school: Ecole du Ski Français

Linked resorts: Méribel, Les Menuires, Val Thorens, Mottaret

Season: December to end April

Kindergarten: *Non-ski:* from 2 years. *With ski:* from 4 years

Prices: *Lift pass:* 6 days Courchevel 625 F (children 437 F); 3 Vallées 825 F (children 650 F). *Ski school:* Group 389 F for 6 half-days (children 315 F); private 140 F per hour.

RATINGS

Skiing Conditions	9
Snow Conditions	8
For Beginners	7
For Intermediates	9
For Advanced Skiers	9
For Children	8
Après-Ski	9
Other Sports	8
Value for Money	7

For map see pp. 138–139.

THE RESORT

Courchevel is the glamour leader of the fabulous 3 Vallées ("Three Valleys"), arguably the most famous ski circus in France—and one of the top in all the Alps. For high style and beautiful people, it has peers but no betters. For skiing, it ranks with the world's best.

There are four centers, generally known by their heights in meters: 1300 (also called Le Praz), 1550, 1650 and the main resort, 1850, which may not be particularly attractive to look at, but is regarded as the most fashionable resort in France. Fur coats abound. Mercedes, too, causing some traffic problems. Pedestrian walkways are separate or fenced off, so car-dodging is not a problem.

The centers at 1550 and 1650 unfortunately do not share 1850's status, amenities or snow at either end of the season. Courchevel 1300 has a relaxed atmosphere and, aesthetically, beats its three big brothers hands down. Courchevel is part of the Savoy Alps and will be staging some of the events in the 1992 Winter Olympics.

THE SKIING

Courchevel's skiing is full of superlatives. As a participant in France's largest ski circus (and the second largest in Europe), it offers a mindboggling lift capacity of 52,000 skiers an hour and boasts the world's largest cable car, the largest ski school in Europe and one of the largest snowmaking installations in the French Alps. But no matter at which level you stay, you will do much of your skiing at 1650 and even more at 1850. Le Signal, above 1650, is the easternmost limit not only of Courchevel but of the entire 3 Vallées. The terrain is relatively easy, and in fact, many of Courchevel's

ski-touring trails also zigzag through the woods in this sector.

To feed into the mainstream of the skiing from Le Signal, it is necessàry either to shuttle over Roc Merlet into the moderately pitched eastern face of the huge Les Creux bowl or to ski down toward 1850 and catch one of the many lifts to the Vizelle/Saulire area. A huge 160-passenger cable car rises from Les Verdons plateau to the Saulire summit, 8,983 ft. (2,738 m.), Courchevel's highest point. The terrain both leading back to Les Verdons and over the other side to Méribel comprises Courchevel's toughest skiing, including three demanding *couloirs*. The Creux Noirs chair, on the Saulire (west) side of the great bowl, also accesses super-steep descents. Col de la Loze, served by lifts from the other side of 1850, offers consistently pitched, moderately challenging terrain.

With 450 instructors, Courchevel is prepared to teach every level of skiing, provide guides for a variety of spellbinding high-mountain tours and offer instruction in pow-

der skiing and some of the new snow sports, such as snowboarding and monoski.

If Courchevel has one disadvantage, it is its location at one end of the 3 Vallées. Strong, fast-moving skiers who aren't much for lengthy lunch breaks can easily make a complete out-and-back circuit in a day—and sample a variety of the splendors en route. Those who are weaker, slower or prone to linger have to make sure they can still complete all the lift connections necessary to return during the afternoon rush. A

taxi from one of the other resorts after the lifts close can cost as much as a week's lift pass.

APRÈS-SKI

There are no bounds in Courchevel (well hardly). You can purchase genuine sophistication among the hotels and rub shoulders with the helicopter set. Often the prices are no higher than those that seem exorbitant at less well-known resorts.

If you have a large quantity of cash to dispose of on luxury products and services, Courchevel offers good value for money. Le Tremplin is lively from close of lifts until the early hours. Half-a-dozen discos throb through the night, peopled by splendidly costumed night-crawlers who may or may not have skied that day. The glitter is brightest in high season, of course, but the Grange and the St. Nicolas always seem to shine.

Courchevel is also a genuine culinary mecca, with French cuisine from *haute* to country style, plus a variety of ethnic offerings. The Fromagerie, as the name suggests, will appeal to cheese-lovers.

There are several movie theaters; and for those only capable of collapsing on the bed, Courchevel has its own radio station.

OTHER ACTIVITIES

There are 30 mi. (50 km.) of cross-country trails, an Olympic-size ice rink and night skiing on the St. Agathe slope once a week, plus ski bikes, street chess, broom hockey, mountain trails, hang-gliding, flying school, parachuting, squash, several swimming pools in hotels open to the public, saunas and two gymnasia. The tourist office organizes frequent classical music concerts, as well as minor exhibitions.

LES DEUX ALPES

mont-blanc 4807 m   grandes jorasses 4208 m   les a
grand paradis
grandes rousses
refuge du rif-tort   plate
besse
en oisans
lac du chamb
fren   ois   mont de ans
bon   cucule

Access: *Nearest airports:* Geneva (3 hrs.); Grenoble (2 hrs.); Lyon (3 hrs.). *By road:* A48 Autoroute to Grenoble, then via Vizille. *By rail:* to Grenoble, then by bus.

Tourist Office: Office du Tourisme, 38860 Les Deux Alpes, France. Tel. 76 79 22 00

Altitude: 5,414 ft. (1,650 m.). *Top:* 11,707 ft. (3,568 m.)

Language: French

Runs: 122 mi. (196 km.)

Lifts: 63

Ski areas: Oisans, Jandri, La Grave

Ski schools: Ecole du Ski Français, Ecole de Ski de St-Christophe

Linked resorts: None

Season: December to May, plus summer skiing

Kindergarten: *Non-ski:* from 6 months. *With ski:* 3–6 years

Prices: *Lift pass:* 6 days 665 F (children 540 F). *Ski school:* Group 440–485 F for 6 half-days; private 150 F per hour.

RATINGS

Skiing Conditions	8
Snow Conditions	6
For Beginners	5
For Intermediates	8
For Advanced Skiers	6
For Children	7
Après-Ski	4
Other Sports	6
Value for Money	4

THE RESORT

Les Deux Alpes, which developed in the fifties, keeps up to date with new lifts and accommodations. Latest is the Dôme Express, the highest funicular in France, built beneath a glacier and an amazing technological feat. Although it is a long trek from one end of the village to the other, there is a bus service. Unlike many other purpose-built ski cen-

res 3510 m
massif de la vanoise
la meije 3983 m
le râteau 3807 m
les écrins 4102 m
col du galibier 2645 m *col du lautaret 2058 m*
dôme de la lauze 3568 m
aiguille du plat de la selle 3597 m
col des ruillans
les vallons de la meije
SKI D'ETE glacier du mont de lans
dôme de puy salié 3418 m
3288 m
le chazelet
villar d'arène
3170 m
parc national des écrins
la grave 1430 m
chalance
lac noir
tête de la toura 2914 m
les gourses
2580 m
le diable
tête moute 2813 m
lac du plan
le rachas
grande aiguille
2185 m
2450 m
stade slalom
les porrons
rochers d'escalade
parc national des écrins
soleil
100 m
vers la bérarde
le vénéon
DAVID
bourg d'arud
venosc

ters, traffic runs along Les Deux Alpes' busy main road.

Ever-popular with French families, the resort can get crowded at weekends with day-trippers from nearby towns. Accommodations to suit all pocketbooks make Les Deux Alpes a versatile destination. Although it has all the convenience and amenities of other new French resorts, it lacks both the harmony of the new and the charm of the old.

Not a pretty spot, but no one seems to mind.

THE SKIING

Les Deux Alpes was so named, not because of the skiing it boasts on two sides of the resort, but because it is set at the point where the Alpes du Nord meet the Alpes du Sud. The western or Oisans side is a limited south-facing hill with mostly easy

terrain. On the other side, closest to most of the accommodations, is a long, steep headwall. A few novice slopes seem to have been pressed onto this mountain base, but the overall impression is truly quite daunting.

At the bottom of a large, multitiered massif called Jandri, more than a dozen lifts, from snail-pace beginner Pomas to four-place chairs, launch skiers onto the slopes. Some rise just a few hundred feet, others climb to a broad terrace where the steep mountain evens out into a wide basin, with mostly midlevel skiing. A series of trams, gondolas and lesser lifts serves this section, which holds Jandri's most varied terrain. There are even some mid-mountain ridges and valleys which ski as long, steep chutes and headwalls, and some challenging off-*piste* skiing, too. Up here, a few lifts serve a relatively tight network of *pistes*, suitable for solid intermediate to advanced skiers.

Above is the Glacier du Mont de Lans, one of Europe's best summer-skiing areas, now reached by the Dôme Express which terminates at 11,237 ft. (3,425 m.). The glacier is also accessible in 20 minutes on the Jandri Express lift, and you can always come down that way if you are too tired to tackle the last leg. This treeless area can be bleak in bad weather and, compared with the size of the village, the on-*piste* skiing is not really extensive. Off-*piste* aficionados appreciate skiing to La Grave—the infamous powder mountain. There are also guided snowcat powder tours.

The Grande Galaxie lift pass entitles you to one day each in Alpe d'Huez, Serre Chevalier, Puy-St-Vincent, Bardonecchia (Italy) or any of the Milky Way resorts (huge area spanning France and Italy).

APRÈS-SKI

This is essentially a skiers' spot. Prices for evening entertainment are high, especially in nightclubs and discos. La Casa is the best of the four discos, if money is no object and you don't object to slightly seedy cabaret shows. There is a pub and a very nice piano bar next to the health club. Watch antics on the ice rink from the windows of the Bar de la Patinoire. Les Deux Alpes offers a wide selection of restaurants or you can eat in hotels. For local specialties (*raclette*, *fondue*), try La Patate and the Igloo bar opposite which charges normal drink prices.

OTHER ACTIVITIES

On the slopes you can learn *parapente* (parachuting off the mountain). At village level, the 2 Alpes Tonic health club has a weight-training gym, dance, acrobic and stretch classes, as well as massage, sauna and Jacuzzi. There is a sauna, too, at the swimming pool and ice rink complex. The outdoor pool is heated. All facilities are either free or discounted with a valid lift pass. Many hotels also have swimming pools for guests. If total relaxation is more your scene after a day on the slopes, try floating in Epsom salts maintained at body temperature in an isolation tank.

A new sports center has opened in Le Village (by bus or a ten-minute walk from town), offering ten-pin bowling, squash, indoor and outdoor pools and table tennis.

Les Deux Alpes lies in the Vallée du Vénéon, one of the six valleys of the Oisans, noted for its lakes and waterfalls, forests and traditional Alpine villages. The Parc National des Ecrins can be explored on foot or cross-country skis.

FLAINE

Access: *Nearest airport:* Geneva (1½ hrs.). *By road:* A40 Autoroute, exit Cluses. *By rail:* to Cluses, then by bus.

Tourist Office: Office du Tourisme, 74300 Flaine, France. Tel. 50 90 80 01

Altitude: 5,250 ft. (1,600 m.). *Top:* 8,203 ft. (2,500 m.)

Language: French

Runs: 93 mi. (150 km.); 161 mi. (260 km.) in Grand Massif

Lifts: 30 (84 in Grand Massif)

Ski areas: Les Grands Vans, Les Grandes Platières, Aujon

Ski schools: Ecole du Ski Français, Ski Ecole Internationale

Linked resorts: Les Carroz, Samoëns, Morillon

Season: December to April

Kindergarten: *Non-ski:* from 6 months. *With ski:* 3–12 years

Prices: *Lift pass:* 6 days Flaine 430–540 F (children 340–420 F), Grand Massif 640 F (children 540 F). *Ski school:* Group 360 F for 6 half-days (children 280 F); private 130 F per hour.

RATINGS

Skiing Conditions	7
Snow Conditions	7
For Beginners	8
For Intermediates	8
For Advanced Skiers	6
For Children	9
Après-Ski	3
Other Sports	4
Value for Money	8

THE RESORT

Flaine is a purpose-built, car-free ski resort located in a sunny bowl with an excellent snow record. It is compact and laid out on three tiers: Forum (first level to be constructed in 1968), Forêt above (linked by lifts day and night) and the Front de Neige below. The resort consists largely of apartments, plus five hotels (Les Lindars is particularly good with nursery and baby-sitting facilities). Designed by Marcel Breuer to blend in with the mountainside, Flaine is loved or hated for its concrete-block appearance.

THE SKIING

Flaine has an image as *the* resort for beginners and families. Indeed facilities for both are excellent, with free beginner lifts and two ski schools, both with English-speaking instructors. But there is also extensive intermediate skiing, some challenging runs and plenty of interesting off-*piste*. Those just starting to venture off marked runs will enjoy wide tracts close by.

There are lifts from all levels into the system, and all the runs in the Flaine bowl lead back to the village, minimizing walking. The quickest way up is by the new *télécabines* (20-plus passengers) from Forum, but "eggs", Pomas and chairs transport you just as high. The Aujon area, at one end of the network, is uncrowded and offers delightful, gentle powder slopes, while at the other end, off the back of Les Grands Vans, the run to Lac de Gers is too steep ever to be groomed.

When safe enough to be opened, it offers perfect powder or spring snow conditions to challenge the most demanding expert.

Intermediate skiers easily yoyo up lifts and down runs along the entire bowl. Most of the *pistes*, designed by the great Emile Allais, are tamed by crossing the fall line. The views from the top stations stretch to Mont Blanc. Skiing to the village from the highest points in the system (such as Les Grandes Platières at 8,137 ft. [2,480 m.] or the saddle below the Tête des Lindars summit) makes for fairly long runs on a relatively modest vertical of just over 3,000 ft. (900 m.). There are also long trails through the trees to the villages below which are partners in the Grand Massif lift system.

The Grands Vans chairlift links into the Grand Massif area comprising Les Carroz (below Flaine, on the road up) and Samoëns and Morillon in the next valley. Limited skiing at Sixt is also covered by the regional lift pass but not linked.

APRÈS-SKI

Après-ski tends to start with a drink on a sunny terrace and, for family types, winds down early. The White Grouse Pub, where you can play darts, is a reasonably sure place to meet other English-speaking visitors. Some prefer relaxing in the comfort of the hotel bars. There are two rather expensive discotheques, plus weekly dancing in the Hotel Aujon bar. Le Desert Blanc, at the

top of the Grandes Platières gondola, occasionally puts on evening entertainment with dancing, followed by a torchlight on-skis descent. A movie theater and music center provide quieter entertainment for those too tired to move.

There are a couple of restaurants which should not be missed. La Trattoria, a Franco-Italian extravaganza, serves exquisite cuisine, to be washed down by smooth house wine. Cook your own meal on the tabletop at Chez Daniel where the specialties are a selection of meats grilled on a hot slate, *fondue* and crêpes. *Fondue* evenings are organized in a couple of mountain restaurants.

OTHER ACTIVITIES

On the slopes you can try hang-gliding or parascending. A small amount of cross-country skiing, 5 mi. (8 km.), is available at the Col de Flaine, and non-skiers can walk in snow-shoes beside the *pistes*. The Topform center has a swimming pool, sauna and weight-training, plus therapeutic massage. Children congregate around the small natural ice rink, and there is a trimoto course for them nearby. Grown-ups can learn to drive a car on an icy circuit. In the evenings, snow-scooter excursions are organized. There is also a contemporary art center at Flaine.

ISOLA 2000

Access: *Nearest airport:* Nice (1½ hrs.). *By road:* A8 Autoroute, St-Isidore exit, then via St-Sauveur. *By rail:* to Nice (TGV), then by bus.

Tourist Office: Office du Tourisme, 06420 Isola 2000, France. Tel. 93 23 15 15

Altitude: 6,562 ft. (2,000 m.). *Top:* 8,563 ft. (2,610 m.)

Language: French

Runs: 75 mi. (120 km.)

Lifts: 24

Ski areas: Pélevos, St-Sauveur, Levant

Ski schools: Ecole du Ski Français, Ski Ecole Internationale

Linked resorts: None

Season: December to April

Kindergarten: *Non-ski:* from 3 months. *With ski:* 3–10 years

Prices: *Lift pass:* 6 days 455–550 F (children 435 F). *Ski school:* Group 415 F for 6 half-days; private 138 F per hour.

RATINGS

Skiing Conditions	7
Snow Conditions	7
For Beginners	8
For Intermediates	7
For Advanced Skiers	4
For Children	9
Après-Ski	7
Other Sports	5
Value for Money	7

THE RESORT

Isola consists mainly of a long, snaking collection of apartments, shops, bars and restaurants, all under one roof and linked by a central corridor, complete with security men and surveillance cameras.

The resort's reputation for good snow and sun (you are awarded a week's free accommodations if the sun doesn't shine for three days) has resulted in expansion up the mountain, so that the original "one-block" concept has been abandoned. A new funicular railway links the Hameau apartments with the main resort.

There can be a problem with cars during peak season on the narrow road up from the Côte d'Azur. This makes the helicopter link attractive. Congestion in the resort itself has been somewhat alleviated by the construction of a 550-place parking lot on the outskirts.

THE SKIING

Few could fault the 75 mi. (120 km.) of *pistes*. Mainly spread out to the south and west, the resort hopes to expand further into Italy (currently *pistes* run along the border) and possibly into a French national park area. Beginners can ski the gentle Grand Tour plateau, an untaxing 3 miles (5 km.). Snow is guaranteed (with a daily refund on the lift pass if it is not possible to ski back to the village), and the resort has held the French snow-depth record for several years.

Closest to the village are the lifts serving the mild terrain on both

sides. There are long easy-to-inter-mediate runs to the Col de la Lombarde and the Combe Grasse on one side and the somewhat more mixed terrain on the lower slopes of a multi-peaked ridge on the other.

The terrain currently spreads to two other interconnected sectors which are not visible from the village. La Cabane has a dense web of novice-to-intermediate *pistes*, their upper portions above the tree line and the lower stretches through the trees, on the village side. Three runs funnel down to the bottom terminals of a trio of chairs—one a detachable quad. These chairs, and two other lifts, serve the great amphitheater formed by the Col de la Valette, Sistron, Mont Mertier and Mont Mene. Here skiers find the resort's most difficult terrain and its greatest vertical, from Sistron's 8,560-ft. (2,610-m.) summit to the bottom of the lowest chair at 5,904 ft. (1,800 m.).

The most crowded area is normally around the top of the single *télé-cabine* at Tête de Pélevos, directly above the main resort. Here snow conditions and crowds can make some of the intermediate runs seem more difficult than the generally quieter Mene area, where some challenging expert runs descend through the trees. Some of the best intermediate skiing is reached by the Génisserie detachable chairlift.

Isola provides excellent children's facilities, with or without ski. Other beginners are taught the *ski-évolutif* (GLM-type) method on a good selection of beginner slopes by the village. The ski school offers every snow sport imaginable.

APRÈS-SKI

Isola does not score highly for its après-ski atmosphere. There are a few very notable exceptions—the Cow Club at the base of the slopes and the Génisserie at the bottom of the four-place chair are excellent restaurants. But the vast majority of bars, discos and restaurants are in the covered ''arcade''. Bars are generally narrow, the discos expen-

ISOLA 2000
115 km de pistes

The tourist office arranges occasional cultural events (classical music concerts throughout the whole season), and the resort has its own 24-hour TV station (sets may be rented). Ski School does its bit with a torchlit display, along with a fireworks display, once a week. Another option is the movie theater where the program changes three times a day. Films are shown in English one day of the week.

OTHER ACTIVITIES

Night skiing (8 till 10 p.m. on Thursdays), monoski, "artistic-skiing", snow-surfing, hang-gliding, parascending, ice-driving, aerobics, rambling are all easily arranged. Alternative sports facilities include snow-buggy track, snow-scooter track, skidoo hire, ice rink, gymnasium and sauna, and an outdoor heated swimming pool open from February. Cross-country skiers have only one tiny loop.

sive. A few of the inside restaurants, however, offer high-quality cuisine, albeit with matching prices. Parties in your apartment are normally the best bet for at least half the week.

MEGÈVE

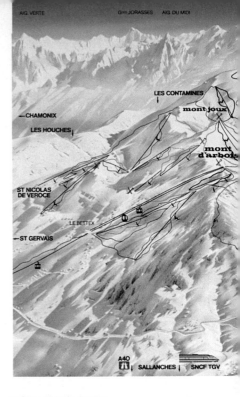

Access: *Nearest airport:* Geneva (1 hr.). *By road:* A40 Autoroute, exit Sallanches. *By rail:* to Sallanches (TGV to Bellegarde), then by bus.

Tourist Office: Office du Tourisme, 74120 Megève, France.
Tel. 50 21 27 28

Altitude: 3,652 ft. (1,113 m.).
Top: 7,710 ft. (2,350 m.)

Language: French

Runs: 186 mi. (300 km.)

Lifts: 43 (89 with linked resorts)

Ski areas: Mont d'Arbois, Roche-brune/Côte 2000, Le Jaillet

Ski school: Ecole du Ski Français

Linked resorts: Combloux, St-Gervais, St-Nicolas-de-Véroce

Season: December to April

Kindergarten: *Non-ski:* from 12 months. *With ski:* from 3 years

Prices: *Lift pass:* 6 days 730 F. *Ski school:* Group 470 F for 6 days (children 400 F); private 150 F per hour.

RATINGS

Skiing Conditions	7
Snow Conditions	5
For Beginners	9
For Intermediates	9
For Advanced Skiers	4
For Children	8
Après-Ski	10
Other Sports	8
Value for Money	6

THE RESORT

Megève is a tasteful and sophisticated town with a well-preserved old center. It has been France's fashionable resort since the thirties, with luxury hotels, smart nightclubs, and fur-clad jet-setters long before there were jets. The opportunity to rub shoulders with the rich and famous pushes prices up, but now there are more apartments and infiltration by non-French clientele. If you shop around, you don't need to spend an arm and a leg.

THE SKIING

Although parts of the town might be some way from the slopes, there is an excellent bus service to the lifts. Mont d'Arbois (where there are also hotels and apartments) is the main skiing area linking with St-Gervais and St-Nicolas-de-Véroce, with plans also to link to Les Contamines.

When snow is plentiful there is a skiing route back to the town.

The Mont d'Arbois sector is the most extensive. Although the *pistes* lack challenge, they are not without interest, winding through trees or cutting across the mountainside. It is a wonderful spot for beginners and intermediates. Les Mandarines is a long, easy run which a third-day skier could tackle, and even the most difficult, La Princesse, could be taken on by any aspiring intermediate. Better skiers will enjoy the moguls on Mont Joux, steep runs down Mont Joly and extensive off-*piste* among the trees.

The Rochebrune area can be reached from two points in Megève, and the recent addition of the Rocharbois cable car means you can ski both areas without crossing the village. On the other side of town Le Jaillet area links to that of Combloux, the next village down the valley. Côte 2000 (linked to Rochebrune)

provides limited but challenging skiing, including a downhill course.

The relatively low altitude makes skiing risky early or late season, although the *pistes* are on pastureland (or a golf course), which means less damage to skis if snow is scant. The *pistes* may seem short to the fast skier. This is partially offset by the abundance of delightful, if sometimes expensive, mountain restaurants at every stop-off point. With most of the skiing below the tree line, visibility is fairly good when the weather is bad.

The Mont Blanc lift pass entitles you to ski in 12 other local resorts (including Chamonix), plus free bus transport in and between these centers.

APRÈS-SKI

For many visitors to Megève the nightlife is as important as the skiing. Some people do not reach the slopes until midday—and some never do. There is fun for everyone and for every pocketbook. Unpretentious bars for an après-ski drink include the Club House du Mont d'Arbois where the ski instructors gather, the Puck by the ice rink and the Coeur de Megève. Excellent restaurants serve local fare, pizzas, seafood or haute cuisine. There are nightspots catering for all age groups and inclinations (Les Enfants Terribles for wealthy youth and five other so-called "American bars" and nightclubs), plus the chance to win enough to afford it all at the casino! Round off the evening by taking a horse-drawn sleigh round the town or back to your hotel or apartment.

OTHER ACTIVITIES

Cross-country enthusiasts will appreciate loops offering a variety of challenge in a breathtaking setting. There are plenty of itineraries for walking in the mountains. Skating outdoors on the centrally situated rink is good fun, with the Puck bar/restaurant to collapse in afterwards. The Palais des Sports houses an Olympic-sized indoor ice rink, curling, swimming pool and saunas, tennis, indoor wall climbing, gym and dance studios.

Megève itself has a lot to offer, with its old church, small streets with quaint buildings, antique shops and boutiques. There are often exhibitions at the Palais des Sports et des Congrès. The Musée du Haut Val d'Arly has a collection of traditional Savoyard art. The road to Calvary runs around the Mont d'Arbois: 14 chapels built by Father Ambroise Martin in 1840 and a reconstruction of the Golgotha of Jerusalem.

There is a regular bus service to Annecy, the capital of Savoie, a beautiful lakeside town with a medieval castle. Chamonix, at the head of the valley, is a must, either to ski the Vallée Blanche (famous 14-mi. [22-km.] off-*piste* route) or just to take the cable car up the Aiguille du Midi to see the Mer de Glace ("Sea of Ice") where this run commences.

LES MENUIRES

Access: *Nearest airport:* Geneva (4–5 hrs.). *By road:* A43 Autoroute to Chambéry, then via Moûtiers. *By rail:* to Moûtiers, then by bus.

Tourist Office: Office du Tourisme, 73440 Les Menuires, France. Tel. 79 00 73 00

Altitude: 5,955 ft. (1,815 m.). *Top:* 9,351 ft. (2,850 m.)

Language: French

Runs: 62 mi. (100 km.); 310 mi. (500 km.) in 3 Vallées

Lifts: 54 (200 in 3 Vallées)

Ski areas: La Masse, Mont de la Chambre, Reberty

Ski school: Ecole du Ski Français

Linked resorts: Val Thorens, Méribel, Courchevel

Season: December to April, plus summer skiing

Kindergarten: *Non-ski:* 3–30 months and 30 months–6 years. *With ski:* from 4 years

Prices: *Lift pass:* 6 days 3 Vallées 742–825 F (children 650 F). *Ski school:* Group 560 F for 6 half-days (children 480 F); private 128 F per hour.

RATINGS

Skiing Conditions	9
Snow Conditions	8
For Beginners	8
For Intermediates	9
For Advanced Skiers	9
For Children	8
Après-Ski	6
Other Sports	5
Value for Money	7

THE RESORT

Lying in the largest valley of the world-famous 3 Vallées complex, Les Menuires has been criticized as one of the most dreary and ugly ski resorts anywhere. The French are not perturbed by such comments and call it the "smile of the three valleys", perhaps because of the semicircular arrangement of the buildings. In reality, Les Menuires is not about architecture. It is about first-rate skiing and is as lively a place as any purpose-built resort.

THE SKIING

The Belleville Valley accounts for two-thirds of the 3 Vallées skiing. It's situated directly beneath Val Thorens, Europe's highest ski resort, where skiing is possible eight months of the year.

From the Reberty area lifts rise directly to the Pointe de la Masse, 9,210 ft. (2,807 m.), providing challenging west-facing descents. From Les Menuires itself *télécabines* ascend to Le Mont de la Chambre, from which medium-steep runs go down to Val Thorens. Méribel is in the next valley. Courchevel can be reached by an intermediate skier in 2 to 3 hours. If you make it a day trip, be careful to check when the lifts close and leave plenty of time for the return.

There are wide, open beginner slopes in the resort's center. As Les Menuires is an altitude resort, problems with snow shortage are rare; nonetheless the resort has invested more than 45 million francs in Eu-

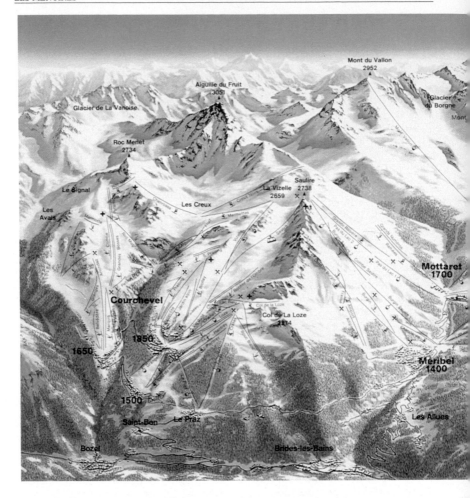

rope's first computer-operated snowmaking machines covering more than 5 mi. (8 km.) of *piste*.

APRÈS-SKI

The main center is at La Croisette, where numerous bars, two discos and a number of restaurants are found. Residents of the Reberty off-shoot have their own facilities, which is just as well, since the shuttle bus stops running in the early evening (they do have the compensation of better access to the skiing,

however). Entertainments include *fondue* evenings, theater, cinema and exhibitions of art and local crafts. Prices are normally lower than in the other 3 Vallées resorts.

OTHER ACTIVITIES

There are 16 mi. (26 km.) of cross-country skiing. Two outdoor swimming pools, two fitness clubs, hang-gliding lessons, snow-scooter rental, snowshoe excursions (escorted), body-building, aerobics, table tennis and ice skating are also available.

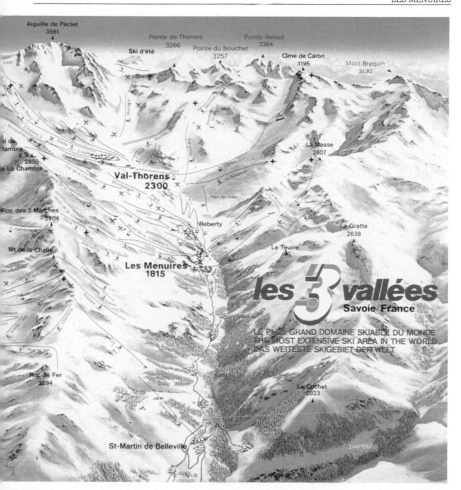

MÉRIBEL

Access: *Nearest airport:* Geneva (4 hrs.). *By road:* A43 Autoroute to Chambéry, then via Moûtiers. *By rail:* to Moûtiers (TGV), then by bus.

Tourist Office: Office du Tourisme, 73550 Méribel, France. Tel. 79 08 60 01

Altitude: 4,593 ft. (1,400 m.). *Top:* 9,686 (2,952 m.)

Language: French

Runs: 62 mi. (100 km.); 310 mi. (500 km.) in 3 Vallées

Lifts: 44 (200 in 3 Vallées)

Ski areas: Mont Vallon, La Saulire, Mont de la Challe

Ski schools: Ecole du Ski Français, Ski Cocktail

Linked resorts: Courchevel, Les Menuires, Val Thorens

Season: December to April, plus summer skiing

Kindergarten: *Non-ski:* 2–8 years. *With ski:* 3–8 years

Prices: *Lift pass.* 6 days 3 Vallées 742–825 F (children 650 F). *Ski school:* Group 840 F for 6 half-days (children 720 F); private 145 F per hour.

RATINGS

Skiing Conditions	9
Snow Conditions	8
For Beginners	7
For Intermediates	9
For Advanced Skiers	7
For Children	7
Après-Ski	7
Other Sports	8
Value for Money	8

THE RESORT

Méribel is 50 years old, but a distinctly "yuppie" resort. A step down from Courchevel, it is more genuine and relaxed. This quite attractive village is very popular with the British. With the coming of the 1992 Olympics to the Savoie region, of which Méribel is a part, road access problems are improving rapidly. Accommodations are mainly in chalets, with no unsightly developments in the main village. Méribel-Mottaret, the higher offshoot, 5,576 ft. (1,699 m.), consists essentially of apartment buildings.

THE SKIING

Méribel is "in the heart of the Three Valleys", between Courchevel and Val Thorens. Some 200 lifts cover 310 mi. (500 km.) of *piste*, covered by one lift pass and easily accessible from Méribel.

Méribel's own skiing is generally divided into two areas, east and west. Advanced skiers use the eastern lifts as a link with superior skiing at Val Thorens. Intermediates, however, will appreciate the immediate area, with most of the skiing accessed by the west-lying lifts to Col de la Loze and Saulire. A new superlift on Mont du Vallon above Mottaret offers more for experts.

All of Méribel's terrain features open snowfields above and runs cut through the trees below. The skiing on both sides of the valley is overwhelmingly for low-intermediate and low-advanced skiers, with the runs from La Saulire being slightly more difficult. The popular runs are

vulnerable to skier traffic and melt-offs, so they are now blanketed with machine-made snow from 240 cannons.

The art of snow-making will be refined over the next several sessions, since Méribel is slated as the venue for the women's Alpine races in the 1992 Olympics. Slalom and downhill stadiums are being built at La Chaudanne, the first time in Olympic history that the speed and technical events will have finished at the same place.

APRÈS-SKI

The best bars and restaurants are in Méribel itself. The Capricorn is one of the liveliest and friendliest, but a bit claustrophobic for non-smokers. English staff and clientele, pop music, beer and the word "Pub" in the name provide a home-away-from-home feel about the bars. Good French restaurants, such as Chez Kiki, abound, and some feature local specialities.

Méribel really doesn't have a huge amount going on after dark. There are two discos, one five minutes' walk down from the village center and another up in Mottaret, two cinemas and a planetarium.

OTHER ACTIVITIES

All imaginable snow sports are possible, with a private ski school offering a "cocktail" of instruction in the various new styles. There's also hang-gliding, an indoor swimming pool, artificial ice rink, fitness rooms with sauna and Jacuzzi, in addition to 12 mi. (20 km.) of marked mountain walks, 20 mi. (33 km.) of cross-country skiing joining Méribel and Courchevel, snowshoe excursions and flying lessons or "flightseeing" rides.

LA PLAGNE

Access: *Nearest airport:* Geneva (4 hrs.). *By road:* A43 or A41 Autoroutes to Chambéry, then via Albertville and Moûtiers. *By rail:* to Aime (TGV to Moûtiers), then by bus.

Tourist Office: Office du Tourisme, 73210 Aime, France. Tel. 79 09 79 79

Altitude: 4,101–6,726 ft. (1,250–2,050 m.). *Top:* 10,663 ft. (3,250 m.)

Language: French

Runs: 124 mi. (200 km.)

Lifts: 100

Ski areas: Montchavin/Les Coches, Plagne Bellecôte/Belle Plagne, Grande Rochette, Biolley, Montalbert/Longefoy

Ski school: Ecole du Ski Français

Linked resorts: None

Season: December to April, plus summer skiing

Kindergarten: *Non-ski:* 2–6 years. *With ski:* 3–7 years

Prices: *Lift pass:* 6 days 730 F (children 550 F). *Ski school:* Group 60 F for half-day; private 140 F per hour.

RATINGS

Skiing Conditions	9
Snow Conditions	8
For Beginners	9
For Intermediates	9
For Advanced Skiers	7
For Children	7
Après-Ski	2
Other Sports	4
Value for Money	7

THE RESORT

French-speakers know that "La Plagne" ought really to be "Les Plagnes" to do justice to the several satellites, from the modern resorts comprising the original Plagne Centre, Plagne Villages, Aime-La Plagne, Plagne Bellecôte, Belle Plagne and Plagne 1800 to the valley villages with rustic origins—Montchavin, Les Coches, Montalbert and Champagny. From the higher resorts you can start the day by going downhill.

Aime-La Plagne is the highest, 6,890 ft. (2,100 m.), and is essentially a huge apartment block with shops and other amenities indoors. Most

accommodations are self-catering, although there are also hotels. Belle Plagne, the newest resort, is still developing. The wood and slate buildings are attractive and the scenery is softened by trees. The lower villages are prettier but, being on the edge of the system, it is harder to appreciate the full skiing potential.

THE SKIING

La Plagne's skiing, designed by the legendary Emile Allais, is complex, multi-layered and as sprawling as the Alps themselves. The scale is awesome. Rising from futuristic villages are endless snowfields with strings of ultra-modern lifts (includ-ing the longest gondola in the world), but the overwhelming impression is that of a vast ski circus— ultimate bliss for muscle-flexing intermediate skiers. Plagne Villages, Plagne Centre and Aime-La Plagne are at roughly the same altitude and lie relatively close together at the bottom of a grand basin. The moderately canted slopes above them form the heart of the ski area. The second concentration of terrain is above Belle Plagne and Plagne Bellecôte, one bowl over. The lifts from these centers access longer *pistes*, but also ones mostly for mid-level skiers.

Experts have endless acres of un-tracked off-*piste* powder to play in,

and many hire a guide to find the best pockets. At least once in every vacation, strong expert skiers should ride to the Bellecôte Glacier (also the site of La Plagne's summer skiing activity) and take the mind-bending, knee-knocking 9½-mi. (15-km.), 6,000-vertical-ft. (1,829-m.) ski route down to Montchavin. It is also possible to ski to Les Arcs and return by bus or taxi.

Although reputed to be an intermediate paradise, La Plagne offers some challenging skiing: vast tracts of open off-*piste*, plus tricky trails through the trees on lower slopes. It is excellent for beginners and children, with a ski school and kindergartens in all villages.

APRÈS-SKI

Because the overwhelming majority of skiers hole up in their apartments, La Plagne is not famed for its wild nightlife, though there is free inter-resort transport well into the night (buses or, in the case of Bellecôte-Belle Plagne, *télécabine*). Some of the bars and restaurants are on the pricey side. Le Vieux Tyrol in Belle Plagne and the Piano Bar in Bellecôte are popular. Most of the discos are in Plagne Centre.

OTHER ACTIVITIES

Cross-country skiers will appreciate a long trail winding through forests from Plagne Montalbert, passing above Les Coches, Montchavin and way beyond toward Les Arcs. At Plagne Bellecôte, there is a heated outdoor swimming pool and a natural ice rink. At Belle Plagne, a new sports center offers fitness facilities, two swimming pools, bowling and indoor golf. Squash enthusiasts can play at Plagne 1800. There are health clubs (at 1800) and saunas (Bellecôte and Centre).

The farming communities on the edge of the system are worth a skiing visit, especially the church at Champagny with its early 18th-century reredos (ornamental screen covering the wall behind the altar). The closest valley town, Aime, also has an interesting old church. Within driving distance is Albertville (host to the 1992 Winter Olympics), a medieval city with castle and museum. Chambéry, the historic capital of Savoie, whose 15th-century castle was the home of the ancient dukes of Savoy, has a wealth of museums, churches and monuments, as well as being a pretty French provincial town.

TIGNES

🎿🎿🎿🎿

Access: *Nearest airport:* Geneva (4 hrs.). *By road:* A41 or A43 Autoroutes to Chambéry, then via Bourg-St-Maurice. *By rail:* to Bourg-St-Maurice (TGV), then by bus.

Tourist Office: Office du Tourisme, 73320 Tignes, France. Tel. 79 06 15 55

Altitude: 5,086 ft. (1,550 m.). *Top:* 11,352 ft. (3,460 m.)

Language: French

Runs: 186 mi. (300 km.) with Val d'Isère

Lifts: 57 (110 with Val d'Isère)

Ski areas: La Grande Motte, Col du Palet, L'Aiguille Percée, Le Lavachet

Ski schools: Ecole du Ski Français, seven private schools

Linked resort: Val d'Isère

Season: late November to early May, plus summer skiing

Kindergarten: *Non-ski:* 3 months–10 years. *With ski:* 4–12 years

Prices: *Lift pass:* 6 days 730 F (children 520 F). *Ski school:* Group 450 F for 6 half-days (children 380 F); private 140 F per hour.

RATINGS

Skiing Conditions	10
Snow Conditions	10
For Beginners	3
For Intermediates	10
For Advanced Skiers	9
For Children	8
Après-Ski	4
Other Sports	7
Value for Money	8

THE RESORT

Tignes was constructed in the early era of the modern breed of French resorts. It is often referred to as "moon station", which is easily understood when you see the apartment blocks rising from a treeless wilderness as you approach. Tignes-le-Lac, 6,890 ft. (2,100 m.), is the nucleus. Newer developments are Val Claret and Le Lavachet. Much farther down the valley lie Tignes-les-Boisses and Tignes-les-Brévières, quiet, rustic villages at the edge of the skiing system.

THE SKIING

The skiing makes up for what the village lacks. This brilliant, extensive ski area is linked to neighboring Val d'Isère. There is an abundance of off-*piste* and day tours (with a guide or ski school) to Les Arcs, La Plagne (a day in each is allowed on the lift pass) and even over to Italy (La Thuile). High glacial slopes at La Grande Motte (above Val Claret) ensure year-round snow cover, with an extensive summer-skiing sector. It's a perfect choice for December, when snow is usually scarce. The area is well networked and lines are minimal. Tignes hosts freestyle skiing championships.

The Bellevarde, rising to 9,275 ft. (2,827 m.), is the linchpin between Tignes' skiing and that of Val d'Isère. Tignes-le-Lac perches on a plateau between a ridge bracketed by Col de Fresse and Pointe du Lavachet on the east (Bellevarde) side and L'Aiguille Percée on the west.

The latter is a huge, sunny sector that is usually less crowded but somewhat less interesting than the rest of the Tignes domain.

Val Claret sits high on the plateau. Lifts climb in two directions. One option is the vast Col du Palet sector, with limited linkage to L'Aiguille Percée and ambitious plans for future expansion. The other is La Balme, another expansive domain capped by summer skiing on La Grande Motte glacier. East-bound lifts from Val Claret and Tignes-le-Lac meet at La Tovière, a popular, often crowded sector.

There is some novice terrain on the fringes of Tignes' turf, in the valley between Bellevarde and Lavachet, but otherwise this is heavyweight skiing for strong intermediate and expert skiers—fabulous long runs and astonishing powder skiing. One splendid option is the

killy

ski route from L'Aiguille Percée to Les Brévières in the valley—nearly 4,000 vertical feet (1,219 meters.), ideal for working up an appetite for lunch.

APRÈS-SKI

Although there are enough bars, restaurants and discos/nightclubs, Tignes is not known for its nightlife. British flock to Harri's Bar in Le La-vachet, which is large and busy, with music and dancing. Hotel bars are very welcoming: the Alpaka (run by an English couple) and Neige et Soleil (with a terrace at the foot of the Tovière slopes and perfect for an après-ski tipple) are both in Tignes-le-Lac. Japanese food is served at the Myako in Val Claret. The smartest club is Les Chandelles in Val Claret, but you pay through the nose in all the discos.

OTHER ACTIVITIES

There are cross-country trails on the frozen lake and between Tignes-le-Lac and Val Claret, but in view of the treeless aspect it is not a spot to be recommended to dedicated cross-country skiers.

Tignes-le-Lac has a comprehensive sports center (Tignespace) featuring exercise and dance studios, weight- and circuit-training gymnasium, squash, indoor tennis and golf-driving range, gymnasium for team games (volleyball, basketball, etc.). In addition there are saunas, Turkish baths, Jacuzzis, massage facilities and sunbeds. Next door is a ten-pin bowling alley and a small natural outdoor ice rink. There is also hang-gliding and parascending off the top of Tovière.

VAL D'ISÈRE

🎿🎿🎿🎿🎿

Access: *Nearest airport:* Geneva (4 hrs.) *By road:* A43 or A41 Auto-routes to Chambéry, then via Bourg-St-Maurice. *By rail:* to Bourg-St-Maurice (TGV), then by bus.

Tourist Office: Office du Tourisme, 73150 Val d'Isère, France. Tel. 79 06 10 83

Altitude: 6,070 ft. (1,850 m.). *Top:* 11,648 ft. (3,550 m.)

Language: French

Runs: 186 mi. (300 km.) with Tignes

Lifts: 53 (110 with Tignes)

Ski areas: Le Fornet/Col de l'Iseran, La Daille/Bellevarde, La Solaise

Ski schools: Ecole du Ski Français, Top Ski, Snow Fun

Linked resort: Tignes

Season: Late November to early May, plus summer skiing

Kindergarten: *Non-ski:* 3 months–10 years. *With ski:* 4–12 years

Prices: *Lift pass:* 6 days 730 F (children 520 F). *Ski school:* Group 441 F for 6 half-days (children 345 F); private 132 F per hour.

RATINGS

Skiing Conditions	10
Snow Conditions	10
For Beginners	7
For Intermediates	9
For Advanced Skiers	10
For Children	6
Après-Ski	7
Other Sports	7
Value for Money	8

THE RESORT

The village of Val d'Isère straddles road and river and now extends almost to neighboring Le Fornet up the valley and La Daille in the other direction. There has been a settlement here certainly since the beginning of the millennium, although the church—a focal point—was not constructed until the 11th century. To recapture some of the old flavor, Val d'Isère has embarked on some reconstruction and traffic-reducing measures in the old town. Skiing was introduced in 1932. Since then the resort has continued to develop in size and increase in popularity. Every new season shows stunning changes, from new granite and timber buildings to exciting lift installations. The village is a hodge-podge of architectural styles but not without character, and is far more attractive than the huge "purpose-built" blocks at La Daille. In contrast, Le Fornet has retained a pretty village atmosphere. Free buses (called *trains rouges*) run regularly along the road between the three centers.

THE SKIING

The Val d'Isère/Tignes area is called "L'Espace Killy" after the 1968 triple Olympic gold-medal winner born in "Val". He has maintained links with the resort and actively supported the bid for Albertville to host the 1992 Winter Olympics. Val d'Isère will organize the blue-ribbon event, the men's downhill. A new run down the face below Bellevarde will replace the OK Downhill at La Daille.

 See also map pp. 146–147.

Val d'Isère's skiing thrusts deep into the mountains south and south-west of town. From west to east along the main road, sectors are La Daille (to the Bellevarde area), La Solaise and Le Fornet (also accessing the Col de l'Iseran and the summer ski area on the Glacier de Pissaillas). At La Daille, the new "Funival" underground railway has almost made redundant the two-stage *télécabine*, for both rise to the top of Bellevarde and there is a chairlift option to mid-station. The Funival takes a mere 4 minutes and can hold a staggering 272 people. From Le Fornet, cable car and subsequent *télécabine* ascend toward the Glacier de Pissaillas.

An excellent network for all levels of skier covers these three sectors. The Tommeuses chairlifts at La Tovière and the Col de Fresse platter-pulls above La Daille link with the equally vast skiing at Tignes, which is covered by the regional lift pass. It is easy to ski to the farthest extremity and back in a day.

Novices enjoy the beginner area close to the village, and there are wonderful altitude easy runs on the Bellevarde side and on the glacier above Le Fornet where good snow is ensured. A new four-place chair-lift is in this sector. There is a vast amount of intermediate skiing with some high-intermediate runs such as the famous "Solaise Bumps". Most of the expert slopes develop giant moguls, particularly the short, sharp "3000" run and the long Bellevarde run back to town.

There is a whole new world of off-*piste* adventure in Val d'Isère. Wonderful routes over wide, open spaces or, lower down, through the trees—occasionally crossing a *piste* to get access to a lift. You must take a qualified mountain guide or special off-*piste* ski instructor. Top Ski has all English-speaking guides and especially solicits Americans for their excellent off-*piste* program.

The only hiccup in *piste* links is the inability to join the Solaise area from Bellevarde without skiing to village level, although it can be accomplished off-*piste* via Tour du Charvet.

APRÈS-SKI

Val d'Isère might not be the prettiest Alpine village, but it is certainly one of the liveliest, with much emphasis on English-oriented après-ski. It starts with a drink straight from the slopes and progresses through fine dining or staying up to dance the night away. There is something to suit all age groups and all pocket-books (although some of the more popular places are pricey).

Dick's Tea Bar (nice pun, but there are no T-bars in the area) shows ski films early in the evening and has a disco (double prices after 10 p.m.). Dick roams the mountains with his camcorder and shows people's antics on the slopes in his bar later on; and the Playback (the Feedback is next door), a piano bar with disco, is busier later on at night.

If you prefer a typically French ambience, try L'Aventure (upmarket piano bar/restaurant) or right at the other end of the scale the Bar des Sports (checked tablecloths, fabulous food and sensible prices). Bar Jacques is a cozy place to eat on chalet girls' night off, and La Taverne d'Alsace has a Teutonic touch. Should no night be complete without gyrations and a little cheek to cheek, head for Club 21 (if that is roughly your age) or Mephisto (if you are still hell-bent but a little older).

OTHER ACTIVITIES

Up on the slopes you can try hang-gliding or parascending. Val d'Isère offers limited cross-country skiing, 10½ mi. (17 km.) at village level and altitude, or walking along prepared trails (snowshoe outings also arranged). There is a municipal swimming pool (free with lift pass) and natural skating rink. Therapeos in the Hôtel Sofitel has a pool, gym, sauna, Jacuzzi, massage (and other therapies) and golf practice. Exercise-to-music classes take place in a small studio in the main street. Snow-scootering and driving on ice are also available.

Whatever your faith or lack of it, the old church cannot fail to move you. Dedicated to those that the mountains have claimed, it has stood the test of time for nearly ten centuries, although parts have been added over the years and a complete restoration took place in the early sixties. The Monday street market with its brightly colored wares is worth a browse.

VALMOREL

Access: *Nearest airports:* Lyon (2 hrs.); Geneva (1½ hrs.). *By road:* A41 or A43 Autoroutes to Chambéry. *By rail:* to Moûtiers (TGV), then by bus.

Tourist Office: Office du Tourisme, 73260 Valmorel, France. Tel. 79 09 85 55

Altitude: 4,593 ft. (1,400 m.). *Top:* 7,884 ft. (2,403 m.)

Language: French

Runs: 100 mi. (162 km.)

Lifts: 46

Ski areas: Col du Gollet, Col du Mottet, Montagne de Tête, Beaudin, Madeleine

Ski school: Ecole du Ski Français

Linked resorts: St-François, Longchamp

Season: Mid-December to mid-April

Kindergarten: *Non-ski:* 6 months–3 years. *With ski:* 3–8 years

Prices: *Lift pass:* 6 days 635 F. *Ski school:* Group 418–813 F for 6 days (children 350–615 F); private 150 F per hour.

RATINGS

Skiing Conditions	8
Snow Conditions	8
For Beginners	7
For Intermediates	8
For Advanced Skiers	6
For Children	9
Après-Ski	5
Other Sports	3
Value for Money	7

THE RESORT

Situated at the head of a protected valley in the Tarentaise region, Valmorel was built a little over a decade ago. It is widely recognized as the most successful in creating an attractive village design with a lively atmosphere, without sacrificing the "ski from your doorstep" ideal.

The resort's center is car-free Bourg-Morel, with ski-in, ski-out accommodations stretching up in three chalet-style "hamlets" above. Bourg-Morel has a cobbled square illuminated by imitation oil lamps which lend a somewhat romantic air.

THE SKIING

Valmorel offers some terrain for everyone, though not in the copious quantities and prodigious verticals found elsewhere in the French Alps.

Beginners have their own gently contoured slopes on the Bois de la Croix, served by a free surface lift, close to the resort and away from the main *pistes*. Later in the week they may progress to the Beaudin area, served by two chairlifts from the center. The Montagne de Tête features some more challenging runs. To the southwest, a two-stage chairlift rises to the Col du Mottet, which at 7,884 ft. (2,403 m.) is the highest point of the resort's skiing. The runs from here suit advancing intermediates and up. Connected to it is the Col du Gollet, with similar runs.

One of the main areas is reached by the Col de Madeleine chair, which is also the access to St-François and Longchamp, old villages

Val Thorens

Le Cheval 2 832

Pointe du Grand Niélard 2 551 m

Les Ménuires

Col du Mottet 2 403 m

Vallée des Belleville

Itinéraire de Roche Blanche

Col du Gollet 1 981 m

1 830 m

NOUVEAU!
Le Télésiège de La Lauzière.
Altitude d'arrivée : 2550 m.
Un nouveau télésiège, un nouveau massif pour la première fois ouvert au ski, quatre nouvelles pistes avec 2 dénivelées de 1000 m.

Valmorel. La Belle.

Le Crey

La Charmette   Le Pré

that have benefited from the ski boom. Around these villages is mostly novice to intermediate skiing on three easily interlinked peaks on one massif. There is night skiing on the Planchamp slope served by the main chairlift.

Children's facilities are especially good in Valmorel, with the ski school taking children from 4 years and the ski kindergarten from 3 to 8 years.

APRÈS-SKI

Nightlife is rather limited, as in other "purpose-built" resorts. Valmorel's "main street" design, however, allows for the area to be livelier than most and there are bars and restaurants to sample (as well as shops, a movie theater and even a library).

Au Petit Savoyard offers local cuisine, while Le Creuset caters to gourmets. Le Petit Prince is a must for pizza-lovers, and Chez Ton Frère specializes in North African food. Le Jean's Club is a popular nightclub/disco.

OTHER ACTIVITIES

One of Valmorel's few serious limitations is its current lack of alternative sporting facilities. There is a toboggan run and the usual snow sports available on the slopes, together with snowshoe trails or hang-gliding. Some 12 mi. (20 km.) of cross-country tracks are a few miles outside town. Otherwise it's aerobics or fitness training at the Club Forme. There is a sauna, and massage can be arranged.

154

Pointe du Mottet
2 592 m

2 016 m

Longchamp

S¹ François
2 550 m

Massif
de la Loupère

Col de la Madeleine
1 993 m

Vallée de Celliers

Quarante Planes

Le Meiller

	Français	English	Deutsch
	Facile	Easy	Leicht
	Moyen	Moderate	Mittel
	Difficile	Advanced	Schwer
	Très difficile	Very advanced	Sehr schwer
	Chemin piétonnier balisé	Surveyed field footpath	Präparierter Fussgängerweg
	Itinéraire non balisé	Unmarked trail	Nicht markierte Piste
	Chalet Accueil-Piste (Information et assistance)	Reception chalet (information and assistance)	Chalet "Pistenempfang" (Information und Rettungsdienst)
	Accueil-Piste (Informations et forfaits)	Information desk (for passes)	Information und Abonnements
	Restaurants d'altitude	Mountain restaurants	Bergrestaurant
	Altisurface	Mountain landing surface	Hohenlandeplatz

155

VAL THORENS

Access: *Nearest airport:* Geneva (2½ hrs.). *By road:* A43 or A41 Autoroute to Chambéry, then via Moûtiers. *By rail:* to Moûtiers (TGV), then by bus.

Tourist Office: Office du Tourisme, 73440 Val Thorens, France. Tel. 79 00 01 06

Altitude: 7,546 ft. (2,300 m.). *Top:* 10,483 ft. (3,195 m.)

Language: French

Runs: 75 mi. (120 km.); 310 mi. (500 km.) in 3 Vallées

Lifts: 36 (200 in 3 Vallées)

Ski areas: Péclet, Mont de la Chambre, La Masse, Cîme de Caron

Ski schools: Ecole du Ski Français, Ski Cool

Linked resorts: Les Menuires, Méribel, Courchevel

Season: October to May, plus summer skiing

Kindergarten: *Non-ski:* from 3 months. *With ski:* 3–8 years

Prices: *Lift pass:* 6 days 3 Vallées 742–825 F (children 650 F). *Ski school:* Group 480 F for 6 half-days; private 145 F per hour.

RATINGS

Skiing Conditions	9
Snow Conditions	9
For Beginners	8
For Intermediates	9
For Advanced Skiers	9
For Children	7
Après-Ski	7
Other Sports	6
Value for Money	7

THE RESORT

Europe's highest resort lies at the top of arguably the world's most famous ski area—the 3 Vallées. Purpose-built, of course, it has more facilities than the majority of its competitors and an almost unbeatable guaranteed-snow/exciting-*piste* combination. Opened in 1973, it is most appealing to those dedicated to dawn-till-dusk skiing, or those who wish for certain snow at the increasingly uncertain extremities of the season. The resort itself comes across as a high-rise island floating in a white sea.

THE SKIING

One of the few resorts that can genuinely "guarantee" snow, Val Thorens is skiable over 8 months a year, thanks to its altitude and glacier. The top station—Cîme de Caron—is reached by what was until recently the world's largest cable car (150-person), normally playing inspirational music by Brahms or Pink Floyd over its PA system. The runs from here include a selection of long advanced and expert *pistes* back to the resort. There is also an intermediate route down a blue run to Les Menuires. Over the other side, numerous lifts ascend from various points offering access across to Méribel, Mottaret and on to Courchevel via Mont de la Chambre and Roc des 3 Marches. The Val Thorens-facing runs, like those of La Masse across the valley, are mostly for strong intermediate and better skiers. Off-*piste* options abound. Summer skiing is on the Glacier de Péclet.

For map see pp. 138–139.

Beginners have three free lifts, their own low-price limited ski pass and a good choice of novice *pistes* running into the resort.

Perhaps the resort's only skiing problem is wind which, due to high altitude and lack of shelter, can be strong and has been known to necessitate closing of the lifts. The children's ski school is run by Marielle Goitschel, former World and Olympic champion.

APRÈS-SKI

Prices tend to match the altitude, and "Alpine charm" rates low, but there are three nightclubs, some good restaurants and about 50 bars. Val Thorens has a well-cared-for feeling about it. The Nectar'Inn offers good food at reasonable prices, and there's a pub, the Lincoln, Champagne Charlie's dishes up French food, and La Pause is a very good bar/restaurant. There are 70 shops and a movie theater in the two main galleries, Péclet and Caron.

OTHER ACTIVITIES

The Pierre Barthès sports club has a fully equipped gym, covered tennis courts (ski/tennis courses available), two squash courts, Jacuzzi, saunas, indoor golf, a swimming pool and an outdoor ice rink. On the *pistes* you can hire a snow-scooter, hang-glide or try all the new styles including snow wind-surfing. There is limited cross-country skiing down the valley to Les Menuires.

BEST OF THE REST

ARGENTIÈRE

This suburb of Chamonix is outgrowing its old town center and expanding, with new apartment complexes being constructed with ferocious speed. The ski area is being improved just as quickly, with new lifts and *pistes* to accommodate the increasing crowds which had created mammoth lift lines. Much of the new terrain is on the low end of the skill scale, but Argentière is also for experts. It is the gateway to the legendary Grands Montets, with extremely challenging terrain peaking at 10,745 ft. (3,275 m.). The Mont Blanc lift pass also includes a dozen other resorts.

LA CLUSAZ

This bustling resort, with long-time family appeal, combines Savoyard charm with skiing on five mountains. Beauregard and L'Etale each have just one cable car and pleasant but limited runs mainly for intermediate and advanced skiers. L'Aiguille, closest to the town center and site of some of France's earliest technologically innovative lifts, has ski terrain fanning out from a mid-mountain restaurant. Novice to intermediate turf is on the Crêt du Merle, and more challenging runs on Crêt du Loup. Outlying Balme has a mid-mountain station at Aiguille de Calvaires, with expert runs and good off-*piste* skiing off two higher peaks, La Roualle and Pointe des Verres.

LES GETS

Around the corner from Morzine, Les Gets is a traditional and informal Alpine village that nevertheless has a huge inventory of new apartments. The skiing, which is connected with Morzine's "non-Avoriaz" side, is also part of the Portes du Soleil lift pass system. Lifts climb directly out of Les Gets via Les Chavannes and Le Ranfolly. From there, the Pointe de Nyon sits across a narrow valley. These sectors comprise the most interesting terrain of the older resorts. The return runs from Morzine are navigable by novice and intermediate skiers. There is also an unlinked local ski area called Mont-Chéry.

LE GRAND-BORNAND

Le Grand-Bornand is in the midst of the ski boom. The village and its chalets surrounding an old church contrast with the new ski village of Chinaillon. The skiing stretches across one side of the mountain above both the old and new villages. La Joyère, at the top of the

gondola terminal, is a good place for beginners and intermediates. Other lifts rise beyond to runs for various abilities. Nightlife is still calm, considering that 15,000 guest beds are available, mostly in apartments.

MONTGENÈVRE

Located less than a mile from the Italian border, Montgenèvre is the sole French member of the resorts grouped under the Milky Way name, which offers 100 lifts in a single interchangeable pass. It is possible to ski across the border into Italy to Clavière, Cesana, Sansicario and Sestrière. Montgenèvre's skiing is primarily for intermediates. For a small resort (just 450 inhabitants), it offers zippy nightlife.

MORZINE

Although it has grown into a substantial resort, the old village still retains some of its traditional atmosphere. It is located at the base of the massif on which high-rise Avoriaz is perched, and it has its own suburb, Super Morzine, tucked into a near-private valley. Morzine has the benefit of close links into the heart of the Portes du Soleil via Avoriaz and also into the Les Gets network on the other side of town. Some of Morzine's own ski terrain is on a long ridge culminating at the Col de la Joux Verte and on a peak called Les Hauts Forts above Avoriaz, and the rest is on Le Pleney and Pointe de Nyon on the Les Gets side.

ST-GERVAIS

It isn't often that North Americans get a chance to ski at a place that has been a resort for centuries, but ancient, atmospheric St-Gervais has been a spa since Roman times. St-

Gervais offers convenience and good neighbors. In addition to the proximity of Geneva (1 hr.), it is interlinked with sophisticated Megève with which it shares the wide, winning precincts of Mont d'Arbois. There is also a cable car to Les Houches, a fairly small ski sector. In addition to the old village center, there are accommodations in outlying Le Fayet, St-Nicolas-de-Véroce and Le Bettex, together accommodating 20,000 guests. St-Gervais is part of the Mont Blanc lift pass, with skiing at 12 resorts including Chamonix.

SERRE CHEVALIER

Serre Chevalier is one resort name that blankets a collection of old and new villages strung along the Ghisane Valley between Grenoble and Briançon. Chantemerle, Villeneuve and the old spa town of Monetier were there first; Serre-Chevalier 1350, 1400 and 1500 followed in the new French mode. The skiing is concentrated in two wide bowls, and the Grande Galaxie lift pass is good at Alpe d'Huez, Les Deux Alpes and Puy-St-Vincent, all in France, as well as Bardonecchia and the other Italian members of the Milky Way group.

FRANCE-INFO

ACCOMMODATIONS

Hotels. In the traditional old French ski towns, accommodations tend to be in equally traditional old hotels. Occasionally, a shiny new property will be found, but these are the exceptions. "Old" doesn't necessarily have a negative sense. Many hotels have individual rooms which are larger than whole apartments in newer resorts. Rooms and public spaces, however, are generally not as exquisite as their counterparts in Austria or Switzerland, and swimming pools, whirlpools and other amenities are less common.

Hotels, motels and inns are classified into five categories, from one-star to four-star luxury. Most hotels in ski resorts fall in the two- to four-star categories; deluxe hotels are rare. All rooms in two-star hotels have private bathrooms, but otherwise they are usually very simple. Top hotels will offer excellent dining and après-ski on the premises, telephones and often television in the rooms, elevators and a full staff. English is spoken at the larger hotels, especially in resorts which attract many British guests. This may not be so in lower categories, which are considerably more modest in all respects.

Some French resort hotels will offer the option of *pension complète* (full board or Full American Plan) with three meals a day, or *demi-pension* (half-board or Modified American Plan), which will include breakfast (usually *croissants* and *brioches,* sweet butter, jam and strong coffee, tea or hot chocolate) and a full dinner (usually a set menu) in the price of the room. In France, far more frequently than elsewhere in the Alps, guests breakfast in their rooms. In the *pension complète* option, guests may often choose whether to return to the hotel for lunch or eat at an affiliated mountain restaurant. In either case, it is comforting to know that all or most meals have been paid for in advance.

Pensions. These small, family-run lodgings—often indicated by one or two stars—are casual and inexpensive, offering a true taste of living with a French family. They are the equivalent of a Bed and Breakfast. Meal plans vary, and the family members probably won't speak English.

Chalets. Especially popular with British groups who find them congenial and economical, chalet-style residences are rented out to groups of six or more. Some can be as elaborate as a hotel with their own bar and disco, and are often staffed with a cook and/or "chalet girl". Meal plans vary with the chalet arrangement.

Apartments. What Americans call condos, the French refer to as *appartements*. The new French resorts, the so-called "purpose-built" places developed for skiing, largely offer apartment accommodations. Units are smaller and less opulent than the typical American ski condo, but what they lack in size or luxury they compensate for in convenience to the lifts and slopes, as well as in price. They are easily available in most resorts.

The per-person, per-day cost can be amazingly low, but there are trade-offs in terms of predictability of cost, as well as space and privacy. Meals, whether home-cooked or eaten out, must be added to base rate, and linen charges are usually additional. If you rent a small French apartment, you'd better do it with family or very, very good friends. Apartments tend to be as compact as ship's cabins and include tiny kitchen units, bathrooms and bedrooms.

Club Med. Club Med started in France, and its ski villages are found in Alpe d'Huez, Les Arcs, Avoriaz, Chamonix, Les Menuires, and Tignes. Their all-inclusive packages cover lodging, meals, lift pass, instruction with Club Med's own ski school and après-ski entertainment. French is the predominant language, but English-speakers among staff and guests are often found.

Room types. France has fewer single rooms than other Alpine countries. A double room might have twin beds or a double bed. What Americans know as double-doubles, pairs of queens or kings, are not found in France.

If a hotel room is described as having a bath, it will have just that—a bathtub, usually with a hand shower. If the room is described as having a shower, it won't have a tub. In older, not-recently-renovated hotels make sure that "bath" also includes a toilet. There will probably also be a bidet.

CUSTOMS AND ENTRY REGULATIONS

Citizens of EEC countries need only a valid passport to enter France. For British nationals, a "British Visitors Passport" (valid for one year) or a "British Excursion Document for Travel to France" (available at the post office for trips of up to 60 hours within a month) is acceptable.

Nationals of other countries require a visa. North Americans will be asked to show their passport when checking in for international flights. France no longer requires a visa for US citizens, a security precaution that had been in effect from September 1986 through June 1989.

DRIVING

Rental cars are available at the airport. Some companies are affiliates of major international chains. The minimum driving age in France is 18, but for car rental it is usually 23 (21 for credit card holders). A valid national license is required and an International Driver's License (obtainable from your home motoring organization), though not required, is advisable.

Insurance. A Green Card as proof of automobile insurance is no longer obligatory for vehicles registered in Western Europe, but comprehensive coverage is recommended. Rental cars come with unlimited public liability, plus fire and theft insurance. Additional collision damage insurance is optional.

Speed limits. Where no specific speed limits are posted, they are 60 kph (37 mph) in town, 90 kph (56 mph) on secondary roads, and 130 kph (81 mph) on *autoroutes* in clear weather with good visibility, and 110 kph (68 mph) in rainy weather or poor visibility.

Rules of the road. Drive on the right, pass on the left. Seatbelts for front-seat passengers are required. Children under 10 may not sit in the front seat unless the car has no back seat. Drinking and driving is a serious offense in France; the permitted alcohol level is 0.8 g. Fines for speeding and exceeding the alcohol level are payable in cash on the spot.

Road information. A road information center in Paris gives 24-hour information on road conditions. The main number is (1) 48 99 33 33. Weather information is given on (1) 45 55 91 88, snow reports on (1) 47 42 23 32 or (1) 42.30.13.13.

Breakdowns. Emergency assistance, including free towing and repairs, is given to members of Touring Secours, which has offices in 14 French cities. The *Automobile Club de l'Ile de France* offers emergency road assistance free to members and for a charge to non-members. The Paris-based 24-hour phone number is (1) 43 80 68 58. Otherwise dial 17, wherever you are in France, and the police will put you in touch with a local garage that will come to your rescue.

Road signs. International pictograms are used for most road signs. The sign *Rappel* indicates a continuation of a previously posted restriction.

Mountain driving. Snow tire and chain laws may be in effect on mountain pass roads. Trucks, buses and vehicles climbing uphill have priority on narrow roads.

ELECTRIC CURRENT

Most of France now runs on 220–230 volts at 50 cycles, though occasionally 110 volts may still be encountered. Sockets (outlets) take round, 2-pin (occasionally 3-pin) plugs. American small appliances and electrical gadgets, which are at 60 cycles, require an adaptor/converter. Dual-voltage appliances require a converter. Bathrooms in French hotels may be equipped with low-wattage outlets suitable only for razors; hairdryers and electric curlers, whether American models used with converters or European models, will not work from these outlets.

GETTING THERE

By air. Geneva is the most convenient transatlantic gateway for the French Alps, less than two hours by bus from most resorts. There are non-stop or direct flights from North America. In recent years Lyon-Satolas Airport has come into its own, with a non-stop service from New York. Nice is the gateway for Isola 2000 and other Alpes Maritimes resorts.

Most skiers from Britain are attached to a tour operator's charter flight. Scheduled services are also discounted through flight sales agencies close to the date of departure.

Regular daily buses operate between Geneva's Cointrin Airport (exit French side) and the resorts of the Savoie and Haute-Savoie regions. The airport also incorporates a railway station, but you have to change at the main Geneva station for destinations in France. "Ski route" buses also connect Lyon-Satolas Airport with many resorts between December and April. Groups traveling with a tour operator are met off the plane by the resort representative and directed to the coach.

By rail. With the advent of the TGV, *Train à Grande Vitesse,* Paris–Alps can take as little as five hours. On arrival, there are buses that meet the train and transport you to the resort. Bourg-St-Maurice is a handy station for Tarentaise resorts (Val d'Isère, Tignes, Les Arcs, La Plagne), Moûtiers for the 3 Vallées, Grenoble or Nice for the southern French Alps. The Haute-Savoie is served by several stations all the way to Chamonix.

HEALTH

If you are taken ill, ask help from your hotel in finding an English-speaking doctor. You will have to settle your bill on the spot and file a claim afterwards with your health insurance company. Keep all official receipts for rescue service, doctor's or hospital fees and chemist (pharmacy) prescriptions, to facilitate your claim.

Citizens of fellow EEC states are entitled to claim the same public health services as those available to resident French people. Britons should obtain the relevant E111 form from their local office of the Department of Health and Social Security before departure.

The Carte Neige, a credit card-sized proof of insurance coverage through the Fédération Française de Ski, provides inexpensive, economical ski-accident and medical insurance. It is available to skiers of all abilities for any length of stay. Coverage includes on- and off-*piste* rescue, medical expenses, liability insurance and transportation to the nearest hospital or, if necessary, back to your home country. Coverage is worldwide, so the card is recommended for skiers who wish to combine a week in France with a week in another country.

The Carte Neige is obtainable from ski schools and sports centers at all French resorts. Rates vary according to length of stay, and family rates are also offered.

HOLIDAYS

The French flock to the mountains, and *pistes* get overcrowded over Christmas, New Year and Easter. French schools have a short break in February, the week varying according to *département.* During this time, resorts are more likely to suffer congestion. Paris week is the worst.

MAIL

Post offices display a sign with a stylized blue bird and/or the words "Postes et Télécommunications" (P&T or PTT). In addition to normal mail service, you can make local and long-distance telephone calls, send telegrams and receive and send money at any post office.

As well as at post offices, stamps may be purchased at the hotel front desk, from tobacconists, postcard and souvenir vendors, and from yellow vending machines. Mailboxes are painted yellow.

Post offices are open 8 a.m. to 7 p.m., Monday to Friday, and from 8 a.m. till noon on Saturdays. Smaller post offices usually have a lunch break between noon and 2 p.m.

MONEY MATTERS

Currency. The unit of currency is the French *franc* (abbreviated F or FF), divided into 100 *centimes.*

Coins: 5, 10, 20 and 50 centimes, 1, 2, 5 and 10 francs.

Notes: 20, 50, 100, 200 and 500 francs.

Credit cards and traveler's checks. Most major hotels and restaurants now accept credit cards, as do an increasing number of shops. Service stations do not accept U.S. credit cards, although those also found in America, such as Mobil, Shell or Texaco, take oil-company cards. Traveler's checks are always welcome.

Banks. Banks offer the best exchange rate on traveler's checks and foreign currency. Banks are open 9 a.m. to 4 p.m. on weekdays (many breaking for lunch between noon and 2 p.m.) and close either on Saturdays (cities and main towns) or Mondays. All banks are closed on Sundays and public (legal) holidays, and most close early the afternoon preceding a public (legal) holiday. Banks in ski resorts tend to stay open later in the evening, sometimes until 7 p.m. Exchange offices at airports and major city railway terminals are open seven days a week.

Value Added Tax. Foreign visitors returning home can have the VAT/sales tax (TVA)—imposed on almost all goods in France—refunded on larger purchases (totalling 1,200 F for visitors from non-EEC countries regardless of number of articles and 2,400 F per article for visitors from EEC countries). Refund documents must be requested from the store, stamped and processed within two hours of departure at the airport customs counter before luggage is checked. Stamped copies of these forms are then mailed back to the store. The refund will arrive a few weeks later or be credited to a specified credit card account.

SKI SCHOOL

The French Ski School (*Ecole du Ski Français*, ESF) has a very good reputation. Some ESF-trained instructors have broken away and set up rival schools. These often specialize in teaching monoski, snowboarding, hang-gliding, *ski fantastique*, etc., while others offer instruction in several languages (the International Ski School—*Ski Ecole Internationale*). You will find ESF instructors who speak English in every French resort.

Normally you will be taught the established method (i.e. snowplow turns through to parallel). In some modern resorts, however, the *ski évolutif* (GLM) method is taught to beginners. Introduced by the French at Les Arcs, it involves starting on very short skis and learning parallel skiing from the start, progressively exchanging the skis for longer ones.

Group lessons are usually from 9 a.m. to noon, so you practice in the afternoon what you learned in the morning. Private lessons are charged by the hour, half-day or full day. It is very expensive on a one-to-one basis, but you learn extremely quickly. If on holiday with a few friends, it may be beneficial to share private lessons (instructors will take up to six people).

More advanced skiers will benefit from occasionally joining class I (or even the competition class), where there is very little hanging around and plenty of fast skiing behind the instructor. Expert skiers are advised to take a private instructor or guide if they want to explore the area off-*piste* or perfect skiing in the bumps.

TELEPHONE

Hotels usually add astronomical surcharges onto phone calls, so these are to be avoided—especially for overseas calls. The most economical calls can be made from post offices or phone booths, which are found at railway stations, airports, outside post offices and in outdoor public spaces.

Coin phones are increasingly rare in Paris and are being phased out all over France. If you expect to be making calls, it is best to purchase a *télécarte* phone card, available from post offices, railway ticket counters and shops recognized by a "Télécarte" sign, and valid for 40 or 120 charge units. This card, which has a line of credit built into it, is inserted into specially equipped public phones and is good for multiple calls until the card's value is used up.

For calls back to the U.S. the best deal is AT&T's USADIRECT program. Insert a coin for access, then dial 19, wait for a second dial tone, then dial 0011. This number connects you directly to an AT&T operator in the U.S., who will then place a credit card or collect call for you.

From Paris to the provinces, it is necessary to dial 16 and then the eight-digit local number. From the provinces to Paris, dial 16, wait for another tone, dial 1 and then the eight-digit local number.

TOURIST INFORMATION OFFICES

The French Government Tourist Office can supply specific resort information, hotel price lists and other useful data.

The main U.S. office is at 610 Fifth Ave., New York, N.Y. 10020; tel. (212) 757 1124 for information services. There are also branch offices in Chicago, Dallas, Los Angeles, San Francisco, and in Montreal and Toronto in Canada.

In Britain, contact the French Government Tourist Office, 178 Piccadilly, London W1V 0AL, tel. (01) 491 7622. There is also a recorded information number (01) 499 6911.

France Ski International is a promotional consortium of 17 leading ski resorts. For information, contact FSI, 2, rue Esnault-Pelterie, Aerogare des Invalides, 75007 Paris; tel. (1) 43 23 94 96.

Local tourist offices can give you very specific and up-to-the-minute information on ski and lodgings, and even suggest a hotel and book your room.

GERMANY AND ITS SKIING

All of the major ski resorts of Germany are in Bavaria, the country's most southerly state. It shares with its neighbor, the Austrian Tyrol, similar dialects, cuisine, customs, architecture and, in many resorts, the same mountains. Yet, while ski tourism from abroad is a major business in Austria, skiing in Germany has been largely confined to the Germans.

Much as Colorado's top resorts attract a mix of day-trip and weekend skiers from Denver and vacationers from all over the U.S., German resorts appeal to weekend skiers from such nearby cities as Munich and Stuttgart and to vacationers from farther north in the country. Thanks to the lavish allotment of annual vacation days and mandatory "cures" enjoyed by German workers, these vacationers may be there for Alpine or cross-country skiing, to partake of assorted light therapies, or simply to walk in the woods and breathe the clean mountain air.

Of all the resorts amid the steep, soaring mountains along the border with Austria, only Garmisch-Partenkirchen, by far Germany's biggest resort, approaches true year-round international stature. This is due to a combination of proximity to large tourist attractions and to the presence of a huge American Armed Forces recreation facility. By contrast, Berchtesgaden is largely a summer spa, with both elegant hotels of a very traditional, mid-European style and rustic chalets, all in the most magnificent of mountain settings. Reit im Winkl and Oberstdorf are more typical Alpine towns, with narrow streets, predominantly chalet-style architecture and a sporty ambience.

Germany's ski terrain is overwhelmingly for solid intermediate skiers, though all resorts do have some novice and beginner slopes, as well as a few runs for advanced skiers. At most resorts, the classic Alpine lift pattern prevails: access via cable car (or occasionally gondola) to the upper mountain, where most of the skiing is found.

165

The majority of accommodations are beyond walking distance from the slopes. A car is useful, although parking areas at the bottom stations of the cable cars tend to be small and can fill up quickly. All resorts included in this guide have ski bus service.

A few state-of-the-art chairlifts have recently been installed, but essentially a few old chairs and a lot of efficient, speedy T-bars provide most of the uphill transport. Still, because lift capacity is geared to the huge weekend crowds (as well as because many beds are filled with visitors who don't ski), week-day waits at the lifts are relatively short.

German snow conditions are similar to those of Austria, with the most reliable cover on the high slopes, which are skiable even when the runs to low-lying resorts have melted off. One weather system which skiers dread is the Föhn, a warm wind from northern Africa, which scoots across the Mediterranean, jeopardizes the snow cover, and may even leave a deposit of fine sand grains on the slopes. The Föhn is usually endured once or twice a winter, and in normal years, snow recovery is swift.

The German ski season cranks up shortly before Christmas and tapers off early in April. Only on the high glacial runs of Garmisch's Zugspitze does the season start earlier and end later. High season is Christmas and February, and low-season discounts are common earlier and later. Combining a ski vacation with Germany's famous Fasching—the pre-Lenten Mardi Gras carnival—is a special treat. Pack a clever costume and get ready to party.

All four of the resorts selected for this guide have lavish winter sports facilities, not just for Alpine and cross-country skiing, but for skating, curling, tobogganing and ski-jumping.

Many other Bavarian mountain towns appear as datelines in the sports pages as the venues of important international sports competitions— Pfronten for slalom racing, Inzell for speed skating, Hochjoch for free-style skiing—but the combination of ski terrain and ancillary facilities in such towns usually does not merit a trip across the Atlantic for a winter vacation.

What makes Germany shine for American skiers is exceptional convenience to Munich and its international airport, which is served by non-stop flights from New York and with convenient connections in Frankfurt for much of the U.S.

While Germany is not cheap, it offers value-packed vacation opportunities. Accommodations are all of a very high standard, meals are generously portioned, and the levels of hospitality are as high as anywhere in the Alps. Except in Garmisch where large hotels are also found, small, cozy, mid-range inns prevail, although all resorts have a couple of super-luxurious and some budget accommodations as well. Many hotels are adding indoor swimming pools, saunas and whirlpools.

Bavarian resorts really provide foreigners with an opportunity to meet the Germans. Because the winter resorts draw mostly skiers from within the country, that's whom visitors from abroad will meet on the pistes and at the lively, merry cafés, bars and nightspots in every town.

BERCHTESGADEN

Access: *Nearest airports:* Munich (1½ hrs.); Salzburg (½ hr.). *By road:* A3 Autobahn, exit Bad Reichenhall. *By rail:* station in Berchtesgaden.

Tourist Office: Kurdirektion, 8240 Berchtesgaden, B.R.D. Tel. (08652) 50 11

Altitude: 1,772 ft. (540 m.). *Top:* 6,148 ft. (1,874 m.)

Language: German

Runs: 25 mi. (40 km.)

Lifts: 31

Ski areas: Jenner, Rossfeld-Zinken, Hochschwarzeck, Götschen

Ski schools: Skischule: Berchtesgaden; Oberau; Margret Aschauer; Allweglehen; Götschen

Linked resorts: Oberau, Rossfeld, Zinken (Austria)

Season: Mid-December to mid-April

Kindergarten: *Non-ski:* none. *With ski:* from 4 years

Prices: *Lift pass:* 6 days DM 140 (children DM 105). *Ski school:* Group DM 75–120 for 6 days; private DM 30–40 per hour.

RATINGS

Skiing Conditions	3
Snow Conditions	4
For Beginners	4
For Intermediates	4
For Advanced Skiers	2
For Children	4
Après-Ski	7
Other Sports	7
Value for Money	8

THE RESORT

Berchtesgaden is not really a ski resort. Rather it is a summer resort and health spa where Germans traditionally take "the cure". Consequently, this large town, while offering limited ski terrain, provides exceptional value both for skiing and lodging of all types from baronial hotel to quaint mountain chalet. Winter is low season in Berchtesgaden, which is therefore also one of the few Alpine ski resorts where lodgings willingly accept reservations for short stays or other than on a Saturday-to-Saturday basis.

Many visitors come to Berchtesgaden simply for the splendid scenery. Those magnificent massifs—the Watzmann, Hochkönig and Steinernes Meer ("Rock Sea")—and the beautiful lake amid the mountains known as the Königssee are among the most scenic attractions in the Alps, whether cloaked in summer's lushness or the white mantle of winter.

As the site of one of the U.S. military's prime recreation centers, including a private seven-lift beginner ski area on Obersalzburg, this resort is especially congenial for American skiers who like to hear familiar voices.

THE SKIING

Berchtesgaden's main ski area, the Jenner, offers a dense concentration of short runs in a high bowl enfolded in razorback ridges and some gentle snowfields below, at mid-mountain. Access to the terrain is via a scenic 22-minute ride in a two-seater gondola. On top, 6,146 ft. (1,874 m.), the ridges form a protective semi-circular bowl with short, easy runs and a few steepish headwalls served by a chairlift and one T-bar. A catwalk winds down to a mid-mountain meadow, where another chairlift is found. Although this upper terrain is not extensive, it offers reasonable shelter from radical weather and is usually snow-sure, even when the 3½-mile (5½-km.) run down to the base of the cable car is not skiable.

Novice and low-intermediate terrain and interconnected skiing with Rossfeld and across the border to Zinken, Austria, is offered on the Ski Ohne Grenzen regional ski pass, which also holds good for ski buses. Most of the runs are short, most of the lifts are T-bars, and most of the skiing is gentle. On cold days during snow-rich winters, many enjoy skiing from the top of the Rossfeld, 5,550 ft. (1,692 m.), 3 mi. (5 km.) to Oberau or 4½ mi. (7 km.) to Unterau and returning by heated bus rather than lift. The regional pass is also valid for some of the smaller villages, including Bischofswiesen, Königssee, Marktschellenberg, Ramsau and Schönau, which each have just one or two lifts and very limited beginner terrain.

APRÈS-SKI

Après-ski actually starts pre-ski, with a ski school orientation in the Kongresshaus each Sunday evening. The Hotel Post in the heart of Berchtesgaden's pedestrian zone and the Auerwirt at the bottom of the run from Rossfeld in Oberau bustle after the lifts close. In the evening, visitors gravitate to such nightspots as the Club Wittelsbach, Kiwi-Tropical and Beverly in Berchtesgaden, the Seimlerkeller on the hill at Maria am Berg, or the Kaserbau on the Königssee. Ice disco takes place each Saturday at the local rink from December to mid-March. The Wittelsbach and a rustic bar called the Holzkäfer are especially popular with Americans. The Berchtesgaden Folk Theater performs weekends during the winter. Gourmets also flock to Berchtesgaden for the fine restaurants, such as the one at the Kur und Kongress Haus.

OTHER ACTIVITIES

There are 35 mi. (57 km.) of cross-country ski trails in and around Berchtesgaden, including a 1½-mile (2-km.) stretch between Riedherrn and Bischofswiesen which is floodlit two nights a week. Some of the higher trails are skiable until April. Non-

170

ski sports, from mild walks in town or along 75 mi. (120 km.) of cleared paths through the woods to challenging winter mountaineering adventures, are on the Berchtesgaden menu.

Ice skating, curling, half-a-dozen sled and toboggan runs, and a ski-bob (on a contraption that looks like a ski-mounted bicycle) headline the outdoor sports, while three fitness centers, swimming, horseback riding, tennis, squash and bowling are leading indoor sports.

Since Berchtesgaden has been designated as a market town for centuries, it offers great shopping, especially for such local crafts as painted wood, cut crystal, silver jewelry and *Dirndls*. Visitors interested in learning some of the crafts may participate in glass and silk-painting courses. A distillery visit to the Enzian Brennerei Grassl, with the opportunity to taste the *Schnaps*, can be made weekdays between 9 a.m. and 4 p.m.

Berchtesgaden is an appropriate choice for vacationers who wish to tour the fabled Bavarian castles, visit Salzburg over the border in Austria, spend time in cosmopolitan Munich—and ski a little. It is the eastern anchor of the famous German Alpine Road, which stretches 295 mountainous mi. (475 km.) to Lindau on Lake Constance. Berchtesgaden's best-known tourist attraction, the Eagle's Nest which was Hitler's fortified mountain retreat, is not open in winter but can be seen from the ski terrain.

GARMISCH-PARTENKIRCHEN

Access: *Nearest airport:* Munich (1 hr.). *By road:* A95 Autobahn, exit Garmisch-Partenkirchen. *By rail:* station in Garmisch-Partenkirchen.

Tourist Office: Verkehrsamt der Kurverwaltung, 8100 Garmisch-Partenkirchen, B.R.D. Tel. (08821) 180-0

Altitude: 2,362 ft. (720 m.).
Top: 9,731 ft. (2,966 m.)

Language: German

Runs: 72 mi. (116 km.)

Lifts: 55

Ski areas: Zugspitze, Alpspitze, Hausberg, Wank, Eckbauer

Ski schools: Skischule: Garmisch-Partenkirchen; Sepp Hohenleitner; Flori Woerndle; Thomas Sprenzel; Olympia-Skischule

Linked resorts: None

Season: October to June

Kindergarten: *Non-ski:* from 3 years. *With ski:* from 4 years

Prices: *Lift pass:* 6 days DM 183 (children DM 121). *Ski school:* Group DM 115–140 for 6 days; private DM 45 per hour.

RATINGS

Skiing Conditions	5
Snow Conditions	6
For Beginners	4
For Intermediates	6
For Advanced Skiers	5
For Children	3
Après-Ski	9
Other Sports	9
Value for Money	6

THE RESORT

The one place in the Alps that has launched more Americans on their skiing careers than any other is Gar-

misch-Partenkirchen, site of the largest U.S. Armed Forces recreation facility in Europe. These twin towns have grown into one megaresort, which offers fine, if oddly laid-out, skiing, and après-ski and non-ski options that rank among the best in the world.

Garmisch, as the duo is usually called, is a bustling small city with sidewalks, traffic lights and pedestrians dressed in business attire.

Only the dominance of the Zugspitze, Germany's highest peak, and the procession of people in ski clothes and ski boots proclaim the proximity of Germany's biggest ski area.

Garmisch hosted the 1936 winter Olympics, the first to include Alpine ski races, and the 1978 World Alpine Ski Championships, plus scores of world-class competitions in every conceivable winter sport.

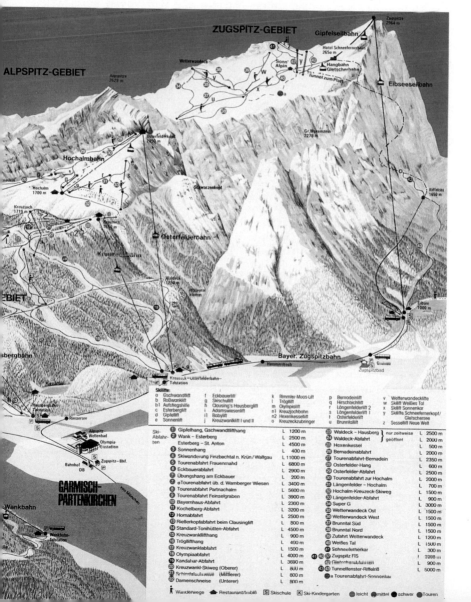

THE SKIING

Garmisch offers a great deal of skiing, but the layout is somewhat fragmented and awkward.

Every skier should—at least once—take the cog railway from Eibsee to the Zugspitzplatt, a large plateau of glacier and eternal snow on the shoulder of the mountain. The leisurely ride takes an hour and a quarter, partially through a tunnel drilled into the rock, but the memory of it will last a lifetime. Still, Zugspitze regulars find it expedient to take the Eibsee cable car, a 10-minute ride.

Threaded among the Zugspitze's rock walls are seven lifts and a handful of runs. Two short cable cars link the Schneefernerhaus, Germany's highest hotel, 8,695 ft. (2,650 m.), and Sonn'Alpin, which are also the upper stations of the cog railway. The Gipfelseilbahn, a third cable car, rises from the Schneefernerhaus to the Zugspitzgipfel, the mountain's highest point and a popular tourist attraction, which affords a four-country panorama (Austria, Italy, Switzerland and Germany).

The Zugspitzplatt's ski terrain weaves through canyons, into chutes and bowls, over snowfields, and down onto the slopes. Though most of the runs are quite short, newer ones, notably the World Cup Super G, are somewhat longer, and all are suitable for solid intermediate skiers. The snow conditions may vary every few hundred yards, but there is always cover. And the scenery is truly spectacular.

There are two long, challenging runs from the Zugspitze. One requires getting off the train at Tunnelfenster, literally "window in the tunnel", and descending via Riffelriss to Eibsee, a run of over 4 mi. (6 km.). Good skiers may also take the 9-mile (15-km.) Gatterl run down the back side of the Zugspitze to Ehrwald in Austria, and return by train.

The Zugspitze massif tilts eastward from the summit. In the middle of the upthrust mountain are the Osterfelder and Kreuzeck cable cars, which comprise the Alpspitze complex, named after an unskiable peak. Their bottom terminals are close to each other, but they respectively unload at the top and bottom of the Hochalm snowfield. A third cable car and seven surface lifts serve the mostly intermediate runs. At the eastern end of the massif is the Hausberg cable car, another handful of lifts and runs from novice through advanced. The Alpspitze and Hausberg terrain is connected, and there are several long runs down to the valley, including the challenging Horn and Kandahar descents.

The entirely separate Eckbauer and Wank sectors each maintain a small web of novice and intermediate runs.

Garmisch also offers a great variety of off-*piste* tours, both of an introductory nature and for the experienced out-of-bounds skier, led by licensed mountain guides.

APRÈS-SKI

Here's where Garmisch really shines. The action starts early, with dancing at the Kongresshaus. After dinner, it continues at places of all styles. Partenkirchen has the more sedate spots, such as the Post-Hotel's Barbarossa Bar for elegant, expensive après-ski, the Gasthof Fraundorfer which puts on a classy Bavarian show, and the Residence Hotel's bar. In Garmisch, popular spots include Bei Kuhti, the best dance bar in town; Heino's Cocktail Bar where there's less dancing and more mingling; the Musik Café and

Evergreen which draw young après-skiers; and Inger am Kamin which appeals to an older crowd. The casino has roulette, baccarat, blackjack, slots, and a more restrained atmosphere than at stateside gambling spots.

OTHER ACTIVITIES

There isn't a winter sport that isn't practiced in Garmisch, from ski-jumping to dog-sledding. Among the most popular are cross-country skiing on 93 mi. (150 km.) of pre-pared touring trails, skating at the Olympic ice arena and curling. All appear on the Garmisch calendar in competition as well as recreational form, as does ice hockey. Tennis, squash, fitness facilities and indoor swimming pools are easy to find, including the Wellenbad with artificial waves that create a sea-like effect. Garmisch also offers a full cultural calendar through the winter, including classical, jazz and pop music, theater, opera and dance. And the shopping ranges from Bavarian folk crafts to high-fashion boutiques.

OBERSTDORF

Access: *Nearest airport:* Munich (2 hrs.). *By road:* Highway 12 to Kempten, then Highway 19 to Oberstdorf. *By rail:* station in Oberstdorf.

Tourist Office: Kurverwaltung, 8980 Oberstdorf/Allgäu, B.R.D. Tel. (08322) 700-0

Altitude: 2,674 ft. (815 m.).
Top: 7,297 ft. (2,224 m.)

Language: German

Runs: 50 mi. (80 km.)

Lifts: 20

Ski areas: Fellhorn, Nebelhorn, Söllereck

Ski schools: Skischule: Erste Skischule Oberstdorf; Exclusiv; Kühberg; Neue Skischule Oberstdorf; Rubhorn; Tiefenbach

Linked resorts: Kleinwalsertal (Austria)

Season: Mid-December to early April

Kindergarten: *Non-ski:* from 4 years. *With ski:* from 3 years

Prices: *Lift pass:* 6 days DM 182 (children DM 129). *Ski school:* Group DM 140 for 5 days; private DM 100 for half-day.

RATINGS

Skiing Conditions	7
Snow Conditions	6
For Beginners	6
For Intermediates	8
For Advanced Skiers	4
For Children	7
Après-Ski	7
Other Sports	9
Value for Money	6

THE RESORT

Tucked in a deep valley hard by the Austrian border, Oberstdorf is the southernmost town in Germany and Bavaria's second largest town, in area, after Munich. It is a major resort by any measure—number and quality of hotels, non-ski pleasures, accessibility and charm.

The downtown area, with an intricate web of narrow lanes that were laid down as paths where livestock could tread, has been turned into a pedestrian zone. The town is set in a broad, flat valley, which is sunny and ideal for the strolling and

176

cross-country skiing which so many guests enjoy.

Oberstdorf is a leading all-round sport center, whose facilities include one of only five 120-m. ski-flying hills in the world, a complex of five smaller jumps, a major hockey and figure skating complex, and an important tennis center, where a local talent named Steffi Memming (touted as Germany's "next Steffi Graf") got her start. But the major local sports celebrity is Hansjörg Tauscher, who stunned the skiing world by winning the prestigious men's downhill at the 1989 World Alpine Championships at Vail.

THE SKIING

The best single ski area in Germany, especially for intermediates, is Oberstdorf's Fellhorn. It has the usual Alpine layout with a high-capacity cable car accessing the upper mountain. However, it adds such unusual features as: alternate access via a double chairlift and two T-bars to nearly the same place; a network of sheltered slopes on the lower mountain; and snow-making at the very bottom to allow good summit-to-base skiing on a vertical of nearly 4,000 ft. (1,220 m.) through most of the season.

The best skiing, however, is on top. The Fellhorn Gipfelbahn is a short cable car leading to the summit, 6,452 ft. (1,967 m.). It is possible to drop down into the bowl beneath the summit to ski the first of a further three expansive bowls. A run along the ridge leads down to the others.

The *pistes* are long and, though most fall easily in the range of the intermediate skier, exceptionally varied. Most are carved into great snowfields which arc across hundreds of feet of mountain, some following sharp ridges, and some even offering opportunities to make a detour among the trees where powder snow may be found. The See-Eck and Fellhorn T-bars serve the best cruising terrain, with occasional headwall or ridgeline as options. The Bierenwang twin T-bars lead part way up the Kanzelwand to the highest point of Oberstdorf's lift-served skiing. This sector attracts the snowboarders who like to maneuver around the rock outcroppings to the left of the lifts.

It is easy to yoyo between these three sectors, but getting from them to the area near the cable car served by the Häflelift (or vice versa) requires a long traverse.

The lower portion of the Fellhorn ridge run drops into the Kleinwalsertal. Skiers have a choice of staying on the upper bowls of the Austrian side, served by the Zwerenalpe triple chair, or skiing all the way down to the village of Riezlern and returning by gondola. On the Oberstdorf side, the skiing is largely on the Fellhorn portion of the massif; from the Kleinwalsertal, it is primarily on the Kanzelwand.

The Nebelhorn is a far smaller total ski area, but in many ways, it is more interesting for advanced skiers—and for powder enthusiasts, because this mountain regularly receives more and lighter snow than either of the others. A large tram from the outskirts of town climbs to a mid-station, where two cable cars—a large, modern one and a smaller parallel tram which is used as a spare at peak times—climb to a high plateau. From there, two old chairlifts and a T-bar rise to bowls on either side of a central ridge. The top lift is used by lovers of bump-skiing and powder hounds who enjoy the short pitches which comprise Oberstdorf's expert terrain. The other lifts and a third chair below the plateau access solid intermediate runs. There is also a short surface for beginners near the mid-

dle station. At the end of the day, strong skiers enjoy skiing from the summit to town—a thigh-burning 7½ mi. (12 km.) and 4,529 vertical ft. (1,380 m.), the longest ski run in Germany.

Söllereck is Oberstdorf's smallest, gentlest ski area with just one chairlift and two T-bars. It is good for novices, families with small children, and for anyone who likes to ski sheltered trails through the trees on snowy days.

APRÈS-SKI

Oberstdorf is a fun town with ample nightlife. Right after skiing, the liveliest spots are the Gasthof Traube on the main street, Altebahnhof zum Dorfwirt near the railway station, and Wirtschaft zum Schmied a short walk away. At night, the Weinklause offers the widest range, with an oompah Bavarian ambience on the main floor and a brash disco in the basement. Intermezzo and Walk-In are other popular discos. The St. James is an exclusive pub, while the Bierhütte and Enzianhütte are rustic. The Bauerntheater puts on folk shows. A popular option is to drive across the border to Kleinwalsertal's casino.

OTHER ACTIVITIES

From indoor tennis to an outstanding *Hallenbad*, an indoor pool complex (with a wave machine that will make you think you're playing in the Pacific surf and aqua-disco evenings every Friday), Oberstdorf offers a profusion of alternative amusements. The *Hallenbad* also has a new fitness center with coin-operated exercise machines and tanning beds, and two other fitness studios are nearby. Skating on one of the three rinks in the mammoth ice stadium, sledding, tobogganing, ski-bobbing, and skiing the valley's 93 mi. (150 km.) of cross-country trails are other options. It is also worthwhile to watch the exciting ski-jumping, ski-flying, figure skating, and hockey competitions which fill Oberstdorf's winter calendar and attract big crowds.

The Heimatmuseum, devoted to local history, is open three afternoons a week. The tourist office puts on an assortment of activities, including a series of torchlight parades. The most spectacular is to a rocky chasm called the Breitachklamm, where torch flames flirt with massive icicles to create an eerie and beautiful scene.

REIT IM WINKL

Alccess: *Nearest airport:* Munich (2 hrs.). *By road:* E54 Autobahn, exit Herrenchiemsee. *By rail:* To Prien, then by post bus.

Tourist Office: Verkehrsamt, 8216 Reit im Winkl, B.R.D. Tel. (08640) 80 020

Altitude: 2,296 ft. (695 m.). *Top:* 6,139 ft. (1,871 m.)

Language: German

Runs: 25 mi. (40 km.)

Lifts: 24

Ski areas: Walmberg, Winklmoos-alm, Kammerköhr, Steinplatte, Dürrnbachhorn

Ski school: Vereinigte Skischule

Linked resort: Waidring (Austria)

Season: Mid-December to late April

Kindergarten: *Non-ski:* none. *With ski:* from 3 years

Prices: *Lift pass:* 6 days full regional pass DM 141–156 (children DM 90–102). *Ski school:* Group DM 135 for 5 days; private DM 40 per hour.

RATINGS

Skiing Conditions	5
Snow Conditions	6
For Beginners	7
For Intermediates	7
For Advanced Skiers	2
For Children	7
Après-Ski	5
Other Sports	5
Value for Money	5

THE RESORT

Reit im Winkl, with its narrow lanes and landmark church, is one of the most pleasant villages along the German Alpine Road. Lying in a broad valley, it retains an air of unspoiled, almost rustic charm. Behind the traditional façades are fine, small hotels, which attract well-heeled German skiers who appreciate a congenial atmosphere, good skiing and warm hospitality.

The town's existence, though conjectured as far back as the 8th century, was first documented in 1160. However, it was so isolated during much of its history that it often fell between the cracks in the power

Großglockner
Großvenediger
Kitzbüheler Horn
Kammerköhrplatte, 1871 m
Fellhorn, 1766 m
Unterberghorn, 1774 m
Scheibelberg, 1462 m
Obere
Hemmersuppenalm
Hindenburghütte
Untere
Sprungschanzen
Deutsche Alpenstraße
L.L. Stadion
Reit im Winkl
Kriegergedächtniskapelle

6 83

struggles of the Bavarian, Tyrolean and Salzburg noblemen. Being thus forgotten has given it an enduring spirit of independence, compounded by the valley's extreme winters which left the village in near-isolation for much of the year until it developed into an important ski resort. Backed up against the Kaisergebirge, with mountains that rank among the steepest in the northern Alps, Reit im Winkl's slopes are blessed with some of the most abundant snow in the region.

Rosi Mittermaier, the triple medalist of the 1976 winter Olympics, hails from Reit im Winkl, which still boasts of the athletic accomplishments of its favorite daughter.

THE SKIING

There is limited novice terrain on the Walmberg, on the outskirts of the village, but the real skiing starts at Winklmoosalm. From this plateau, reachable by ski bus, a pair of parallel T-bars leads over the gentle, sunny Rossalm slopes to two peaks of 6,000 ft. (1,830 m.) and more, high for this region of the Alps.

Although this range includes steep and radical rock walls, the skiing is concentrated in gentle bowls and meadows near the mountain summits. The terrain, though overwhelmingly for intermediate skiers, provides a great deal of variety. There are sweeping bowls scooped

181

out of mountain flanks, wide, white highways shooting straight down the fall line, and short, curvy routes. Serving this terrain, which Reit im Winkl skiers share with those from Waidring in Austria, are two high-speed quad chairlifts—one covered with a plexiglass bubble—plus a gaggle of surface lifts.

The state-of-the-art chairlifts are just part of a skiing experience which is long on comfort, even by European standards. Five mountain restaurants provide abundant space to enjoy a leisurely lunch or a nap on a sun terrace. The congenial Möseralm's specialty drink is Möserschnee, a sweet liqueur served hot and topped with whipped cream.

The most challenging run in the Reit im Winkl orbit is the Nordhang, from the summit of the Steinplatte, 6,000 ft. (1,829 m.), nearly a mile long and densely moguled on its steepest pitches. The longest cruising runs are off the Bäreck covered quad, which zips up the Kammerköhr, 6,129 ft. (1,868 m.), in eight minutes.

From the Winklmoosalm, it is also possible to take a chairlift up the Dürrnbachhorn, 5,827 ft. (1,776 m.), with one long intermediate run and access to the Sonntagshorn, slated for major expansion in the early to mid-90s, but currently offering limited off-*piste* skiing.

New skiers may wish to save a few marks by purchasing the Winklmoosalm ski pass, valid for lifts on the German side. The Steinplatte facilities, which include the quad chairs and some of the more challenging runs, are actually across the border on the Austrian side and skiable on the regional lift pass.

APRÈS-SKI

Compact Reit im Winkl is ideal for strolling, an easy activity popular with the middle-aged, middle-class, mid-skiing level Germans for whom this is a favorite resort. Après-ski activities begin with a stop at the Milchbar or the Kur-Café. At the former, little milk is drunk, and at the latter, the activity is considerably livelier than that normally associated with a spa.

In the evenings, the Woipadinger disco attracts a young crowd. Bavarian music can be found at the Almsrauschkeller, which offers dancing and is popular with older folks, and the Kuhstall, whose house yodeler is known throughout Germany. The Kutscher Bar in the Hotel Post is a lively beer pub. A folk theater in the Gasthof zur Post gives entertain-

ing Bavarian-country performances.

Regularly scheduled après-ski activities include a welcome evening, hosted by the tourist office, with live entertainment and dancing and a weekly ski ball, hosted by the ski school, for students and their guests.

OTHER ACTIVITIES

Reit im Winkl is part of the splendid 100-mi. (160-km.) Dreieck cross-country trail network, largely paralleling the German Alpine Road to Inzell, 22 mi. (35 km.) away by car. Many of the routes are flat and easy, but there are also two World Cup loops with challenging climbs and downhills. Fine touring trails for novices are found on the scenic Hemmersuppenalm.

There are four sled runs from the Hindenburghütte to Blindau. Indoor tennis courts are at the Tennispark, and the modern *Hallenbad* offers indoor swimming, children's pool, sauna, massage, solarium and tanning beds. Two natural ice surfaces are available for skating and curling. Bowling is offered at the Kupferkanne restaurant. Sleigh rides and a new indoor riding arena provide equine amusements. Competitions are periodically held at the town's ski jumps.

GERMANY-INFO

ACCOMMODATIONS

Germany has no official hotel rating system, but the standards of accommodations are very high. The types of hotels and other lodging options in Bavaria are similar to those in neighboring Austria; see Austria-Info p. 92 for information on accommodations and room types.

AIRPORT

Munich is the most convenient transatlantic gateway for all the Bavarian ski resorts. There are daily non-stop flights between New York and Munich, as well as services via Frankfurt from a variety of North American gateways.

CUSTOMS AND ENTRY REGULATIONS

For a stay of up to three months, a valid passport is sufficient for citizens of the U.S.A, Canada, Australia, New Zealand and South Africa. No visa is required. Visitors from the United Kingdom and Eire need only an identity card to enter West Germany.

DRIVING

Rental cars are available at Munich airport. Some firms are affiliates of major international companies. The minimum driving age in Germany is 18, but rental firms may impose their own minimum, which will probably be higher. You'll need an International Driver's License (obtainable from your home automobile association) or a valid national license (held for at least half a year).

Insurance. Third-party insurance is compulsory. Visitors from abroad, except those from EEC and certain European countries, will have to present their international insurance certificate (Green Card) or take out third-party insurance at the German border.

Speed limits. Although there are no official posted speed limits on Germany's *Autobahn* network, the recommended limit is 130 kph (81 mph) for cars without trailers. Elsewhere, speed limits are 50 kph (31 mph) in towns and 100 kph (62 mph) on secondary roads.

Road regulations. Drive on the right, pass on the left. On an *Autobahn*, passing on the right is prohibited and "keep right except to pass" is the rule. Children under 12 may not sit in the front seat. Seatbelts for front-seat passengers are required. Studded snow tires are prohibited. Drinking and driving is a serious offense in Germany. The permissible blood alcohol level is 0.8 per mille.

Automobile associations. In Germany, these are the *Allgemeiner Deutscher Automobil Club* (ADAC), based in Munich; the *Automobilclub von Deutschland* (AvD), based in Frankfurt; and the *Deutscher Touring Automobil Club* (DTAC), also based in Munich. The ADAC Highway Patrol provides free breakdown service (except for spare parts) on the *Autobahn* and federal highways. They can be summoned from emergency call boxes placed at regular intervals along highways, marked by a small arrow on the roadside reflectors. Dial 192 11 round-the-clock. When calling, request "Strassenwachthilfe". The ADAC City Service provides emergency service in the cities.

Road signs. International pictograms are used on all road signs.

ELECTRIC CURRENT

West Germany operates on 220–250 volts 50 cycles AC. British and American small appliances and electrical gadgets require an adapter/converter, though many electric clocks, record players and tape recorders will not work properly even with such devices. Bathrooms in many German hotels are equipped with low-wattage outlets suitable for razors; hairdryers and electric curlers, whether American models used with converters or European models, will not work from these outlets.

HEALTH

If you become ill or are injured, you will find that most resort doctors are multilingual and accustomed to arranging payment from patients from abroad. If there is a problem, your hotel can help straighten it out. You must settle your medical bill while in Germany and submit the claim to your health insurance company on your return home.

Citizens of European Community countries may use the German Health Services for medical treatment. Ask for a copy of the requisite form at your local Health and Social Security Office.

In Garmisch-Partenkirchen, the cost of rescue and medical treatment up to DM 50,000 is paid for by a *Kurtax* which is automatically part of your hotel costs. In other resorts, rescue services are extra, and insurance coverage is recommended.

MAIL

Stamps may be purchased at post offices, at the hotel front desk, or normally any place that sells postcards, as well as from yellow vending machines near mail boxes. Mail boxes are painted yellow with a black post-horn.

Post offices generally open from 8 a.m. to 6 p.m., Monday to Friday, and till noon on Saturdays.

MONEY MATTERS

Currrency. The unit of currency in West Germany is the *Deutschmark* (abbreviated DM), divided into 100 *Pfennig*.

Coins: 1, 2, 5, 10 and 20 Pfennigs and DM 1, 2, 5 and 10 Marks.

Notes: DM 5, 10, 20, 50, 100, 500 and 1,000 Marks.

Credit cards and traveler's checks. Most major hotels and restaurants now accept credit cards, as do shops. However, German service stations do not accept U.S. credit cards, although those found also in America, such as Mobil, Shell or Texaco, take oil-company cards. Traveler's checks are always welcome.

Banks. Banks offer the best exchange rate on traveler's checks and foreign currency. Banking hours are 9 a.m. to 12.30 p.m. and 2.30 to 4 p.m., Monday to Friday (Thursdays until 5.30 p.m.). Exchange offices at airports and major city railway terminals are open seven days a week from 6 a.m. to 10 p.m.

Value Added Tax. *Mehrwertsteuer* (M.W.S.) is imposed on all goods and services and is included in posted prices.

For skis, skiwear and other large purchases, it is often worthwhile for visitors to apply for a refund. This program is offered at the shop's discretion. You must request and fill in a form from the store where the purchase was made. When you leave the country, have the customs officer at the airport validate the forms. Mail the original validated form to the stores where you purchased merchandise (or to a service office, if the store says it uses one). You will receive your refund by mail.

TELEPHONE

The postal service also runs the telephone. Hotels usually add astronomical surcharges onto phone calls (up to triple the unit cost of a pay phone), so these are to be avoided—especially for overseas calls. The most economical calls are from public phones at railways stations, airports, outside post offices and in public places.

For local calls, insert several coins and dial. The unit charge is 20 Pfennig. When the other party answers, the phone will automatically consume the money as long as you stay on the line, and there will be a digital display to indicate that your money is running out. When it does run out, the call will be disconnected without warning. Unused coins will be returned, but no change is made for time left when large-denomination coins are used.

Germany is introducing a phone card system, which is used for long-distance calls, but this is currently available only in major cities.

TOURIST INFORMATION OFFICES

The German National Tourist Board— Deutsche Zentrale für Tourismus e. V. (DZT)—can supply specific resort information, hotel price lists and other useful data.

In the United States, it maintains offices at 767 Third Ave., New York, N.Y. 10017; tel. (212) 308 3300 for information services. There are branches in Los Angeles and Toronto.

In Britain, the DZT is at 61, Conduit Street, London W1R OEN, tel. (01) 734 2600.

For specific information about a resort, contact the local tourist office directly.

ITALY AND ITS SKIING

Italy offers very good skiing—in a uniquely Italian way. There is less intensity, perhaps, but more joie-de-vivre, and less emphasis on performance, more on enjoyment than in its Alpine neighbors. And along with the relaxed approach to life, you'll find the inimitable style that Italians bring to everything from ski clothes to macaroni.

Internationally renowned resorts include Courmayeur, Cortina d'Ampezzo and Cervinia, which combine exceptional skiing with an air of chic and elegance. Lesser-known villages, tucked away from the crowds (and, in the past, the tax man) up inaccessible mountain roads, retain a more genuine Latin flavor—but the really obscure ones are usually too inconvenient for North Americans to reach. Few Italian resorts are "purpose-built" in the French sense. Most tend to be designed to look rather "non-purpose-built", with hodgepodge construction that may mix old and new in one busy scene.

If Italy is not as readily associated with big-league skiing as Austria or Switzerland, remember that it has the lion's share of the Alps, with its own access to Europe's most famous peaks—Mont Blanc (Monte Bianco, 15,781 ft. [4,810 m.]) and the Matterhorn (Monte Cervino, 14,692 ft. [4,478 m.]). The country's northern border stretches along southeastern France, southern Switzerland and Austria, then north western Yugoslavia, with ski resorts all the way.

Italy has long enjoyed a reputation as Europe's bargain-skiing capital for Americans. The "big three" resorts—Cervinia, Cortina, Courmayeur—traditionally provided more skiing and better living for the dollar than elsewhere in the Alps. In the seventies, Bormio—aggressively promoted—gained popularity, reaching the pinnacle of its international stature in 1985, when it hosted the World Alpine Ski Championships. However, the bargain image is

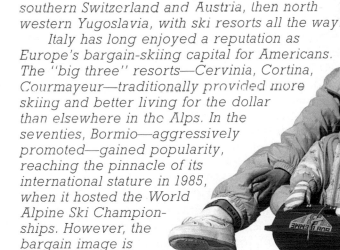

187

being eroded, as prices have risen more sharply in Italy than elsewhere in the Alps. In addition to normal inflation, some of these increases can be attributed to hotel renovations and lift improvements, which have shifted into higher gear. But whatever the price, Italy offers spectacular scenery and ineffable charm.

The mountain scenery varies as you go. In the west are the towering white peaks of the French and Swiss Alps, while in the east is the main Dolomite range including the precipices and pink-gray pinnacles of the Brenta Dolomites (west of the Trento Valley). The regions change too: Piedmont in the west includes the Aosta Valley resorts such as Courmayeur and La Thuile, plus the Milky Way resorts of Sauze d'Oulx, Sestrière, Sansicario and Italy's oldest ski resort, Clavière. Lombardy comprises Bormio, Santa Caterina, Livigno and half of the Passo Tonale. Trento takes in much of the Dolomites, including Madonna di Campiglio and the other half of tiny Passo Tonale; the Alto Adige in the center of the Dolomite mountains contains Selva and the Val Gardena, the Fassa Valley and San Martino di Castrozza. In the northeastern corner, the Veneto, above Venice, covers the eastern Dolomites, including Cortina d'Ampezzo.

The Dolomites are one of Europe's most interesting areas. Their geologically unique structure was discovered in 1788 by French mineralogist Dieudonné Dolomieu, after whom the range was named. Jagged, straight-sided pinnacles tower high in the sky. The bare precipices expose beautiful, ancient rock, which glows in the morning and evening sun.

The Dolomites are as interesting politically as they are geologically. Much of the region is also called Südtirol (South Tyrol), and was ceded to Italy at the end of World War I when the Austro-Hungarian empire collapsed. Attempts to Italianize the region in the past 70 years appear to have failed. Most towns and villages have two names—for instance, among the ski resorts, Selva is also Wolkenstein, Ortisei is also St. Ulrich. The architecture is distinctly Austrian, or rather Tyrolean—with wood and stone chalets. Most road signs are in German and Italian, and the local people speak both languages.

For skiers, the Dolomiti Superski Pass is more important than geology, politics or history. Revolutionary when it was created two decades ago, this "ski credit card" covers almost 500 lifts and nearly 700 mi. (over 1,000 km.) of pistes in 35 resorts and 11 valleys—mind-boggling especially in the context of Italy, a country not normally associated with organization. The pass is inserted into a terminal at the bottom of each lift. When the device beeps, the skier may board the lift—and the lift owner is credited for the ride. It is most impressive in ski areas like the Sella Ronda (Corvara, Colfosco, La Villa, Fassa Valley, Arabba) and Val Gardena (Selva, Ortisei, Santa Cristina) where it enables you to ski on and on from one resort to the next and be assured of lift access wherever you go. The most recent joint lift pass, finally introduced in 1988-89, is the long-awaited interchangeable ticket for the Via Lattea (Milky Way) resorts—Clavière, Sestrière, Sauze d'Oulx, Borgata, Cesana Torinese, and Montgenèvre in France.

This success story highlights the contradictions of Italian business sense: here a large number of resorts have gotten together; elsewhere the limited number of lifts in just one resort may be owned by different companies (or families) and require different lift passes.

The disadvantage in the Dolomites' structure is that the mountains tend to have gentle lower slopes, suddenly developing into quasi-precipices toward the summit. Much of the skiing, therefore, is near the bottom, with skiable passes between the fortress-like high peaks a rarity. The skiing around the Sella Ronda is not challenging for experts, but that makes it all the more enjoyable for intermediates. Many advanced skiers, however, are happy to trundle around the easy slopes just for the experience of being able to ski without lift pass limitations.

If skiing hard all day is not your primary objective, Italy has many alternative pleasures to savor, not the least being the food and wine. Meals are several leisurely courses of sheer culinary delight, whether on a sunny terrace at lunchtime or in a cheerful trattoria in the evening.

189

DOLOMITI SUPERSKI REGION

MERANO
MERAN

BRENNERO/BRENNER

GITSCH

CALDARO
KALTERN

VELTURNO
FELDTHURNS

FORTEZZA
FRANZENSFESTE

MARANZA
MERANSEN

TRENTO

BOLZANO/BOZEN

PONTE GARDENA
WAIDBRUCK

AUTOBAHN

BRESSANONE

10 LOSE M 2447

ORA / AUER

AUTOSTRADA

CARDANO
KARDAUN

FIE
VÖLS

CASTELROTTO
KASTELRUTH

CHIUSA
KLAUSEN

BRIXEN

FUNES
VILLNÖSS

SECEI

GNA
FUMARKT

ALDINO
ALDEIN

NOVA PONENE
DEUTSCHNOFEN

SIUSI
SEIS

M 2005

M 2163

ORTISEI
ST. ULRICH

INTANEFREDDE
ETENBRUNN

ALPE DI SIUSI

M 1800

S. CRISTINA
ST. CHRISTINA

PASSO OCLINI
JOCHGRIMM

OBEREGGEN

TIRES
TIERS

SEISER ALM

MONTE PANA

SELVA
WOLKENSTEIN

SAN LUGANO

P.SO LAVAZE

04

NOVA LEVANTE
WELSCHNOFEN

M 21

M 2100

CIAMPINOI

PL

08

ALPE PAMPEAGO

CATINACCIO
ROSENGARTEN

SASSOLUNGO M 515
LANGKOFEL

P.SO SELLA M

DAIANO

VARENA

STAVA

CIAMPEDIE M 1998

05

COL RODELLA

CARANO

CAVALESE

P.SO CAREZZA M 1753
KARERPASS

CAMPITELLO

PEC

ASTELLO

LANZADA

MASI

TESERO

VIGO DI FASSA

PERA

MAZZIN

CANAZEI

LAGO

PANCHIA

MOENA

POZZA DI FASSA

BUFFAURE

PENIA

ZIANO

SORAGA

CIAMPAC

ALBA

ALPE CERMIS

PREDAZZO

CIAMPEDIE

P.SO S. PELLEGRINO M 1910

BELLAMONTE

ALPE DI LUSIA M 2242

11

PANEVEGGIO

COL MARGHERITA

TOGNOLA

P.SO ROLLE M 1782

MALGA CES

09

COL VERDE

PASSO VALLES

PIAN DE SALINE

ALPE TOGNOLA

S. MARTINO DI CASTROZZA

© copyright by CORMAR bolzano

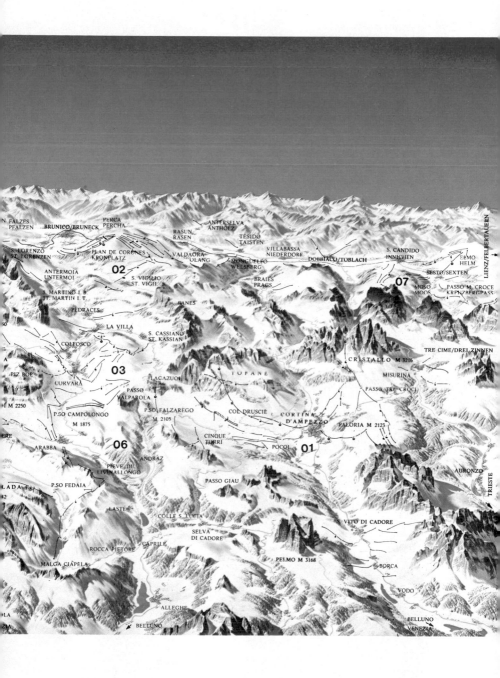

Italian cuisine needs no introduction (pizza and pasta in all their infinite variations have achieved worldwide popularity), but you can be sure that it will taste better on its home ground. Despite the plethora of sauces for pasta, the essence of Italian cooking is simplicity: fish cooked with perhaps a touch of fennel, other seafood served straight as cold hors d'oeuvre, charcoal-grilled Florentine steak, or vegetables sautéed without elaborate disguise, at most marinated in lemon, olive oil, salt and pepper.

Popular wines come from around Verona and Lake Garda, notably the velvety Valpolicella and the light Bardolino. Piedmont boasts some of Italy's finest reds, particularly the powerful, full-bodied Barolo. From south of Turin comes the sparkling Asti Spumante. The South Tyrol also has excellent local vintages, including Riesling and Traminer in the whites, Lagrein-Kretzer and Santa Madalena in the reds.

While skiing in Italy, it's well worth taking a day off to sightsee. Some of Italy's cultural splendors are accessible from the resorts. Turin, less than an hour away by rail from the Milky Way, is best known for the giant Fiat automobile works, but the proud Piedmontese capital is far from being a dull or dismal factory town. The Ligurian coast, also known as the Italian Riviera, is not a difficult day trip from the more southerly resorts. From the Val di Sole in the Brenta Dolomites, you can visit Milan, Verona, Trento or Bolzano. This area is also near the Italian Lake District, with Como close at hand (though not really worth it in winter unless the weather is fine). Farther north, in Lombardy, options include famous Swiss resorts such as St. Moritz, just over the border, or Bolzano again. From the Dolomites visit Innsbruck, Bolzano and, of course, Venice, particularly accessible from eastern resorts such as Cortina d'Ampezzo.

If you don't fancy a full day away, the local town is always worth a visit. Those keen on a bargain will have fun shopping around, and the prices for liquor are often much lower than the duty-free prices at the airport.

Wherever you eventually decide to go, it's unlikely that you won't enjoy a skiing holiday in Italy. Many of the resorts are genuinely unspoiled in a way that the more famous French, Swiss and Austrian resorts cannot claim to be. English may not be widely spoken, but non-Italian/German speakers can always get by, thanks to the friendliness of the Italian mountain folk.

BORMIO

🎿🎿🎿🎿

Access: *Nearest airport:* Milan (4 hrs.). *By road:* N2 Autostrada to Lugano, then via Sondrio and Tirano. *By rail:* to Tirano, then by bus.

Tourist Office: Azienda di Promozione Turistica, 23032 Bormio, Italy. Tel. (0342) 90 33 00

Altitude: 4,019 ft. (1,225 m.).
Top: 9,882 ft. (3,012 m.)

Language: Italian

Runs: 53 mi. (85 km.)

Lifts: 23

Ski areas: Monte Vallecetta/Cima Bianca, San Colombano Valdisotto/ Valdidentro

Ski schools: Scuola Nazionale di Sci Bormio, Scuola di Sci Anzi, Scuola di Sci Duemila, Scuola di Sci Capitani, Scuola di Sci Sertorelli

Linked resorts: None

Season: December to April; summer skiing at Passo di Stelvio

Kindergarten: None

Prices: *Lift pass*: 6 days L. 145,000 (children L. 120,000 for 7 days). *Ski school:* Group L. 70,000 for 6 half-days; private L. 27,000 per hour.

RATINGS

Skiing Conditions	7
Snow Conditions	7
For Beginners	7
For Intermediates	8
For Advanced Skiers	6
For Children	5
Après-Ski	7
Other Sports	7
Value for Money	7

THE RESORT

Bormio is a picturesque market town that came to the fore in 1985 when it hosted the World Alpine Ski Championships, a fact that is likely to be promoted well into the next century. The practical manifestations for today's tourists are good sporting facilities and the little extras that most Italian resorts lack—such as card telephones.

Bormio's importance as a key trading center between Germany and Italy has been documented since the 12th century (nearby rock carvings date back much further). Situated in the Stelvio National Park, at the junction between three valleys, the resort is relatively compact, but loosely divided into old town—complete with cobbled streets—and new development. It's also a thermal spa town (the Roman Bath is still open), and there are mud baths and a new Olympic-size thermal swimming pool.

THE SKIING

Most of Bormio's skiing on the north face of the Cima Bianca is for intermediates. A cable car climbs to Bormio 2000 (a second cable car goes on to the top), where there are a number of snow-sure, gentle slopes. An old gondola from Ciuk bypasses Bormio 2000 and leads directly to sky-high, wide-open slopes. Below, a dense network of lifts covers the slopes, which are equally densely tree-covered. It's possible to ski from top to bottom on an 8-mi. (12½-km.) run with a vertical drop of 6,000 ft. (1,800 m.).

There is a second ski area on Masucco linking Oga (Valdisotto) and Isolaccia (Valdidentro), a ten-minute bus ride from town. It has recently been expanded, with 11 lifts serving 22 mi. (35 km.) of *pistes*.

Plenty of snowmaking (thanks to the World Championships) helps cure the old problem of snow-shortage on the lower slopes—provided the temperatures remain low enough. Advanced skiers whoop it up enjoying the long mogul-covered Stelvio *pistes*, created for the World Championships. Summer skiing is on the Stelvio Glacier (from late May to October).

The lift pass also covers nearby Santa Caterina and not-so-near, duty-free Livigno (both linked by bus during the day). The ski school organizes race training and ski touring.

APRÈS-SKI

Convivial charm rather than rollicking nightlife is Bormio's style, though it has plenty of restaurants—notably the Taula, a converted 16th-century stable, or the renowned Baiona outside town—as well as pizzerias, bars, discotheques and a pub. The Palazzo Pentagono, opened for the 1985 Championships, arranges film shows and performances of folk groups.

OTHER ACTIVITIES

There's 19 mi. (30 km.) of cross-country skiing in the valley, but this is often better up at Santa Caterina. The Olympic-size thermal swimming pool also boasts a sauna (quaintly translated as "sweating grotto"), massage and Jacuzzi. The Palazzo del Ghiaccio houses a covered ice-rink. Additional activities include tobogganing, tennis, and horseback riding at nearby Val Zebru and in the Parco Nazionale dello Stelvio.

The outdoor markets are fascinating and fun. Two museums and an interesting library depict the geological and social history of Bormio. There are a total of nine thermal springs in the area, already in use as far back as the 1st century A.D.

Local buses run to Lake Como, Milan and Bolzano, and day excursions are usually available to St. Moritz.

PRESANELLA

CORNO TRE SIGNORI m 3359

CO TRESERO m 3602

Rif. Bernasconi

M. SOBRETTA m 3296

Rif. Berni

COSTA SOBRETTA m 2725

VALLECETTA m 3148

PLAGHERA

CIMA BIANCA m 3012

CIMINO

a

b

m

c

o

l

d

h

i

p

n

RIGO

12

16

CIUK

g

S. PIETRO

f

e

COMBO

225

PIATTA

MASSUCCO m 2205

q

r

S. LUCIA

CERVINIA

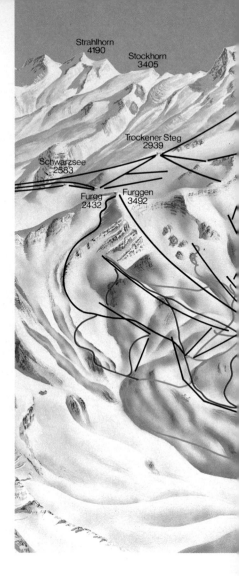

Strahlhorn 4190
Stockhorn 3405
Trockener Steg 2939
Schwarzsee 2583
Furgg 2432
Furggen 3492

Access: *Nearest airports:* Turin (2 hrs.); Milan (2½ hrs.). *By road:* Grand St. Bernard Tunnel to Aosta, then via Châtillon. *By rail:* to Châtillon, then by bus.

Tourist Office: Azienda Autonoma di Soggiorno, 11021 Breuil-Cervinia, Italy. Tel. (0166) 94 91 36

Altitude: 6,726 ft. (2,050 m.).
Top: 11,457 ft. (3,492 m.)

Language: Italian

Runs: 65 mi. (105 km.) with Valtournenche

Lifts: 27 (36 with Valtournenche)

Ski areas: Plan Maison, Furggen, Plateau Rosà, Carosello

Ski schools: Scuola di Sci del Cervino, Scuola di Sci Cieloalto, Scuola Sci e Tecnica Agonistica

Linked resorts: Zermatt (Switzerland), Valtournenche

Season: Late October to mid-May, plus summer skiing

Kindergarten: None

Prices: *Lift pass:* 6 days L. 155,000. *Ski school:* Group L. 120,000 for 6 days; private L. 28,000 per hour.

RATINGS

Skiing Conditions	7
Snow Conditions	9
For Beginners	6
For Intermediates	8
For Advanced Skiers	6
For Children	5
Après-Ski	7
Other Sports	6
Value for Money	5

THE RESORT

It is perhaps because of its three claims to fame—the longest *piste* in Europe, the highest *piste* in Europe (from Piccolo Cervino at nearly 11,500 ft. [3,500 m.]), and its position on the other side of the Matterhorn from Switzerland's jet-setting Zermatt—that Cervinia's failure to live up to its international status is so disappointing.

Ahead of its time 50 years ago

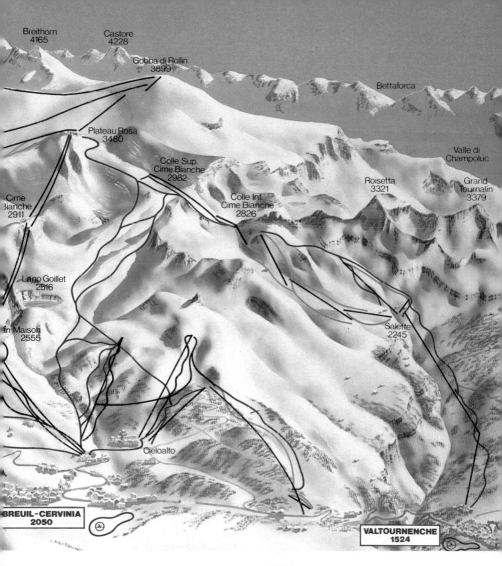

when Mussolini changed its named from Breuil because it sounded too French (and boosted his ego by building there what was, at the time, the world's longest and highest cable car), the town is now a collection of aging "modern" buildings. It survives on its obvious skiing potential (though with an increasingly inadequate and outdated lift system) and its lively nightlife. The town is cheerful but charmless, and appears to have based its reputation and prices on Zermatt, without providing the facilities. Even the best view of the Matterhorn isn't visible from the Italian side.

THE SKIING

The terrain is vast, particularly compared to other Italian resorts, but it is flatter and less interesting than it appears from below. The pluses include good and reliable snow—and some of the best spring skiing in the

199

Alps. Wind is a problem on the southern side of the Matterhorn and outdated lifts are sometimes closed as a result.

One cable car from the village takes you to Plan Maison, 8,383 ft. (2,555 m.), the starting point for a number of gentle runs back down. The "real skiing" is farther up on the Plateau Rosà, 11,418 ft. (3,480 m.), the main skiing area shared with Zermatt accessed by two consecutive pairs of parallel cable cars. Easy options are still available, but the Ventina run back to Cervinia is for the more adventurous. A left fork off the Ventina takes you down Europe's supposedly longest *piste*— 13½ mi. (22 km.) all the way to the little village of Valtournenche.

Another cable-car option takes you from Plan Maison to Furggen, 11,457 ft. (3,492 m.), a notable spring skiing site. At the top, you have to carry your skis down some 300 steps through a tunnel to the starting point of an expert run back down to Plan Maison.

The one alternative to the main mountain is Carosello, 8,137 ft. (2,480 m.), a small area of mainly medium-level runs reached by a couple of chairs from the village.

Europe's most famous cross-border excursion is the one between Cervinia and Zermatt, best reached from Plateau Rosà. For the return trip, with a supplement to your regular pass, you take the lift from Trockener Steg to the top of the Piccolo Cervino (known as the Klein Matterhorn on the Zermatt side), walk through a cool tunnel cut through the tip of the mountain and then descend Europe's highest *piste* back to Italy. Strong intermediates can do it easily.

APRÈS-SKI

The Perroquet Bar and the Dragon Bar—the latter serving fast food and draught beer—are both popular with northern Europeans. Video bars (Yeti's), Italian ice-cream cafés (Dandalo's) and cocktail bars all put in an appearance alongside numerous pizzerias. There are very few establishments that could be described as top class, though the Café des Guides is a quite sophisticated restaurant. In any event, prices remain high, especially by Italian standards.

Discotheques include La Chimera and the Etoile. It's very easy to have an excellent night out, especially if you finish off with a drink of *grolla*, black coffee mixed with liqueurs, sugar and fruit, and served in a wooden bowl.

OTHER ACTIVITIES

There are natural ice rinks (where hockey matches are played), motor bobs for hire and two short cross-country ski tracks. One of the world's fastest natural bobsled runs (not open to the public) is at Lac Bleu, at the east end of town. Swimming is a ten-minute bus ride away in Cieloalto or in the private Olympic-size pool at the Hotel Cristallo.

CORTINA D'AMPEZZO

Access: *Nearest airport:* Venice (3 hrs.). *By road:* A22 Autostrada, exit Bressanone, then via Dobbiaco. *By rail:* to Calalzo di Cadore or Dobbiaco, then by bus.

Tourist Office: Azienda di Promozione Turistica, 32043 Cortina d'Ampezzo, Italy. Tel. (0436) 32 31

Altitude: 4,016 ft. (1,224 m.). *Top:* 10,640 ft. (3,243 m.)

Language: Italian

Runs: 100 mi. (160 km.)

Lifts: 52

Ski areas: Falzarego/Cinque Torri, Tofana, Cristallo/Forcella, Faloria

Ski schools: Scuola di Sci Cortina, Scuola di Sci Azzurra Cortina

Linked resorts: None

Season: Early December to late April

Kindergarten: *Non-ski:* none. *With ski:* from 3 years

Prices: *Lift pass:* 6 days L. 145,000–174,500 (children 30% discount). *Ski school:* Group L. 110,000-180,000 for 6 days; private L. 38,000 per hour.

RATINGS

Skiing Conditions	6
Snow Conditions	7
For Beginners	7
For Intermediates	8
For Advanced Skiers	7
For Children	6
Après-Ski	9
Other Sports	9
Value for Money	6

THE RESORT

Ranking alongside Switzerland's Wengen for history and St. Moritz for style, Cortina is one of the grand old breed of ski resorts. The "Queen of the Dolomites" has been famous for more than half a century and for all the right reasons. A wide

variety of skiing is matched by a vast selection of non-ski alternatives; in short, a resort with all the facilities required for a well-rounded vacation. Since it is traditionally home of the chic, ski-scruffs will feel out of place in Cortina, where skiing prowess is respected but is definitely not the be-all and end-all. The resort was the Olympic host in 1956.

THE SKIING

If you ski just one Italian resort in your life, it must be Cortina. This great, lively village has the most varied terrain in the country—spread out over several mountains. Italy's most famous ski resort lies at the eastern end of the Dolomiti Superski Pass area. Cortina has plenty of skiing of its own, in spectacular mountain scenery, though not necessarily close to the town or hotels.

Cortina's fragmented skiing encircles the town with a ring of lifts and *pistes* that are not interconnected. Because of the cliff-like outcroppings at the mountain tops, the summits often offer a limited choice of

routes down, and these are rarely easy. Lifts and *pistes* tend to appear in greater density at mid-mountain, above the trees and below the rocks. Only where the forests have been shaved are there ski slopes near town.

The most famous sector is Tofana, rising to 10,640 ft. (3,243 m.), reached by two cable cars. The summit runs, including one that starts with a steep drop through a red-rock chute, are challenging by anyone's measure. The lower slopes and those on the interlinked Duca d'Aosta/Pomedes sector even out considerably and offer Cortina's best beginner terrain.

Across a narrow valley leading to Passo Falzarego is the Cinque Torri/ Falzarego sector, which offers lots of wide upper snowfields for great cruising, plus a cable car to the summit of Lagazuoi, 9,187 ft. (2,800 m.), with a rock-rimmed descent that is easier than Tofana. Across the valley in the other direction are the gentle slopes of Col Tondo and Miètres, both close to town.

Continuing to yet another valley toward Passo Tre Croci, there are lifts on either side of the road. One leads to the Cristallo sector, named for the too-rocky-to-be-skied landmark peak. The skiing from the Forcella/Staunies saddle also launches skiers into a tough chute, and below, among the red-hued cliffs, is a small, fairly demanding area. Across the way, a long cable car sails over unskiable woods to the Faloria plateau, 6,966 ft. (2,123 m.), above which are the wide, mostly intermediate slopes of Tondi, 7,750 ft. (2,362 m.). There are also several very small, very easy little areas in outlying hamlets.

Snow-making installations (including on the Tofana Olympic men's downhill run) and new lift construction are being undertaken with determination to catapult this old resort into line with modern skiers' expectations.

APRÈS-SKI

Cortina is a lively town with an awful lot going on. There are beautiful people swathed in furs, chic international jet-setters and trendy young Italians—and all find places to party. There are simply too many bars and restaurants to make it fair to single any out. Nightclubs and possibilities for dancing to live music are endless. What you will need is money: drinks can be exorbitant, but if you shop around, it is possible to avoid breaking the bank.

OTHER ACTIVITIES

Virtually incomparable facilities for cross-country skiers include a recently opened, well-marked trail stretching 130 mi. (210 km.) and crossing the regions of Veneto, Alto Adige, East Tyrol and Carinthia before arriving in Villach, Austria. The route can be completed in six stages, and there is an arrangement for luggage to be forwarded to par-

ticipating hotels. In addition, there are 45 mi. (74 km.) of local cross-country trails.

The resort has many cultural and "extra-curricular" activities organized throughout the year. January is a particularly busy month, with a veteran car race, a horse race on snow and a dogsled race—all attracting international competition.

The Olympic legacy has left an ice rink (with ice disco on occasions), ski jump and bobsled run. There is a public indoor swimming pool, and the Hotel Miramonti opens its pool to non-residents. Indoor tennis courts and horseback riding are also available.

The Cortina Card gives visitors discounted access to most sporting facilities, savings in many other establishments and on services.

There's a local history museum, art gallery and library, and for further diversion, you can take a trip down to Venice.

COURMAYEUR

Access: *Nearest airport:* Geneva (2 hrs.). *By road:* Via Chamonix and Mont Blanc Tunnel. *By rail*: to Pré-St-Didier, then by bus.

Tourist Office: Azienda Autonomo di Soggiorno e Turismo, 11013 Courmayeur, Italy. Tel. (0165) 84 20 60

Altitude: 4,016 ft. (1,224 m.). *Top:* 11,385 ft. (3,470 m.)

Language: Italian

Runs: 62 mi. (100 km.)

Lifts: 32

Ski areas: Chécrouit-Val Veny, Col du Géant

Ski school: Scuola di Sci del Monte Bianco

Linked resort: Chamonix (France)

Season: December to April, plus summer skiing

Kindergarten: *Non-ski:* none. *With ski:* 5–10 years

Prices: *Lift pass:* 6 days L. 142,000–169,000. *Ski school:* Group L. 120,000 for 6 half-days; private L. 29,000 per hour.

RATINGS

Skiing Conditions	6
Snow Conditions	8
For Beginners	6
For Intermediates	9
For Advanced Skiers	7
For Children	5
Après-Ski	8
Other Sports	3
Value for Money	6

THE RESORT

One of Italy's most popular skiing destinations, Courmayeur wins on its traditional village atmosphere, welcoming residents and easy accessibility. All it has lost during its 50-odd years of popularity is the duty-free status it once had. Situated in the historic Aosta Valley, it is at the Italian portal to Mont Blanc, and views from the ski slopes to the surrounding range are particularly spectacular.

THE SKIING

The lion's share of the skiing wraps around a peak called Chécrouit, 7,402 ft. (2,256 m.). Day-trippers

from Geneva reach it by a series of lifts from Entrèves, at the mouth of the Mont Blanc Tunnel. Those staying in Courmayeur hike to the main cable car from town or take an antique gondola from Dolonne to the Plan Chécrouit, which has all the facilities one would find at a U.S. ski area base—beginner terrain, ski rental and repair and restaurants and cafeterias.

From here the skiing opens up, with mainly intermediate runs another lift ride or two away. On the front face of the mountain, one gondola and a gaggle of surface lifts climb to the Chécrouit summit and offer mostly intermediate skiing. Two more cable cars climb to Cresta Youla, 8,609 ft. (2,624 m.), and Cresta

d'Arp, 9,039 ft. (2,755 m.), offering more demanding terrain, but these lifts are extremely weather-vulnerable. An exciting adventure for advanced skiers is the 6-mi. (10-km.) descent from Cresta d'Arp to Dolonne.

The Entrèves side of the area has lots of interesting twisty trails through the trees—some very challenging. Scattered all over the mountain are two dozen of the best restaurants in skidom. From Plan Chécrouit, skiers ride back to town by cable car.

The three-stage cable car from La Pallud (just out of town) takes you to one of the most beautiful runs, a spectacular off-*piste* descent of 11 mi. (18 km.) from Punta Helbron-

ner down the Vallée Blanche to Chamonix, from which you take the bus back. Neither this action-packed descent nor the one back on the Italian side over the Toula Glacier should be undertaken without a guide. Summer skiing is in this area.

There are also once-weekly lift pass swaps, when those in Courmayeur can ski for a day in Cervinia, and vice versa. Although the Aosta Valley (Courmayeur, Cervinia, La Thuile, Pila and others) is promoting itself collectively, lift passes are otherwise still limited to individual resorts.

APRÈS-SKI

The main street, Via Roma, is the après-ski center. The American Bar and neighboring Caffè della Posta are friendly rivals, with the former offering interesting cocktails and the latter serving various traditional and sometimes unique beverages. For "real English beer on draught" and lots of British guests, the Leone Rosso is across the way.

As the town boasts many restaurants with high standards and fairly reasonable prices, it is very worthwhile to take up one of the bed-and-breakfast accommodations packages offered by some of the small hotels. Absolutely everyone goes to the Maison de Filippo restaurant at nearby Entrèves, where dinner is both Lucullian and theatrical. There are also two movie theaters.

OTHER ACTIVITIES

With 13½ mi. (22 km.) of prepared tracks at nearby Val Ferret, cross-country facilities are adequate. Indoor and outdoor pools can be found at two hotels, but these are not often open to the public. There are sauna facilities and an artificial ice rink (with ice discotheque).

The Wednesday street market should not be missed, and there's a good selection of shops. If you have a few free hours, visit the fascinating museum of local culture and history. If you have a day, take the bus to Chamonix.

LIVIGNO

Access: *Nearest airports:* Milan (5 hrs.), Zurich (5 hrs.). *By road:* N3 Autobahn, exit Landquart, then via Zernez and Drossa Tunnel. *By rail:* to Tirano, then by bus.

Tourist Office: Azienda di Promozione Turistica, 23030 Livigno, Italy. Tel. (0342) 99 63 79

Altitude: 5,958 ft. (1,816 m.).
Top: 9,138 m. (2,785 m.)

Language: Italian

Runs: 53 mi. (85 km.)

Lifts: 28

Ski areas: Lago Salin, Monte della Neve, Costaccia

Ski schools: Scuola Italiana di Sci: Livigno Inverno/Estate; Interalpen; Livigno Italy; Livigno Soc. Coop.

Linked resorts: None

Season: December to April, plus summer skiing

Kindergarten: None

Prices: *Lift pass:* 6 days L. 125,000–145,000 (children L. 90,000–110,000). *Ski school:* Group L. 60,000–68,000 for 6 days; private L. 30,000 per hour.

RATINGS

Skiing Conditions	4
Snow Conditions	7
For Beginners	7
For Intermediates	5
For Advanced Skiers	4
For Children	5
Après-Ski	8
Other Sports	2
Value for Money	6

THE RESORT

Livigno is rapidly gaining in popularity with the British and Swedes, since this is Italy's top duty-free resort. The town itself, once three separate villages, is spread out along a narrow street lined for 5 mi. (8 km.) with grocers selling literally hundreds of brands of alcohol, tobacco, perfume and tea at incredibly low prices (and very little actual food). With a rather spaced-out ski area, Livigno provides an extensive, if not varied, week of ski exploration for the intermediate skier.

Livigno's duty-free status is rumored to be the result of its inaccessibility. Whenever the government sent out tax collectors, the town helpfully returned them minus their lives. The advent of modern transport hasn't made Livigno much more accessible, as you need to count on a five-hour transfer from Milan or Zurich.

THE SKIING

The remarkable thing about Livigno's 28 ski lifts is that 14 of them are approximately 300-ft. (100-m.) beginner surface lifts, mainly stretching up the resort's western side. Yet what might be considered a plus for beginners or families is canceled out by the fact that, by all accounts, the ski school hasn't got much going for it, and there isn't a kindergarten.

Slightly more serious skiing is concentrated in three areas, a small network beneath the Cantone peak in the southwest, a still smaller one on Costaccia in the northwest, and the biggest across the valley beneath Monte della Neve in the east. The western sectors are linked by a windy ridge run, so moving between them means skiing down to the bottom, walking across the busy road, then riding up the other side to reach Monte della Neve. However, the numerous wide mid-grade runs make excellent ego-boosting skiing for the progressing intermediate. More advanced skiers may find the greatest test to their ability in negotiating the bald patches or ice rinks on the runs down to the village (it is possible to ski back to most hotels).

It's best to concentrate a day in each area, because the lifts are poorly laid out and the free ski bus irregular. There's invariably a few sizable walks to the skiing, so many people end up satisfied with the area nearest to their hotel or apartment.

There are regular buses to Bormio, which is included on the lift pass along with Santa Caterina and two other small resorts.

APRÈS-SKI

For those interested in a pub crawl, a certain amount of stamina is needed, due to the length of the valley. So it's normally a choice between staying home with duty-free booze, going to the local bar or taking a taxi down (or up) to the town center. Since taxis here are in the form of very cheap and reliable minibuses, this is not a huge problem (they can also be called when the ski bus fails to turn up).

The dispersed layout of the village results in a large number of places to eat and drink—atmospheric cellar bars and excellent restaurants and pizzerias, all with noticeably friendly management and extremely reasonable prices. The central disco/pub, Foxi's, is lively every night.

OTHER ACTIVITIES

There is cross-country skiing along the valley, plus a small natural ice rink, tobogganing, and snow scooters for rent. The Hotel du Lac opens its swimming pool to non-residents in the afternoons. St. Moritz is just over the border.

MADONNA DI CAMPIGLIO

Access: *Nearest airport:* Milan (3½ hrs.). *By road:* A22 Autostrada, exit San Michele, then via Malè. *By rail:* to Trento, then by bus.

Tourist Office: Azienda di Promozione Turistica, 38084 Madonna di Campiglio, Italy. Tel. (0465) 42 00 0

Altitude: 5,086 ft. (1,550 m.). *Top:* 8,235 ft. (2,510 m.)

Language: Italian

Runs: 56 mi. (90 km.); 93 mi. (150 km.) with linked resorts

Lifts: 31

Ski areas: Cinque Laghi, Monte Spinale, Grostè, Pradalago, Campo Carlo Magno

Ski schools: Scuola Italiana di Sci Campiglio, Scuola di Sci Cinque Laghi, Scuola di Sci des Alpes

Linked resorts: Folgarida, Marilleva

Season: Early December to late April, plus summer skiing

Kindergarten: *Non-ski:* none. *With ski:* from 5 years

Prices: *Lift pass:* 6 days L. 180,000. *Ski school:* Group L. 108,000 for 6 days; private L. 32,000 per hour.

RATINGS

Skiing Conditions	8
Snow Conditions	8
For Beginners	6
For Intermediates	8
For Advanced Skiers	5
For Children	6
Après-Ski	7
Other Sports	7
Value for Money	6

THE RESORT

At the beginning of the century Santa Maria di Campiglio—as it was called then—was rated one of the best climbing resorts in the Alps, second only to a few Swiss resorts for ice-climbs, but unbeaten for its

212

rocky Brenta Dolomites scenery; the town nestles among thick pine woods. Since 1932 "Campiglio" has been a successful and expanding ski resort. Today it is linked by lifts to Marilleva and Folgarida; combined they boast more than 90 mi. (150 km.) of *piste*. This bustling, attractive town with a modern central complex and plenty of facilities is popular with the Italians—particularly the well-heeled variety—who make up the vast majority of its clientele.

THE SKIING

Skiing is possible in almost every direction from Campiglio, owing to four cable cars from village level. To the southeast a long gondola climbs from Campo Carlo Magno, a 10-minute bus ride from the resort, to Passo del Grostè, the highest point for skiing. The runs back are long, often busy but very enjoyable cruises—assuming the bitter winds that cut across the exposed area above the trees aren't blowing.

Lower down, the *piste* narrows to a long path through the firs, and from here a few more challenging options open up.

Another southeast ascent is possible on the small, old-fashioned Spinale cable car which departs near the center of town and usually has lines, even off peak-season. From here the runs are very different from those from Grostè, shorter but steeper. The Grostè skiing can also be reached by a long chair from near the top of Spinale.

The southwest is accessed by the Pancugolo cable car, with another lift to the start of the popular 3-Tre (or Tre Tre) *piste*. This is also the World Cup run and the only one featuring snowmaking facilities. It is quite steep, especially by Campiglio's standards, and is linked to several more advanced and expert runs.

Another cable car ascends to Pradalago and a chair to Monte Vigo, 7,153 ft. (2,180 m.), and the descents to Marilleva and Folgarida. These two are covered by the lift pass, and some options also offer Pinzolo in the Val di Sole beyond them.

Campiglio's beginner slopes are

scattered around the village outskirts and are generally good. There are numerous alternative lifts (usually chairs) to all the areas mentioned. The skiing is extensive and offers plenty of alternatives for the intermediate and advancing skier. It's generally best to stick to one area a day. Only a third of the total number of lifts are surface lifts, and many of the *pistes* are carved through the trees, above which the Brenta Dolomites appear particularly spectacular.

APRÈS-SKI

A slightly chic atmosphere prevails in Campiglio. The old center has some attractive architecture, the new precinct is well laid out, and both areas are packed with shops selling largely luxury or high-quality goods. There are also plenty of piano bars, tea bars and a colorful ice-cream parlor. Nightspots include the Stork Club combining pizzeria, restaurant, discotheque and "country club", while Contrasto is a trendy discotheque. Theatrical and cabaret performances are occasionally staged.

OTHER ACTIVITIES

The total length of cross-country loops is 18½ mi. (30 km.), the best being at Campo Carlo Magno. The racing trails are Malga Mondifra and Malga Dare. There is an indoor swimming pool, high-speed Olympic ice circuit, ice motor-biking, and skating on a large area of the frozen lake. The ski schools offer instruction in all the new snow sports, especially snowboarding.

Campiglio is on the borders of Val Rendena and the Val di Sole for excursions to towns like Trento, Bolzano or Verona—even Venice is sometimes proposed.

ORTISEI (ST. ULRICH)

Access: *Nearest airports:* Milan (3 hrs.); Innsbruck (1½ hrs.). *By road:* A22 Autostrada, exit Chiusa, then via Val Gardena. *By rail:* to Chiusa or Bolzano, then by bus.

Tourist Office: Azienda di Soggiorno, 39046 Ortisei-St. Ulrich, Val Gardena, Italy. Tel. (0471) 76 32 8

Altitude: 4,055 ft. (1,236 m.).
Top: 8,262 ft. (2,518 m.)

Languages: Italian, German, Ladin

Runs: 109 mi. (175 km.) in Val Gardena

Lifts: 6 (85 in Val Gardena)

Ski areas: Seceda, Alpe di Siusi, Rasciesa

Ski school: Scuola di Sci Ortisei

Linked resorts: Arabba, Campitello, Canazei, Colfosco/Corvara, San Cassiano, Santa Cristina, Selva, La Villa

Season: December to April

Kindergarten: *Non ski:* from 2½ years. *With ski:* from 5 years

Prices: *Lift pass:* 6 days L. 152,000–183,000 (children L. 106,500–128,500). *Ski school:* L. 105,000 for 3 days; private L. 33,000 per hour.

RATINGS

Skiing Conditions	5
Snow Conditions	7
For Beginners	7
For Intermediates	6
For Advanced Skiers	5
For Children	6
Après-Ski	7
Other Sports	5
Value for Money	5

THE RESORT

Ortisei, or St. Ulrich (the name of the village for several centuries before the South Tyrol came under Italian rule), is one of the bilingual towns of Val Gardena (Gröden). Most signposts give both names, and the Tyrolean influence remains very strong. It has a charming old town, decorated with ice sculptures, and is more attractive than its more famous neighbor, Selva. Prices tend to be lower here, too.

THE SKIING

Of all the major Val Gardena towns, Ortisei, situated between basically unimpressive ski areas, has the least fortuitous setting for skiing. Alpe di Siusi (Seiser Alm) is a remarkable plateau known for excellent cross-country trails and walking paths, sleigh rides, a sunny, rustic atmosphere—but marginal skiing which is best for beginners who are as awed by the scenery as by their first tracks. On the plus side, some runs have snow-making, and there is one long run down to Santa Cristina, which in turn links into other Val Gardena ski areas.

Ortisei's highest skiable mountain, Seceda, 8,262 ft. (2,518 m.), is also generously endowed with good views, but provides skiing that is only somewhat more extensive and interesting. A long two-stage cable car climbs Seceda, accessing several long intermediate runs that are vulnerable to sun-melt. One easy, exceedingly pretty run leads from the summit terrain back to Ortisei, and one more challenging, un-

215

For map see pp. 220–221.

groomed route takes skiers to the edge of Selva (Wolkenstein).

The whole Val Gardena area is covered by the Dolomiti Superski Pass, including the Sella Ronda, which is more convenient for skiers staying in resorts other than Ortisei.

APRÈS-SKI

Après-ski has a distinctly Tyrolean flavor, but is relatively low-key. Ortisei is a sizable resort, with plenty of bars, cafés and restaurants, and a movie theater. There are four discos, and dancing to live music. Concerts are organized occasionally, as are folklore evenings.

OTHER ACTIVITIES

Ortisei has over 60 mi. (100 km.) of cross-country tracks, and skiers can go from Siusi across to Montepana above Santa Cristina. Other loops have been marked out in the valley between the two resorts. There is an ice-skating rink (popular local ice-hockey league), a large covered indoor pool, a small heated outdoor pool, bowling, toboggan runs, plus tennis, squash and horseback riding. A sleigh ride up on the Alpe di Siusi is an enjoyable experience.

The museum of local history houses displays of religious wood-carving. In fact, Ortisei is famed for its wood-carving industry (the same is true of Selva and Santa Cristina), and visitors are welcome in most shops to watch the craftsmen and women at work. It is also worth a visit to the Chiesa di San Antonio (1676) and the even older Chiesa di San Giacomo (1181) with exquisite 14th-century frescoes.

SANSICARIO

Access: *Nearest airport:* Turin (2 hrs.). *By road:* Fréjus Tunnel, then via Bardonecchia. *By rail:* to Oulx, then by bus.

Tourist Office: I.A.T., 10054 Cesana, Italy. Tel. (0122) 89 202

Altitude: 5,627 ft. (1,715 m.).
Top: 8,842 ft. (2,695 m.)

Language: Italian

Population: 30

Runs: 24 mi. (38 km.); 186 mi. (300 km.) in Milky Way

Lifts: 13 (100 in Milky Way)

Ski areas: Fraitève, Monti della Luna

Ski school: Scuola di Sci Sansicario-Cesana

Linked resorts: Clavière, Sestrière, Cesana Torinese, Montgenèvre (France)

Season: December to late April

Kindergarten: *Non-ski:* 3–13 years. *With ski:* 3–13 years

Prices: *Lift pass:* 6 days L. 130,000–140,000. *Ski school:* Group L. 100,000–120,000 for 6 days; private L. 26,000 per hour.

RATINGS

Skiing Conditions	7
Snow Conditions	7
For Beginners	6
For Intermediates	7
For Advanced Skiers	6
For Children	7
Après-Ski	6
Other Sports	5
Value for Money	6

THE RESORT

Straight off the Italian designer's drawing board, Sansicario is one of Europe's most attractive purpose-built resorts. Completed in 1973, it remains a cleverly structured, stylish collection of small apartment blocks, with a good selection of designer-fashion and sports shops. Most of the lodging is ski-in, ski-out—or at most a short walk from the lifts. Just down the road is the original old village, equally appealing for its unspoiled character. Cesana, part of the same municipality, is a bus ride away, but does not offer great skiing of its own.

THE SKIING

Occupying center stage in the Via Lattea (Milky Way), Sansicario offers some decent, close-in terrain on three mountains which link into the Milky Way and with each other. Roccia Rotonda, 8,184 ft. (2,495 m.), and Colle Bercia, 7,546 ft. (2,300 m.), provide the routes down from Sestrière's terrain, and are challenging on top, milder in the middle and meet with a novice trail above lower-lying Cesana down at the bottom. High above is Monte Fraitève, 8,862 ft. (2,701 m.), which has intermediate runs leading down to Sestrière and steep, ungroomed routes (most for experts but one less intimidating) to Sauze d'Oulx with a vertical of nearly 4,600 ft. (1,400 m.).

Sansicario offers challenging skiing possibilities for the intermediate and advanced skier. Strictly speaking, Sansicario's ski area has only 13 lifts and 24 mi. (38 km.) of *piste*, but

more realistically the immediate area, including neighboring Cesana, Grangesises and Clavière, offers more than twice that much. Just over the Fraitève mountain are Sauze d'Oulx and Sestrière, and in the other direction, you can ski to Montgenèvre in France (snow permitting), to come nearer to the Milky Way's full potential. In its entirety, the Milky Way, which claims to be the "largest ski area in Europe" (though it's not clear what the measure is), can be a challenge to intermediates and provides a great deal of off-*piste* for experts.

Beginner slopes are next to the village and there are a number of novice runs up at the Soleil Bœuf

area. Intermediates and experts have a choice of more difficult runs from Fraitève, where the off-*piste* is usually good.

APRÈS-SKI

Après-ski ranges from beer halls and wine cellars to dance places, and comfortable and spacious modern bars are popular from close of lifts through to the small hours. The Drugstore in European fashion isn't a pharmacy or sundry shop but a lively crêperie/bar/pizzeria with photo prints on the wall. There is a disco, the Black Sun, complete with flashing dance floor in the Hotel Sansicario. Other dancing is in the Hotel

Rio Envers Gallia. In addition to the choice of modern restaurants in the resort, more traditional fare is found down in the original village, a 20-minute walk away. There is also a movie theater.

OTHER ACTIVITIES

A short cross-country loop past picturesque old villages is available, plus all the variations of downhill skiing—monoski, snow-surf, parascending and heli-skiing. Although very much a skier's resort, there is an indoor swimming pool, sauna, fitness gym with weight-training and indoor tennis courts. There are plenty of browseworthy shops.

SELVA (WOLKENSTEIN)

Access: *Nearest airports:* Innsbruck (1½ hrs.); Milan (3 hrs.). *By road:* A22 Autostrada, exit Chiusa. *By rail:* to Bolzano or Chiusa, then by bus.

Tourist Office: Azienda Soggiorno e Turismo, 39048 Selva Gardena, Italy. Tel. (0471) 75 1 22

Altitude: 5,128 ft. (1,563 m.). *Top:* 7,540 ft. (2,298 m.)

Languages: Italian, German, Ladin

Runs: 53 mi. (85 km.); 109 mi. (175 km.) in Val Gardena

Lifts: 60 (110 in Val Gardena)

Ski areas: Ciampinoi, Danterceppies, Plan de Gralba, Seceda

Ski school: Scuola Nazionale Italiana di Sci Selva Gardena

Linked resorts: Arabba, Campitello, Canazei, Colfosco/Corvara, San Cassiano, Santa Cristina, Ortisei, La Villa

Season: mid-December to mid-April

Kindergarten: *Non-ski*: 2–4 years. *With ski*: from 4 years

Prices: *Lift pass*: 6 days L. 158,000 (children L. 111,000). *Ski school:* Group L. 102,000 for 14 hours per week; private L. 29,000 per hour.

RATINGS

Skiing Conditions	7
Snow Conditions	7
For Beginners	7
For Intermediates	8
For Advanced Skiers	7
For Children	7
Après-Ski	7
Other Sports	5
Value for Money	6

THE RESORT

Selva is famous for its stunning Dolomite scenery, lively atmosphere, and for being host to an annual pre-Christmas FIS World Cup men's downhill race. More a small town than a village, it is spread out in a mixture of rustic old buildings and newer hotels. Skiing began here in the first decade of the century, prior to Italian rule, when the village was called Wolkenstein. Today it is considered the major resort of the Val Gardena (Gröden) region. The locals maintain their Ladin culture and language, together with a mixture of Austrian and Italian influences.

THE SKIING

Quantum improvements have been made in the last several years in the region's lift system—a new 12-passenger stand-up *télécabine* on Ciampinoi, a large cable car on Piz Sella, new triple chairs on Passo Sella and so forth.

Lifts ascend to the north, south and east. The main area for beginners is Danterceppies, which is also the access route to the Sella Ronda—its

ridge overlooks Colfosco and Corvara—by way of a beautiful 6-mi. (10-km.) cruise. The beginner slopes are on a wide sunny plateau at the bottom of the mountain, but up above the village. A modern, efficient six-passenger gondola goes up the whole slope. Intermediates will find a number of long, angled, fast descents cutting down through the trees—even advanced skiers should find these entertaining at a higher speed.

From Ciampinoi on the south side, there are several steep runs back to Selva or Santa Cristina (including the World Cup course). There are numerous surface lifts and chairs above, in a vaguely southerly direc-

tion, toward Canazei. This is the southwest corner of the Sella Ronda. Selva is thus well placed for the best of Val Gardena skiing, excursions to Alta Badia and for access to the Sella Ronda. This wonderful excursion begins over the ridge and leads—eventually—to resorts such as Arabba. It is not difficult skiing. Selva is one of the resorts where the Dolomiti Superski lift pass is most useful.

The scarcely used Seceda area to the north is best reached from Santa Cristina and Ortisei. The runs are generally novice to intermediate.

APRÈS-SKI

Selva is the liveliest resort on the Sella Ronda circuit, with tea dances in two establishments after the lifts close, several popular discos—two with live music—continuing throughout the evening. The Bar Stella, a roomy place in the center of town, never stops buzzing, and at night the Stella Club draws a young crowd. So do 'L Medèl (disco) and 'L Ciulè (live music). The Laurinkeller and Ustaria de Luisl have their fun, too. The Speckkeller is just as popular, particularly straight after skiing, though it keeps on going into the small hours. There are many other equally good establishments and plenty of restaurants and pizzerias, such as the Ciampinoi.

OTHER ACTIVITIES

Although there are less than 10 mi. (15 km.) of cross-country trails in Selva itself, there are more than 30 mi. (50 km.) in Val Gardena. The Hotel Gran Baita has a games room, sauna, solarium and large indoor pool open to the public. Hotel Antares has a pool, sauna and Jacuzzi. There's also indoor tennis, bowling, ice skating and hockey in a new stadium, curling and billiards.

SESTRIÈRE

Access: *Nearest airport:* Turin (2½ hrs.). *By road:* Grand St. Bernard Tunnel, then via Aosta. *By rail:* to Oulx, then by bus.

Tourist Office: Azienda di Promozione Turistica, 10058 Sestrière, Italy. Tel. (0122) 76 04 5

Altitude: 6,677 ft. (2,035 m.). *Top:* 9,262 ft. (2,823 m.)

Language: Italian

Runs: 75 mi. (120 km.); 186 mi. (300 km.) in Milky Way

Lifts: 26 (100 in Milky Way)

Ski areas: Monte Fraitève, Grangesises, Monte Sises, Monte Banchetta, Borgata

Ski schools: Scuola di Sci: Sestrière; Borgata Sestrière; Grangesises

Linked resorts: Sauze d'Oulx, Sansicario, Jouvenceaux, Cesana, Clavière, Montgenèvre (France)

Season: November to April

Kindergarten: *Non-ski:* none. *With ski:* none; ski school from 4 years

Prices: *Lift pass:* 6 days L. 155,000. *Ski school:* Group L. 30,000 for 3 hours; private L. 30,000 per hour.

RATINGS

Skiing Conditions	8
Snow Conditions	7
For Beginners	5
For Intermediates	8
For Advanced Skiers	6
For Children	5
Après-Ski	7
Other Sports	5
Value for Money	7

THE RESORT

The world's first purpose-built ski resort (by Fiat founder Giovanni Agnelli in 1934) was treated then— as its French descendants are now— with a certain amount of distrust. Skiers sometimes hesitate to enjoy a vacation in a resort that cannot claim to have once been a charming little Alpine village. Sestrière was created on a piece of extremely barren mountain. It's not the most hospitable place on earth even now, but the skiing is extensive and wide ranging, the après-ski likewise, and the prices are reasonable for what is a well-appointed Italian resort. Italy's beautiful people no longer flock to Sestrière, but instead it is now populated by ordinary skiers who enjoy the extraordinary scope of the Milky Way.

THE SKIING

If you wanted a resort between three mountains, linked to several others on a famous ski circuit (the Milky Way) and with one of Europe's largest snowmaking facilities, you'd be directed to Sestrière. The season is long, from November to April, and the lift pass also now extends all the way to France.

Before the recent institution of a single Milky Way pass, Sestrière had a two-resort deal with Sauze d'Oulx, and the two still form the heart of skiing for Sestrière guests, for it is at the end of the ski circus—a long distance from Montgenèvre on the other end. From the original resort, lifts rise to the south to Monte Sises, 8,531 ft. (2,600 m.), which

For map see pp. 218–219.

224

draws good skiers to its short, steep upper runs. Connected with it, above the Borgata Sestrière development, is Banchetta, with lifts up to 9,262 ft. (2,823 m.) and more tough stuff up on top—plus easy novice and intermediate runs below.

North of the resort is Monte Fraitève, 8,826 ft. (2,691 m.), Sestrière's most famous mountain. The runs back to the resort are good intermediate standard, and the gully route known as Rio Nero provides nearly 6 mi. (10 km.) of steepness down to the road between Cesana Torinese and Sauze d'Oulx. Fraitève is also the link with Sauze—and on to the rest of the Milky Way, as well as to Sansicario, roughly to the northeast.

Beginners will find slopes near the village. Before deciding to ski at Sestrière, however, they should consider how much they'll actually get from what is, for the first-timer, an expensive lift pass. On the plus side, a well-designed lift system means that lines are rarely long, except at the odd holiday weekend.

APRÈS-SKI

Night times are normally lively but not loud. The crowd receives a boost at weekends and Italian holidays when the residents of Turin, for whom the resort was built, pour in. For the early evening there is a wide selection of good quality bars, pizzerias and restaurants. Later on, the Tabata discotheque normally fills first, but perhaps only because the Black Sun is so large. The resort also has a movie theater.

OTHER ACTIVITIES

Club Colombière has sauna, gymnasium and an open-air heated swimming pool, while the Palazzetto Sport has tennis, squash, basketball and a sauna. It's possible to manipulate your hotel/lift pass package to include ice driving. There's also a tiny cross-country loop in the resort, not to mention a go-kart track. Skating, too, is available, and there is a ski jump.

LA THUILE

Access: *Nearest airports:* Turin (2½ hrs.); Geneva (2 hrs.). *By road:* Mont Blanc Tunnel, then via Pré-St-Didier. *By rail:* to Pré-St-Didier or Chamonix, then by bus.

Tourist Office: Azienda Autonoma di Soggiorno e Turismo, 11016 La Thuile, Italy. Tel. (0165) 88 41 79

Altitude: 4,728 ft. (1,441 m.). *Top:* 8,668 ft. (2,642 m.)

Languages: Italian, French

Runs: 50 mi. (80 km.); 84 mi. (135 km.) with La Rosière

Lifts: 14 (30 with La Rosière)

Ski areas: Les Suches, Chaz Dura, Belvedere

Ski school: Scuola di Sci Rutor

Linked resort: La Rosière (France)

Season: December to April

Kindergarten: *Non-ski:* none. *With ski:* from 5 years

Prices: *Lift pass:* 6 days L. 131,000–151,000. *Ski school:* Group L. 93,000–100,000 for 6 half-days; private L. 24,000–28,000 per hour.

RATINGS

Skiing Conditions	7
Snow Conditions	8
For Beginners	7
For Intermediates	8
For Advanced Skiers	8
For Children	5
Après-Ski	5
Other Sports	5
Value for Money	6

THE RESORT

La Thuile is an interesting combination of an "abandoned" mining town, predictable semi-smart new ski developments and even a barracks for the Italian Army Corps. It is also one of the few Italian resorts with a definite French connection. La Rosière over the border can be included on the lift pass, extending the ski area from 50 mi. (80 km.) to 84 mi. (135 km.) and doubling the number of lifts available. You can reflect on history as you ski the region, as the pass below some of the ski slopes was supposedly traveled by Hannibal and his elephants in their famous crossing of the Alps. Those who want a picturesque setting have probably the best Italian view of Mont Blanc from the resort, which is dominated by the Rutor Glacier.

THE SKIING

Among the high peaks at the Franco-Italian border south of Mont Blanc stands Mont Valaisan, 9,485 ft. (2,891 m.), and canting off from its craggy peak is a long ridge which forms a Y, leading to Belvedere, 8,668 ft. (2,642 m.), in Italy and Col de la Traversette, 7,819 ft. (2,383 m.), in France. Between them is a huge powder field above the Col du Petit St. Bernard, thought to be the pass Hannibal used. This snowfield and two lifts provide the link between La Thuile and La Rosière.

La Thuile's skiing, which culminates in the Belvedere peak, rises up in stages on one side of the village. The first stage is Arnouvaz/Les

Suches, steepish valley walls with runs through the trees. A new high-capacity cable car now serves Les Suches. Above is a series of chairs and surface lifts to such mid-massif sectors as Chaz Dura, Ponteille and Cerellaz—all with gentle to moderate terrain. Lifts continue to Belvedere. One side features a steep run (plus a handful of easier ones) toward the Col du Petit St. Bernard, from which the return is by chairlift. On the other is the traverse into the bowl which leads to the connection with La Rosière. The French resort also offers a mix of runs for various ability levels (including several challenging chutes), but more of the terrain is above the tree line.

La Thuile has a reputation for less than meticulous grooming, so a higher ability level than a *piste*'s steepness would indicate is sometimes called for, especially when the snow has gotten choppy. Off-*piste* is a far better bet.

APRÈS-SKI

A good sampling of restaurants and pizzerias is the most La Thuile can boast of. Otherwise things tend to be quiet, especially mid-week. La Bricole, at the junction of the old and new parts of the village, combines bar, restaurant and cellar disco in a well-converted old building.

OTHER ACTIVITIES

Limited cross-country skiing consists of an easy ½-mi. (1 km.) loop, two runs that are medium in length and difficulty, and a trail of around 5 mi. (7½-km.) with more challenge. Most sports other than skiing are concentrated in the Planibel complex and include indoor swimming pools and ice rink, squash courts, sauna, massage, gym, bowling, basketball and other facilities. The ice rink puts on an ice disco every night. There's also tobogganing.

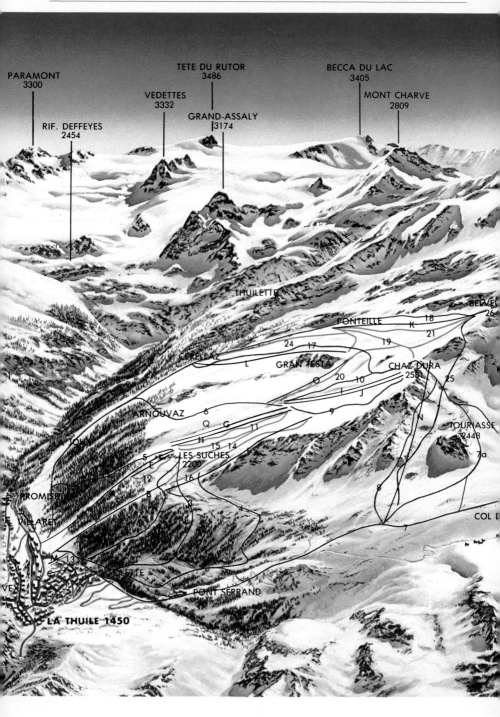

PARAMONT
3300

RIF. DEFFEYES
2454

VEDETTES
3332

TETE DU RUTOR
3486

GRAND-ASSALY
3174

BECCA DU LAC
3405

MONT CHARVE
2809

THUILETTE

BELVE
264

PONTEILLE   K   18
                              21
                         19

CERELLAZ   L   GRAN TESTA
24   17

CHAZ DURA
258   25

O   20   10

ARNOUVAZ   6   9

Q   G   11   J   N

TOURIASSE
2448

H   15   14   7a

5   LES SUCHES
E   2200

12   16   8

PROMISE   B   8

VILLARET   4   7

COL D

M   13   COLETTE

VEX   PONT SERRAND

LA THUILE 1450

228

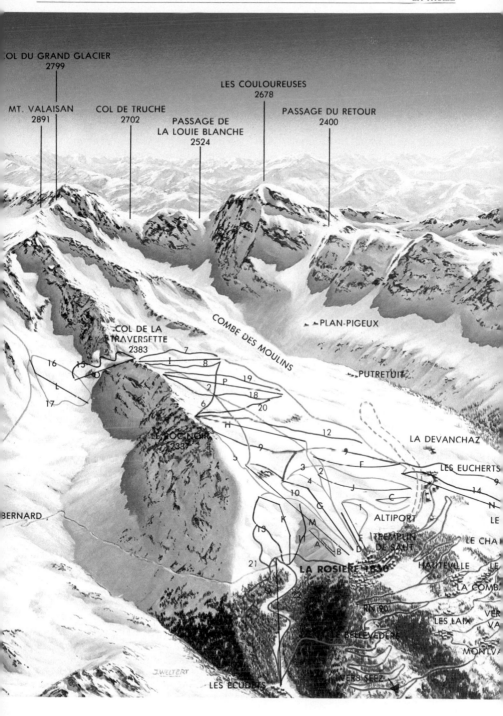

COL DU GRAND GLACIER
2799

MT. VALAISAN
2891

COL DE TRUCHE
2702

PASSAGE DE
LA LOUIE BLANCHE
2524

LES COULOUREUSES
2678

PASSAGE DU RETOUR
2400

COMBE DES MOULINS

PLAN-PIGEUX

COL DE LA
TRAVERSETTE
2383

PUTRETUIT

LE ROC NOIR
2337

LA DEVANCHAZ

LES EUCHERTS

BERNARD

ALTIPORT

TREMPLIN
DE SAUT

LA ROSIÈRE 1850

HAUTEVILLE

LA COMB

LES LAIX

LES ÉCUDETS

VERS SEEZ

BELLEVEDERE

RN 90

LE CHA

LE

MONTU

J.WELTERT

229

BEST OF THE REST

BARDONECCHIA

One of Italy's oldest, most atmospheric and most traditionally elegant resorts, Bardonecchia was favored both by King Umberto, Italy's last monarch, and Benito Mussolini, the dictator who ruled the country during World War II. Today, it is a popular weekend destination for skiers from Turin (2 1/2 hrs.). The skiing is in two main sectors. Monte Jafferau has good intermediate runs and nifty, challenging skiing among the trees on the lower slopes. Colomion/Malezet is also best for better skiers. Heli-skiing excursions and mountain tours are popular in spring.

CLAVIÈRE

Clavière claims to be Italy's oldest ski resort and is definitely part of its newest joint ticketing offer, the Via Lattea or Milky Way. This relaxed and low-key town on the French border offers the best access to the lifts and runs of this newly joined group. These resorts, when combined, offer a good range of skiing and a novel off-the-beaten-track flavor.

MARILLEVA

There are two Marillevas—an undistinguished one at a very low elevation along the Val di Sole and a newer, more attractive development nearly 3,000 ft. (900 m.) higher on the mountain. Located in the scenic northwest corner of the Brenta Dolomites, this twin resort, along with Madonna di Campiglio and Folgarida, forms a sizable ski circus with some 90 mi. (145 km.) of *pistes*. Easy to medium-steep terrain is found at Marilleva, a sunny resort which sometimes resembles a snowy beach dotted with sunbathers more than a ski center.

PIANCAVALLO

Located in a basin set among the contoured hills of the Veneto region, this compact, modern resort offers good family facilities, mostly intermediate skiing, a startling view of the Adriatic and easy access to Venice, 60 mi. (96 km.) away. The ski terrain is on two mountains on either side of the resort, Monte Tremol and Monte Suac. There is a high proportion of interesting skiing among the trees. Piancavallo has welcomed Americans from a nearby Air Force base almost since opening day, and the sightseeing and shopping possibilities in nearby Venice and Verona are hard to beat for non-skiers and sometime-skiers.

SANTA CRISTINA

The smallest of the big three Val Gardena resorts (the other two being Ortisei and Selva), Santa Cristina is a charming town spread out along a lovely hillside. Each of the resorts has a cable car to Ciampinoi, portal to an extensive high plateau with access to skiing on Piz Sella (Sellajoch) and down to Canazei in the Val di Fassa. Santa Cristina also has smaller ski areas at Monte Pana/Mont de Seura and Col Raiser, which also gets traffic linked with Ortisei's Seceda. All of these areas are skiable on the Dolomiti Superski Pass.

SAUZE D'OULX

This oddly spelled resort (pronounced "sew-zay doo") is a bustling village with economical lodging, a lively ambience and many British skiers. It participates in the new Milky Way pass program. Beginners make a beeline for the Sportinia plateau, from which the skiing branches out to miles of largely intermediate runs. Monte Triplex is the more demanding mountain, with the odd mogul field. Sestrière is an easy connection, and a day-trip to Montgenèvre, France, is on many skiers' itinerary.

VAL DI FASSA

Val di Fassa and its resort village of Canazei perch in the Dolomites and offer proximity to the Sella Ronda, a full-day, four-valley ski circus. There are nine small ski areas in the valley including Passo Sella, Passo Pordoi and Passo Fedaia, served by 63 lifts. There is a Val di Fassa pass, as well as the more wide-ranging Dolomiti Superski Pass. Val di Fassa is also the site of the famous Marcialonga cross-country marathon.

ITALY-INFO

ACCOMMODATIONS

The standards of accommodations vary greatly throughout Italy—and substantially in the Italian Alps. Star ratings are set on a province-by-province basis. Accommodations in the Alto Adige (South Tyrol) are not only Austrian in style, but the standards are generally higher than in other parts of the Italian Alps.

Hotels. Top hotels offer the amenities and service you would find elsewhere in the Alps. The lower end of the scale usually designates small, family-run hotels which can range from dreary to quaint, and there is less chance of English being spoken. Half-board (MAP or Modified American Plan) accommodations are usually offered. This includes breakfast (usually a light meal of rolls and coffee, except in the South Tyrol, where buffet breakfasts are becoming more common) and a full, set-menu dinner in the price of the room.

Pensioni. These small, family-run lodgings are casual and inexpensive. They are the equivalent of a Bed and Breakfast (B&B) in the U.S. or Britain. Plumbing standards might not be high, and meal plans vary.

Chalets and apartments. These economical accommodations for families and groups, very popular with British skiers, are increasingly found in Italian resorts. Unlike in many other European resorts, Italian apartments are dispersed among numerous small buildings and tend to be more spacious and individual, owned by families rather than companies.

Room types. A single room will have one single bed; a double room will have two single beds (placed next to each other, but with separate sets of bedclothes).

If a room is described as having a bath, it will have just that—a bathtub, usually with a hand shower. If the room is described as having a shower, it won't have a tub.

AIRPORTS

Milan is the most common transatlantic gateway for the Italian Alps and the most convenient for the central resorts. The city has two airports, *Malpensa,* 30 miles (46 km.) northwest of the city center, for intercontinental traffic, and *Linate,* about 6 miles (10 km.) to the east, mainly for domestic and European flights. There are non-stop flights to Milan from Boston, Chicago, Los Angeles and New York, and there is a service between New York and Venice, the closest gateway to Cortina, Piancavallo and other resorts in eastern Italy.

Munich and Innsbruck are good bets for the resorts in the Alto Adige (South Tyrol), just south of the Brenner Pass. Turin is a convenient jumping-off point for west-central Italy, but this requires a change of planes. The commute from Geneva to Italy's westernmost resorts is short.

CUSTOMS/ENTRY REGULATIONS

For a stay of up to three months, a valid passport is sufficient for citizens of the U.S. and Canada and most western European countries. Visitors from the United Kingdom and Eire need only a visitor's identity card to enter Italy.

Non-residents may import or export up to L. 500,000 in local currency. In foreign currencies, you may import unlimited amounts, but to take the equivalent of more than L. 5,000,000 in or out of the country, you must fill out a V2 declaration form at the border upon entry.

DRIVING

Rental cars. Rental cars are available at major airports. Some are affiliates of international chains. The minimum driving age in Italy is 18, but rental firms may impose their own higher minimum. An International Driver's License (obtainable from your home automobile association) is required. Motorists crossing a border without an international license may obtain a declaration of validity for a U.S. license.

Gasoline Discount Coupons. Discount coupons for gasoline are available to tourists driving cars with non-Italian registration, including rental cars from other countries. They may be purchased at any ACI *(Automobile Club d'Italia)* office or at Italian Government Tourist Office (E.N.I.T.) locations in Europe. Payment must be made in foreign currency.

Gasoline is available in super (98–100 octane), unleaded (95 octane)—still rare, normal (86–88 octane) and diesel. Gasoline stations—most have a self-service pump—generally provide full service in winter from 7 a.m. to 12.30 p.m. and from 3.30 to 7.00 p.m. Many close on Sundays. Stations along the *autostrada* are open 24 hours a day. Attendants expect a tip for special attention.

Insurance. Fully comprehensive insurance is mandatory. If you are taking your own car into Italy, you must have a Green Card, proof that your regular insurance policy has been extended to include foreign countries.

Speed limits. In cities and towns, the limit is 50 kph (31 mph). Outside built-up areas the limit is 90 kph (56 mph); on the *autostrada* maximum speed is 130 kph (81 mph), 110 kph (68 mph) on weekends. Occasionally the speed limit on the *autostrada* may be significantly dropped by the police in a temporary crackdown against flagrant speeding, so pay attention to the posted limit and avoid a fine.

Fines for speeding are high. Always pay on the spot; if you don't, you'll be charged considerably more later.

Rules of the road. Drive on the right, pass (overtake) on the left. Traffic on major roads has right of way over that entering from side roads. Where roads of similar importance intersect, the car from the right has priority. Passing on the right is prohibited, except when the car ahead has signaled its intention to turn left. On the *autostrada*, "keep right except to pass" is the rule. On three lane roads, the middle lane is reserved for passing, which must always be signaled in advance with the directional signal (which must also be kept on while passing).

Drivers entering Italy in a car not their own must have the owner's written permission.

In addition to the usual car documents and driving license, drivers should be equipped with a national identity sticker on the car and carry a red warning triangle for breakdowns and accidents.

Automobile associations. The *Automobile Club d'Italia* (ACI) maintains offices all over Italy. It offers 24-hour breakdown assistance (dial 116) and other services. Their multi-lingual personnel can give information on road and weather conditions, gasoline coupons and hotels.

ACI charge for any breakdown assistance, so it's a good idea to take out international breakdown insurance before leaving home. Spare parts are available for all popular makes of car; ACI will give you the address of the nearest supplier.

Accidents and breakdowns. In the case of a breakdown, switch on the flashing warning lights and place a warning triangle 150 feet (50 m.) behind your car, or at an even greater distance on the *autostrada*. In addition to ACI, you can dial the all-purpose emergency number 113 to report an accident or breakdown. There are emergency telephones on the motorways. Some have separate buttons for technical problems (indicated by a monkey wrench) and injuries (a red cross); press the button until a lamp lights up and wait for help. Other telephones give information in four languages on how to request police, first-aid and breakdown assistance. It's wise to ask for an estimate (with VAT added) *before* undertaking repairs.

Road signs. International pictograms are used for road signs. Specific road and traffic condition information is given by English-speaking operators from the ACI's Phone Assistance Center, dial (06) 42112.

Mountain driving. Snow tire and chain laws may be in effect on mountain pass roads. Chains come in various tire sizes and vary in price according to the sophistication and ease of handling. In Britain, major ski shops hire them out, as does the AA (Dover branch). Practice putting on chains *before* you get stuck in heavy snow.

Studded tires are subject to restrictions: there is a speed limit of 90 kph (55 mph.), and they can only be used between November 15 and March 15 and on vehicles weighing less than 3,500 kg.

Trucks, buses and vehicles climbing uphill have priority on narrow roads. Some Alpine passes are closed in winter, for as long as six months. However, the following routes are normally kept open by snow plows: Bracco (Italy), Brenner (Austria–Italy), Fugazze (Italy), Mauria (Italy), Mendola (Italy), Monte Croce di Comelico (Italy), Montgenèvre (France–Italy), Resia (Austria–Italy), Sestrière (Italy), Tenda (Italy–France) and Tonale (Italy).

There is a special art to driving on ice and in snowy conditions. The golden rule is always to drive more slowly than you think you should. Avoid sharp reactions or sudden braking; it's better to anticipate well in advance. Keep a good distance from the car in front (two or three times the normal braking distance). When starting off or going uphill, put the car in the highest possible gear to avoid wheel spin. Never drive in ski boots.

Roofracks. Skiing luggage, if you have all the equipment, can be excessively unwieldy. Boxes which fit onto the roof are excellent (though expensive) and protect skis and other belongings from the elements. Regular ski roofracks cost less and in Britain can also be hired from some ski hire shops or the AA.

ELECTRIC CURRENT

The current in Italy is 125 or 220 volts, 50 cycles AC. American and British small appliances and electrical gadgets require an adapter/converter, though many electric clocks, record players, and tape recorders will not work properly even with such devices. Travelers are advised to check the voltage with the hotel before using any appliances.

HEALTH

Citizens of fellow EEC states are entitled to claim the same public health services as those available to resident Italians. Britons should obtain the relevant E111 form from their local office of the Department of Health and Social Security.

Italy has no health insurance for North American visitors. If you become ill or are injured, you may find resort doctors to be reasonably multi-lingual and accustomed to arranging payment from patients who are visitors from abroad. If there is a problem, your hotel can help straighten it out. You must pay your bill on the spot and submit your claim to your insurance company.

On-*piste* rescue is usually free. Off-*piste* may be expensive. Short-term insurance may not be available at the resort, so skiers are advised to obtain such coverage before leaving home. (If combining France and Italy on one vacation, remember that French *Carte Neige* coverage is international for the duration of the policy, see p. 162.)

HOLIDAYS AND SPECIAL EVENTS

Italian holidays falling during the ski season are: Immaculate Conception (Dec. 8), Christmas Day, St. Stefano's Day (Dec. 26), New Year's Day, Epiphany (Jan. 6), and Easter Monday.

Resorts in Italy are busy over Christmas and the New Year, and if the snow is still good, at Easter. Italian schoolchildren have no February break as in other European countries, but it is traditional for Italian families to head for the Alps over Carnival week in February, the exact dates varying from year to year, depending on the date set for Easter.

MAIL

Stamps may be purchased only at post offices and tobacco shops. Post offices are open from 8.30 a.m. to 2 p.m.; on Saturdays and the last day of each month, they close at noon. The main post offices in large cities and at major airports are open longer—including some with 24-hour service for registered mail and telegrams.

Letter boxes are painted red. The slot marked "Per la Città" is for local mail; the one labeled "Altre Destinazioni" is for all other destinations. Mail to and from Italy can be slow.

MONEY MATTERS

Currency. The unit of currency in Italy is the *lira* (abbreviated L.).

Coins: 10, 20, 50, 100, 200 and 500 lire
Notes: 1,000, 2,000, 5,000, 20,000, 50,000 and 100,000 lire.

Credit cards and traveler's checks. Major hotels, restaurants and shops may accept credit cards. Traveler's checks are welcome. Take your passport or national identity card along when you go to cash a traveler's check.

Banks. Banks and exchange offices (*Ufficio di Cambio*) offer the best exchange rate on traveler's checks and foreign currency. Banking hours are 8.30 a.m. to 1.30 p.m. and from 3 to 4 p.m., Monday to Friday; banks are closed weekends and holidays. Exchange offices at airports and major city railway terminals are open seven days a week.

Sales tax. A VAT or sales tax of 9 to 38% is imposed on most goods and services in Italy.

Tax refunds. Foreign visitors residing outside the EEC will be refunded the IVA paid on larger purchases made in shops displaying the "Italy Tax Free" symbol—a red package attached to a balloon. Goods valued at L.525,000 or more qualify for the refund. Obtain a receipt from the shop, to show on departure together with the goods to a customs officer. Post the receipt in one of the special boxes to be found past the customs area at most international airports in Italy. Or send it by mail within 50 days of the date of purchase. A small service charge will be deducted from the refund.

SKI SCHOOLS

The Italian Ski School (Scuola Nazionale Italiana di Sci) is recognized by its distinctive snowflake logo.

Generally speaking you will be taught the traditional method of learning through snowplows progressing to parallel turns. After that there is usually some specialist instruction available in racing or, in some resorts, monoskiing, snowboarding and perhaps even ski hang-gliding and para-skiing.

You can either go into group lessons or take a private instructor. If you choose to go in a group, make sure it is of the right level. Often in Italy there is a ski-off for those who are not complete beginners to establish their level—a short, shallow descent with perhaps one or two turns. The instructors will then allot you a class. If you feel that you are in either a too-slow or too-advanced group, it is easy to move up or down, though it is best to check that your instructor agrees.

There can be up to six different ability levels in a normal Italian ski school. Try to get an instructor who speaks English. Most groups have around seven or eight members. Lessons normally last about two hours in the morning or afternoon.

Private lessons are available by the hour, half-day or full day. It costs considerably more, but you do learn faster.

TELEPHONE

The postal service also runs the telephone. Hotels usually add astronomical surcharges onto phone calls, so these are to be avoided—especially for overseas calls.

A local call from a public telephone requires a 200-lire token (gettone) or two 100-lire coins. Gettone may be purchased at newsstands, tobacco shops or coffee bars. Be sure to buy enough tokens to cover the call. Place the token(s) in the slot, but do not release them until the party answers. The phone consumes the money as long as you stay on the line, and any unused coins will be returned.

Some newer telephones are card-operated. Phone cards (scheda telefonica) are available at SIP (Società Italiana per l'Esercizio Telefonico) offices, where you can also make long-distance and international calls; they are usually open from 7 a.m. to around 10 p.m.

Long-distance (interurbano) calls may be dialed directly between major cities. To reserve or make a telephone call to another European country, dial 15. To reserve or make an intercontinental telephone call, dial 170.

International calls can be made from phone boxes marked "Teleselezione". Alternatively, you can book a call at the local public telephone office (Posto Telefonico Pubblico).

To make a direct international call, dial 00 and wait for a change of tone before dialing the country's code, area code and subscriber's number. Some country codes:

Australia (00) 61   U.K. (00) 44
Eire (00) 35   U.S.A. (00) 1

To telephone Italy from abroad, dial the international access code, followed by 39.

Charges for international phone calls are reduced by about 30% between 11 p.m. and 8 a.m. on weekdays and all day on Sundays.

For calls back to the U.S., the best deal is AT&T's USADIRECT program, but it is currently available only from Milan and Rome. Insert a coin for local access, dial 172 1011 and wait for up to 30 seconds for a direct connection to an AT&T operator, who will then place a credit card or collect call for you.

TOURIST INFORMATION OFFICES

The Italian National Government Tourist Office (E.N.I.T.) has resort information, hotel price lists and other data, although some of their material is available only in Italian.

In the U.S. the main office is at 630 Fifth Ave., New York, N.Y. 10111; tel. (212) 245 4822. There are also branch offices in Chicago, San Francisco and Montreal. Some are open during normal business hours and others are open only in the mornings.

In the U.K. the office is at 1, Princes Street, London W1R 8AY; tel. (01) 408 1254.

For specific information about a resort, contact the local tourist office directly.

SWITZERLAND AND ITS SKIING

Even before the invention of skiing, the Swiss were already exploiting the tourist potential of their mountains in summer. Switzerland is also the oldest winter-vacation country, welcoming the first group of British sportsmen to St. Moritz over a century ago, and that sense of tradition cannot fail to strike the visiting skier today.

As a nation, the Swiss are firmly resolved to give visitors to their country the best possible service during their stay. Almost invariably this service is reflected in the price. Switzerland is not cheap for foreigners, but the strength of the Swiss franc and Switzerland's minimal inflation rate means that many hotel and restaurant prices remain stable for years at a time. And, although visitors to Switzerland may grumble about prices being higher than in other Alpine countries, they seldom have cause to complain about value for money or quality of service.

The Swiss are undoubtedly the world's best hoteliers and, although many of them now ply their trade abroad, there are still plenty of them left at home. Whether you choose a five-star or a one-star hotel for your Swiss holiday, you can be sure that standards of cleanliness and service will be the best in that category. Many Swiss hotels in ski resorts are still run as family businesses, so the manager and/or chef may well also be the owner.

Switzerland is a country that is synonymous with cleanliness, efficiency and honesty. It is a matter of national pride that any advertised service is provided, regardless of freak snowstorms or any other obstacles. In other words, the trains run on time and the ski lifts work, as long as it is safe for them to do so. Reliable public transportation and efficient, safe lift systems are obviously a great attraction to ski vacationers, who praise the heavens for such competence.

The Swiss public transportation system is the envy of the world. Both the country's major international airports, Zurich and Geneva, have mainline railway stations attached to the terminals. The remarkable Fly/Rail program, in cooperation between Swissair and the Swiss Federal Railroads, enables travelers to check their baggage in for a Swissair flight anywhere in the world directly through to their resort. Upon return, they may check their bags in at the resort railway station directly through to the airport in their home country.

Many Swiss resorts are served by mountain railways which connect with ordinary trains at mainline stations. (From Geneva to Zermatt, for instance, you take a through train from Geneva airport to Visp, where you change onto a narrow-gauge train to Zermatt.) But even those resorts not served by railways are regularly served by reliable yellow post buses.

Travel by car is also easy in Switzerland. Access roads to all ski resorts are kept open throughout the winter except in very severe weather. It is always advisable to carry chains—better still have a four-wheel-drive vehicle. Switzerland's autoroute (Autobahn) system, available to all vehicles displaying a specially purchased sticker, is one of Europe's best. Particularly useful are the networks running from Geneva airport, close to the French border, all the way along the north side of Lake Geneva and then the Rhône valley to important towns like Aigle, Martigny and Sierre, and from Zurich to Chur.

Uphill transportation for skiers is as good as regular ground transportation for everybody. Switzerland has had funiculars for decades, and some historic rack-and-pinion railways are still in operation in great old mountaineering villages turned into even greater ski resorts, such as Wengen and Zermatt. They may be slow by the standards of modern cable cars, gondolas, and high-speed chairlifts, but they are peerless in terms of safety, reliability and charm.

While the best of the old lifts continue a service that is as dependable as a Swiss timepiece, there are ultra-high-tech new conveyances as well. Zermatt's new Klein Matterhorn cable car, for instance, has a top terminal built into the mountain, and each car of Verbier's new tram, called Le Jumbo, holds 150 skiers.

Just because Switzerland is efficient does not mean that it lacks character. The character is just a little hard to define since the country has something of a split personality. Switzerland is at once intensely nationalistic yet incredibly cosmopolitan. With borders adjoining Europe's other three main skiing countries, Switzerland inevitably has some similarities to each of them.

There are four official languages: German (spoken in a curious Swiss-German dialect, though all Swiss-Germans can also speak high German), French, Italian and Romansch (which like the Ladin of Italy's Alto Adige is closely derived from Latin). German is the first language of about 70 per cent of the Swiss who live in eastern and central Switzerland. French is the mother tongue of about 27 per cent of the population who live in western Switzerland, while 2–3 per cent in sunny southern Switzerland, near Lugano, speak Italian first. However, it is rare that a Swiss employed in the tourist industry will not speak a handful of other languages as well. Naturally, skiers who are francophiles will probably be happiest in the French-speaking resorts, while those who are attracted to the German or Austrian character will prefer the German-speaking parts. But whatever its language, every Swiss ski resort, no matter how close to the border it may be, remains defiantly and proudly Swiss. To prove it: no other nation in Europe is as keen on displaying its national flag.

Switzerland's three greatest international resorts— the trio consistently most popular with North American skiers—transcend specific regional characteristics and have taken on a unique image. St. Moritz in south- eastern Switzerland, not far from Italy's Trento, is the ultimately pricey, ultimately elegant, ultimately chic ski resort. The richest, most famous, most titled Europeans who could afford to go anywhere tend to choose St. Moritz—in high season, naturally. Even the most luxurious hotels, the most sought-after ski instructors, the smartest dining spots and après-ski watering holes welcome the rest of us at other times—often with prices that, while still high, are relative bargains.

Davos is a big, bustling but not particularly pretty town in eastern Switzerland, but its skiing ranks with the best in the world. Long runs on fabulous mountains and a lively atmosphere make everyone forget the undistinguished architecture.

Down in southwestern Switzerland, over the border from Italy's Aosta Valley, Zermatt is a dramatic contrast. This quintessentially picturesque town in the shadow of the Matterhorn has retained a rustic, old-fashioned air, despite the fact that authentic rusticity never was as elegant as the Zermatt version.

Other eastern Swiss resorts are very traditional, often in a staid, formal Germanic style but with a sporty overlay—and always with first-rate services on every front. Andermatt, Arosa, Engelberg, Flims/Laax and Lenzerheide/Valbella tend to attract Swiss and German skiers, many of them regulars winter after winter. Klosters, which shares its ski terrain with Davos, is more elegant, more charming and more expensive. Grindelwald, Mürren and Wengen in the Jungfrau region are younger, sportier and have an overwhelming sense of being in the heart of the mountains. Gstaad, charming in the sense that Zermatt is (though with neither the isolation nor the mountain grandeur), sits on the border of the French- and German-speaking parts of Switzerland and is favored by international stars. Moving westward toward Geneva, Crans-Montana is French in language and cuisine, as are Château d'Oex, Les Diablerets, Verbier and Villars.

Many of Switzerland's resorts, especially the traditional ones, are winter resorts more than ski resorts. Miles of touring trails and walking paths, a variety of non-ski sports and, usually, fine shops prevail. Excellent accommodations, clean air, the probability of sunshine and fine food are enough to lure non-skiers to the Swiss Alps in winter. Many of them board the lifts right along with the skiers to reach mountain restaurants with great food and greater views.

In fact, Switzerland has some of the best mountain restaurants to be found anywhere—consider La Marmite in St. Moritz or Enzo's Hitta in Zermatt. The cuisine is usually international, borrowing from France, Germany and Italy, yet also boasting uniquely Swiss dishes like potato rösti, raclette (melted cheese eaten with potatoes boiled in their jackets) and various types of fondue. Down in the villages, most Swiss resorts offer a wide range of eating places, from pizzerias to gourmet restaurants.

Switzerland's best-known wines are Dôle (red) and Fendant (white). Clear, potent Schnaps, especially that made from the Williams pear, is served as an apéritif or for a toast. And Swiss beers are robust and excellent.

When it comes to après-ski activities, the usual rule for Switzerland applies: it may not be cheap, but it is good value. The Swiss do not insist on making their guests have fun in the evenings; they allow you to participate as much or as little as you like. In general the après-ski scene is sophisticated. There is not much yodeling, and oompah bands are scarce. Nightspots such as the King's Club in St. Moritz, the GreenGo in Gstaad, the Farm Club in Verbier and the Post in Zermatt, some of the smartest in Europe, are often mentioned in gossip columns.

The Swiss provide a warm welcome for visitors of all nationalities, but in many resorts there is always a particular affection reserved for the British. The two nations go back a long way together as far as Alpine activities are concerned and a mutual respect born a hundred years ago or more still endures. Americans are the country's number-two-ranked visitors on a year-round basis.

In the end, the only way to appreciate properly the very special attractions of Switzerland is to go there and discover the country and meet the people. It would be surprising if the service and hospitality you received and the skiing you enjoyed on such a visit did not make you resolve to make a return to the slopes of Switzerland very soon.

ADELBODEN

Access: *Nearest airport:* Zurich (2½ hrs.). *By road:* N6 Autobahn, exit Spiez. *By rail:* to Bern, connection to Frutigen, then by bus.

Tourist Office: Verkehrsbüro, 3715 Adelboden, Switzerland. Tel. (033) 73 22 52

Altitude: 4,593 ft. (1,400 m.). *Top:* 7,645 ft. (2,330 m.)

Language: German

Runs: 74 mi. (120 km.) with Lenk

Lifts: 29 (44 with Lenk)

Ski areas: Engstligenalp, Boden, Schwandfeldspitz, Hahnenmoos

Ski school: Schweizer Skischule Adelboden

Linked resort: Lenk

Season: December to April

Kindergarten: *Non-ski:* from 1 year. *With ski:* 4–6 years

Prices: *Lift pass:* 6 days Sfr. 162 (children Sfr. 97). *Ski school:* Group Sfr. 93 for 6 days; private Sfr. 40 per hour.

RATINGS

Skiing Conditions	4
Snow Conditions	6
For Beginners	6
For Intermediates	6
For Advanced Skiers	4
For Children	6
Après-Ski	6
Other Sports	7
Value for Money	7

THE RESORT

Adelboden, in the Engstligen Valley of the Bernese Oberland, is one of the most charming Alpine villages in Switzerland. Dominated by the impressive Wildstrubel mountain, the resort is full of character, with lots of beautiful old wooden chalet buildings. It is a popular tourist destination in summer as well as winter. The skiing links with the neighboring resort of Lenk, which has a rather different character. While the skiing is not the most convenient, the prettiness of the village makes up for it.

THE SKIING

Adelboden's skiing is spread among four separate areas, some quite minor, linked by road (though by 1990/91 they should also be lift-linked): Geils/Hahnenmoos, Kuonisborgli/Fleckli, Dirg/Engstligenalp, and Tschentenegg/Schwandfeldspitz. For all except the Tschentenegg area, it is necessary to take a long walk or a bus from the center of Adelboden. A car can be as much of a hindrance as a help, since the drives are relatively short and parking at the bottom lifts can often be a problem.

There is not much in the way of difficult skiing, but there are plenty of good, sunny slopes for intermediates. The Tschentenegg area rises up to the Schwandfeldspitz, 6,359 ft. (1,938 m.), and offers a single advanced run all the way back down to Adelboden.

The lifts from Boden up to the

Höchsthorn, 6,244 ft. (1,903 m.), serve fairly easy runs, while the lift on the Fleckli system rises to 6,109 ft. (1,862 m.), offering more challenging skiing.

From Birg, a cable car goes to the top of the Engstligenalp, 6,444 ft. (1,964 m.), but you also have to return by this cable car, and the skiing off a series of short surface lifts to Dossen, 7,645 ft. (2,330 m.), while the resort's highest, does not really justify the laborious journey.

Geils accesses the most interesting and challenging skiing in the Adelboden region and also provides the link with Lenk. The best runs are those from the top of the Laveygrat chairlift, 7,218 ft. (2,200 m.).

APRÈS-SKI

Adelboden is not as quiet after dark as it sometimes seems. The illusion is created principally because most of the après-ski activity goes on inside hotels. The Alte Taverne near the Nevada-Palace Hotel is the largest and most exciting nightspot. Those in search of cheaper, more informal nightlife should find it at the Hotel Kreuz, particularly in the pizzeria. There is also a movie theater, with films in English.

OTHER ACTIVITIES

Cross-country skiers can enjoy 25 mi. (40 km.) of tracks along easy and intermediate trails, and there are 25 mi. (40 km.) of walking paths. Skating and curling take place on indoor and outdoor rinks, with instruction available, and there is swimming, riding, sleigh rides, hang-gliding from the Schwandfeldspitz, and skibobbing. A ski jump occasionally stages competitions. For a taste of local culture and history, visit the Heimatmuseum.

ANDERMATT

← Unteralp

← Oberalppass

Stöckli 236

Access: *Nearest airport:* Zurich (2 hrs.). *By road:* N2 Autobahn, exit Göschenen. *By rail:* to Göschenen, then Oberalp railway to Andermatt.

Tourist Office: Verkehrsbüro, 6490 Andermatt, Switzerland. Tel. (044) 6 74 54

Altitude: 4,738 ft. (1,444 m.). *Top:* 9,722 ft. (2,963 m.)

Language: German

Runs: 34 mi. (55 km.)

Lifts: 13

Ski areas: Gemsstock, Nätschen-Stöckli, Winterhorn

Ski school: Schweizer Skischule Andermatt

Linked resorts: None

Season: December to May

Kindergarten: *Non-ski:* none. *With ski:* ski school from 4 years

Prices: *Lift pass:* 6 days Sfr. 160. *Ski school:* Group Sfr. 37 per day (children Sfr. 35); private Sfr. 43–48 per hour.

RATINGS

Skiing Conditions	5
Snow Conditions	7
For Beginners	6
For Intermediates	4
For Advanced Skiers	7
For Children	5
Après-Ski	3
Other Sports	5
Value for Money	7

THE RESORT

Often described as being at the "crossroads of the Alps", the tiny, traditional village of Andermatt is the major ski resort in the small, scenic Swiss canton of Uri. The St. Gotthard Pass into Italy runs by Andermatt, which also lies between the Furka and Oberalp passes.

Andermatt is reminiscent of more famous resorts Zermatt and Saas-Fee, although it is much smaller and more compact than either of them. The resort is not car-free, but private vehicles are discouraged, and the streets are narrow. Despite being at a "crossroads" and being just 2 hours from Zurich, Andermatt has a sense of isolation, of apartness amid rugged mountains.

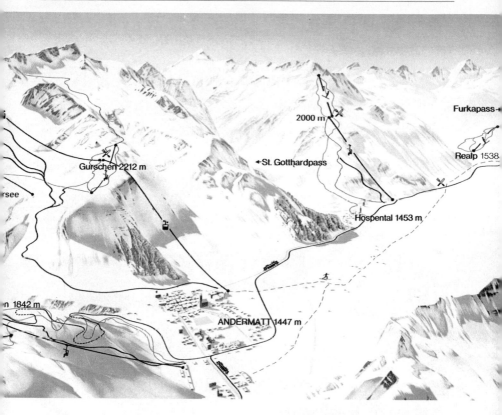

THE SKIING

Andermatt has a reputation for having some of the most reliable snow conditions in Switzerland. There is some very demanding skiing on the principal ski area, the Gemsstock, including steep runs straight down the front of the mountain. The summit affords an awesome panorama of 600 peaks. Getting up this mountain tends to be rather less fun. The two-stage cable car often stacks up with long lines at peak times. The two other lifts on the Gemsstock—a chairlift and a surface lift—are relatively short, so the cable cars constitute the main means of getting back uphill.

The other principal ski area is Nätschen-Stöckli, a relatively low mountain, 6,044 ft. (1,842 m.), reached from the opposite end of the village, either by a fairly new chairlift or by the traditional train to Nätschen station. There are a couple of good mountain restaurants at Nätschen, and the runs down to Andermatt are mainly wide, easy and sunny; the exception is the expert run under the chairlift.

The Andermatt lift pass also covers the installations in the neighboring villages of Hospental and Realp, reached by road or rail. The former offers the better skiing—a chairlift followed by a surface lift ascending to a saddle on the Winterhorn, 8,731 ft. (2,661 m.). Realp is really not of interest to anyone other than beginners.

Andermatt is a major center for

mountain tours, with top guides such as Martin Epp and Alex Clapasson based here.

APRÈS-SKI

Andermatt by night is a quiet place. Low-key eating and drinking take place mainly in hotels, but there is one disco, the Downhill, and a movie theater showing English films.

OTHER ACTIVITIES

You'll find 13 mi. (20 km.) of cross-country tracks, skating on an outdoor rink, curling, tobogganing, sleigh rides and bowling.

AROSA

Access: *Nearest airport:* Zurich (2½ hrs.). *By road:* N13 Autobahn, exit Chur-Nord. *By rail:* express to Chur, then by Rhaetian railway to Arosa.

Tourist Office: Kurverein, 7050 Arosa, Switzerland. Tel. (081) 31 16 21

Altitude: 5,906 ft. (1,800 m.). *Top:* 8,704 ft. (2,653 m.)

Language: German

Runs: 43 mi. (70 km.)

Lifts: 16

Ski areas: Weisshorn, Hörnli

Ski school: Schweizer Skischule Arosa

Linked resorts: None

Season: December to April

Kindergarten: *Non-ski:* 3–8 years. *With ski:* from 2½ years

Prices: *Lift pass:* 6 days Sfr. 167 (children Sfr. 84). *Ski school:* Group Sfr. 160 for 6 days (children Sfr. 140); private Sfr. 45 per hour.

RATINGS

Skiing Conditions	6
Snow Conditions	7
For Beginners	6
For Intermediates	7
For Advanced Skiers	4
For Children	6
Après-Ski	7
Other Sports	7
Value for Money	7

THE RESORT

Arosa is one of those classic, old-fashioned ski resorts that could only be found in Switzerland. A village has existed on this site at the head of the Schanfigg Valley in the Grisons canton since the 13th century. The Arosa Ski Club was founded in 1903, the ski school was established 30 years later, and the first three lifts were built in 1938. Accommodations are mostly in hotels, of which there is a great variety, ranging from several that are very grand to some that are very simple.

Arosa is an ideal resort for mixed groups of vacationers, with non-skiers as well as skiers. Indeed, nearly half the winter visitors to Arosa do not ski. The variety of activities is such that non-skiers are unlikely to get bored.

THE SKIING

Arosa is certainly a resort for beginners and especially intermediate skiers rather than for experts. It is a beautiful place in which to learn and a splendid place to lunch in a fabulous collection of mountain restaurants. Arosa itself is fairly high up in a sweeping, south-facing bowl which invites zigzagging back and forth between the well-interlinked sectors. The skiing stretches up to the peak of the Weisshorn, 8,704 ft. (2,653 m.), almost all of it above the tree line. The lifts are well laid out, and there are some good long, broad runs and some fine off-*piste*.

The Weisshorn is the highest point in the area, from which the most difficult run to the mountain chapel,

249

with a variation to the Carmenna-hütte, begins. Others are of intermediate standard.

The Hörnli, 8,242 ft. (2,512 m.), offers wide, sunny *pistes* perfectly suited to the early intermediate skier. There is also an off-*piste* descent down the back, all the way to the nearby resort of Lenzerheide. When snow conditions permit, there is also a long, challenging run down the Schanfigg Valley to Chur.

APRÈS-SKI

With so many non-skiers in the resort, there are always plenty of people with energy for après-ski (or après-non-ski) activities. Nevertheless, the average age of the clientele is older than in resorts with more demanding skiing. One of the most popular centers for nightlife is the Kursaal, which has two bars, a restaurant, a disco and a movie theater.

With so many hotels, it is not surprising that much of the après-ski revolves around them. The much-loved bar of the Arosa Kulm Hotel was transplanted from the 1929 version of the hotel after it was rebuilt in 1975. The Hotel Park is fairly lively and boasts a bowling alley, while the Tschuggen Grand Hotel is a good place for more traditional dancing and even some black-tie (optional) evenings every week.

OTHER ACTIVITIES

Arosa offers about 19 mi. (30 km.) each of cross-country loops and paths for walkers, plus skating (artificial and natural rinks), curling, squash, indoor tennis, sleigh rides, indoor golf, horseback riding, swimming, bowling, tobogganing snowboarding and hang-gliding. There are weekly concerts, exhibitions and a regional museum at Innerarosa, open twice a week.

CRANS-MONTANA

Access: *Nearest airport*: Geneva (2½ hrs.). *By road*: N9 Autoroute, exit Sion, then via Sierre. *By rail*: to Sierre, then funicular or bus.

Tourist Office: Office du Tourisme, 3962 Montana, Switzerland. Tel. (027) 41 30 41. Or, 3963 Crans, Switzerland. Tel. (027) 41 21 32

Altitude: 4,922 ft. (1,500 m.).
Top: 9,843 ft. (3,000 m.)

Language: French

Runs: 77 mi. (125 km.)

Lifts: 34

Ski areas: Petit Bonvin, Cry d'Err/ Bella Lui, Les Violettes/Plaine Morte, Chetseron

Ski schools: Ecole Suisse de Ski Montana, Ecole Suisse de Ski Crans

Linked resort: Aminona

Season: December to April, plus summer skiing

Kindergarten: *Non-ski*: 2 months– 12 years. *With ski*: 3–7 years

Prices: *Lift pass*: 6 days Sfr. 169 (children Sfr. 101). *Ski school*: Group Sfr. 95 for 7 days (children Sfr. 80); private Sfr. 42 for 50 min.

RATINGS

Skiing Conditions	8
Snow Conditions	5
For Beginners	6
For Intermediates	8
For Advanced Skiers	6
For Children	7
Après-Ski	7
Other Sports	7
Value for Money	6

THE RESORT

Historically Crans and Montana were two separate resorts that sprawled into each other, and they have now officially amalgamated. Each retains its distinctive character, Crans being the more upscale of the two, with expensive boutiques, pricey hotels and nightspots and many fur coats in evidence. Spread along a south-facing plateau above

Sierre in the Rhône valley, Crans-Montana is the sunniest resort in Switzerland.

THE SKIING

Crans-Montana was the venue for the 1987 World Alpine Ski Championships, and new lift facilities—and even new *pistes*—installed for this event have enhanced the skiing possibilities here. Essentially, the ski area is a mini "3 Vallées", with lots of interconnected (though considerably less interesting) terrain. The different sectors are: Cry d'Err/Bella Lui, Les Violettes/Plaine Morte and Petit Bonvin. Access to the system is provided at four points along the plateau: Crans, Montana, Les Barzettes and Aminona. All these bottom stations are linked by a free shuttle bus.

Crans-Montana has masses of fine intermediate skiing, but it also offers a fair number of taxing runs for the expert, including the mogul-ridden slopes below the Bella Lui summit, the top section of the Piste Nationale downhill course, the run down from Plaine Morte and the steep mogul slopes next to the Toula lift.

A cable car from Les Violettes serves the upper section of the ski area. There are spectacular panoramic views from the top of the Plaine

Morte Glacier, 9,843 ft. (3,000 m.), and the run down offers a combination of great skiing and superb scenery. A limited amount of easy summer skiing is available on the glacier itself. This sector is often closed during severe weather or after heavy snowfalls, and in high season there can be longish lines for the cable car.

Because so many of its slopes are south-facing, Crans-Montana suffers from poor snow cover and icy runs, particularly lower down, at either end of the season. The most atmospheric mountain restaurant is at Merbé, between Cry d'Err and Grand Signal, and the more modern restaurants at Les Violettes and Plaine Morte also serve good food.

APRÈS-SKI

Après-ski is a curious mix of high-style, high-action, high-price discoing (Crans) and low-key, family-oriented dining. Crans also has a casino, and the resorts boast no shortage of smart nightclubs, those in Crans being generally more expensive than those in Montana. Tearooms are very popular après-ski rendezvous points; among the best are the Constellation in Crans and Gerber in Montana. The hotel bars are fashionable but expensive; the bar of the Crans-Ambassador is usually well patronized. But there are cheaper drinking places, such as La Grange in Montana and Le Pub in Crans. Au Gréni in Montana is one of the best restaurants, specializing in Valaisan fare, while Au Vieux Moulin (Montana) is a good pizzeria. Crans has a movie theater.

OTHER ACTIVITIES

You'll find 25 mi. (40 km.) of cross-country tracks, skating, curling, swimming (hotel pools and spa swimming pool), tennis, bowling, squash, horse riding, 31 mi. (50 km.) of marked walks, tobogganing, ski-bobbing, snowboarding, fitness centers, indoor golf and hot-air ballooning.

DAVOS

⛷ ⛷ ⛷ ⛷ ⛷

Access: *Nearest airport*: Zurich (2½ hrs.). *By road*: N3 Autobahn, exit Landquart, then via Klosters. *By rail*: station in Davos.

Tourist Office: Kur- und Verkehrsverein, 7270 Davos, Switzerland. Tel. (083) 3 51 35

Altitude: 5,118 ft. (1,560 m.). *Top*: 9,331 ft. (2,844 m.)

Language: German

Runs: 171 mi. (276 km.) with Klosters

Lifts: 55 with Klosters

Ski areas: Schatzalp/Strela, Parsenn, Jakobshorn, Pischa, Rinerhorn

Ski schools: Schweizer Skischule Davos Platz, Schweizer Skischule Davos Dorf

Linked resort: Klosters

Season: December to mid-April

Kindergarten: *Non-ski*: for all ages. *With ski*: 3–10 years

Prices: *Lift pass*: 6 days Sfr. 200 (children Sfr. 120). *Ski school*: Group Sfr. 22 for half-day (children Sfr. 17); private Sfr. 44 per hour.

RATINGS

Skiing Conditions	9
Snow Conditions	7
For Beginners	5
For Intermediates	9
For Advanced Skiers	8
For Children	5
Après-Ski	9
Other Sports	9
Value for Money	7

THE RESORT

Davos is a big, brassy town and year-round tourist center composed of Davos Dorf and Davos Platz, now grown into one lively whole. It may lack Alpine charm, but it offers easy access, a great range of sports and non-sports activities, terrific nightlife, a truly international clientele and some of the best cruising terrain in the Alps.

THE SKIING

The main ski area is the Parsenn region, a fabulous massif which links with the Schatzalp/Strela sector to the west and the Klosters/Gotschnagrat sector to the east. This is a popular area for intermediate and advanced skiers, with many long, challenging runs, especially those leading back to Davos-Dorf. There are plenty of broad, open *pistes*, a variety of off-*piste* options and some good mogul skiing. The Parsenn is not only an end unto itself, but also the stepping-stone to the Weissfluhgipfel, 9,328 ft. (2,844 m.), Davos's highest skiable point. One of the classic routes of the Alps leads from the summit to the Küblis railway station—a 7-mi. (11-km.) run which even a strong intermediate can handle (and one of the Alps' few ultraruns which requires strength rather than a really advanced level of skiing). Most skiers elect to stop at a mountain *Schwendi* for refreshment en route.

The Schatzalp/Strela sector is on the same side of Davos as the Parsenn, but an unskiable valley between the mountains prevents the

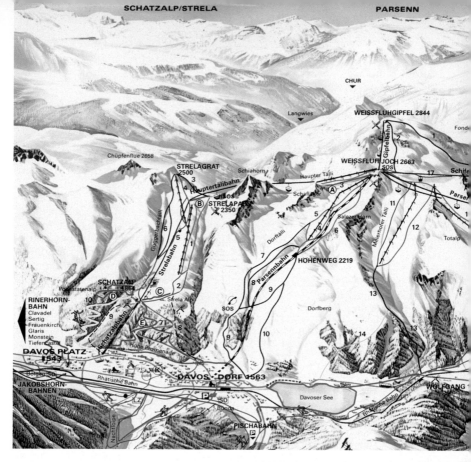

skiing from being interlinked. (There is a high cable car from the Strela Pass to the Weissfluhjoch, so that skiers can move between them without having to return to town.) The Schatzalp/Strela layout is long and steep rather than broad, and some runs tend to mogul up into good bump skiing.

Across the valley are three smaller sectors which are not interconnected but which do offer relief from Parsenn crowds. The biggest is the Brämabüel/Jakobshorn, which has lots of wide, sunny slopes for intermediate skiers and some good mogul terrain. The Rinerhorn area, peaking at the Nüllisch Grat, has short runs—easier on top and more difficult ones through the woods at the bottom—but its north-facing ori-

Glattwang 2376
29
LANDQUART
horn 2460
Arflinafurgga 2247
Arflina
Fideriser Heuberge
Strassberger
Furggli
Chistenstein
28
Girenspitz
Plandagrez
FIDERIS 747
27
JENAZ 728
SOS
Val Maiderschi
SOS
Barga
Seehorn
KÜBLIS 813
SOS
Schutzhütte
Kreuzweg 2305
Gauderloch
SOS
24
Conterser Schwendi
1682
24
CONTERS
1088
SAAS 938
18
Obersäss 2014
Schifer 1567
26
gen 2443
Casanna 255
22
25
19
20
52
PRÄTTIGAU
31
30
21
Casanna Alp
940
SOS
22
PARSENNHÜTTE
2200
41
49
Serneuser
Schwendi 1622
SERNEUS 1032
Gruobenalp
49
51
16
42
43
GOTSCHNAGRAT
2285
SOS
50
21
23
Bad Serneus 981
44
SOS
45
47
Gotschnaboden
Cavadürli
1355
SOS
46
KLOSTERS
DORF 1127
Schwarzseealp
48
Midrisabahn
T 1525
45
21
48
Rhätische Bahn
SOS
KLOSTERS 1194

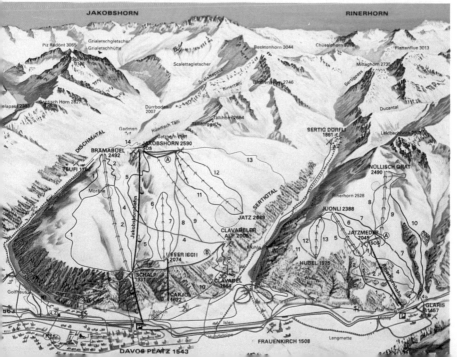

JAKOBSHORN
RINERHORN
Piz Radönt 3065
Grialetschgletscher
Grialetschhütte
Beckenhorn 3044
Chüealphorn 3076
Plattenflue 3013
Scalettagletscher
Mittaghorn 2735
lapass 2385
ontisch Horn 2827
Scalettahorn
Rinertälli
Bladnerhorn 2746
Sertigpass
Ducantal
Dürrboden
2007
Tällihorn 2684
Gadmen
Rüedisch Tälli
Tällifurga
Leidbachhorn 280
DISCHMATAL
14
JAKOBSHORN 2590
SOS
SERTIG DÖRFLI
1861
BRÄMABÜEL
2492
13
NÖLLISCH GRAT
2490
TEUFI 1710
A
12
Mörtsch
5
11
Rinerhorn 2528
4
SERTIGTAL
JUONLI 2388
2
7
8
9
JATZ 2069
6
JATZMEDER
2045
A
SOS
CLAVADELER
ALP 2005
5
12
13
ISSER IGGU
2074
B
Mühli
11
HUBEL 1975
ISCHALP
1931
C
CLAVADEL
1864
LARJOL
1622
10
Bolgen
1825
GLARIS
1457
P
Golfhaus
Islen
Hundeloipe
Lengmatte
DAVOS PLATZ 1543
FRAUENKIRCH 1508

entation makes it snow-sure when other sectors might have conditions problems. Finally the Pischa deep in the Flüela Valley, reached by bus, has easy, wide-open skiing, plus a couple of good off-*piste* options.

APRÈS-SKI

Davos is a sophisticated town. The Pöstli Corner bar of the Posthotel Morosani and the Chämi bar with its surreal decor are always popular after skiing. The Davoserhof has the finest hotel restaurant, while the Gentiana is a good place for *fondue*. The Padrino pizzeria has bargain eating, and Chinese restaurants flourish here—the newest and smartest being the Zauberberg in the lavishly refurbished Hotel Europe. Dinners at Teufi or Schatzalp outside Davos are popular too. The Pöstli Club in the Posthotel and the Cabanna Club (also in the Europe) are the most popular nightclubs, but there are many others. The two movie theaters show films in English.

OTHER ACTIVITIES

Davos is immensely proud of its 1½-mi. (2½-km.) floodlit cross-country track for night touring. There are another 46 mi. (75 km.) of trails in the area, as well as 37 mi. (60 km.) of cleared walks. The resort, which is one of Europe's major winter sport capitals, has a calendar full of spectator events, and offers skating (on the largest natural ice rink in Europe, and indoors too). Curling, swimming, horseback riding and hang-gliding, paragliding, tennis, squash, bowling, tobogganing and sleigh rides are also possibilities.

Davos is rich in history. Several museums provide insights into the area, including the cantonal mining museum. Thomas Mann's *Magic Mountain* was set here, and it is a bit ironic that the German title of his masterpiece, *Der Zauberberg*, is now the name of a Chinese restaurant. Robert Louis Stevenson stayed at the Hotel Belvedere, but there isn't yet an establishment called Jekyll and Hyde.

LES DIABLERETS

Access: *Nearest airport*: Geneva (2 hrs.). *By road*: N9 Autoroute, exit Aigle. *By rail*: station in Les Diablerets.

Tourist Office: Office du Tourisme, 1865 Les Diablerets, Switzerland. Tel. (025) 53 13 58

Altitude: 3,937 ft. (1,200 m.).
Top: 9,745 ft. (2,970 m.)

Language: French

Runs: 25 mi. (40 km.); 56 mi. (90 km.) with Villars

Lifts: 16 (39 with Villars)

Ski areas: Isenau, Meilleret, Glacier des Diablerets

Ski school: Ecole Suisse de Ski Les Diablerets

Linked resort: Villars

Season: December to April, plus summer skiing

Kindergarten: *Non-ski*: 1–5 years. *With ski:* 2–11 years

Prices: *Lift pass:* 6 days Sfr. 188 (children Sfr. 132). *Ski school*: Group Sfr. 17 for half-day; private Sfr. 40 per hour.

RATINGS

Skiing Conditions	6
Snow Conditions	6
For Beginners	5
For Intermediates	6
For Advanced Skiers	5
For Children	5
Après-Ski	7
Other Sports	5
Value for Money	7

THE RESORT

Les Diablerets is basically a pretty, old-fashioned mountain village, cleverly incorporating a number of new large chalet-style buildings without losing any of the atmosphere. Lying above the valley town of Aigle in the canton of Vaud and surrounded by high mountain peaks, including the Diablerets Glacier itself, the resort is dramatically situated. Although it is small, Les Diablerets is fairly smart, and the quality and variety of accommodations and après-ski reflect this. The village itself is quite low, so skiing down to resort level at either end of the season is not always possible.

THE SKIING

The Diablerets ski region consists of two main areas: Isenau and Meilleret. Meilleret, 6,395 ft. (1,949 m.), connects with the Villars lift system, but this liaison is not perfect and involves quite a bit of poling and plodding. Most of the terrain on the Diablerets side is on trails and slopes cut through the trees. Only the section above Les Mazots, 5,633 ft. (1,717 m.), is open. There are some reasonably challenging runs on the Meilleret side, some to Les Diablerets itself and others to Vers l'Eglise along the valley.

The Isenau area, which can be reached by a gondola from the center of the village, rises to Floriettaz, 6,956 ft. (2,120 m.). It offers very easy, pleasant skiing and links into the glacier area via the Pillon–Pierres Pointes gondola.

The much-publicized Diablerets

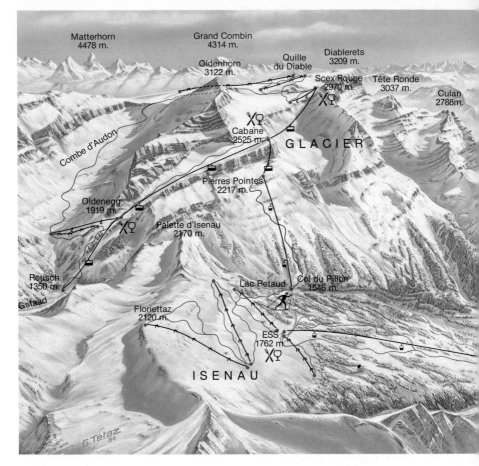

Glacier is in fact principally intended for summer skiing. It is often closed in December and January because of too much snow. However, in the case of poor snow cover lower down, the glacier is sometimes opened to ensure that there is at least some skiing available. Even later in the season, the glacier can often be closed for days on end due to bad weather and/or avalanche danger. The lifts on the glacier are not included on the local lift pass, but are part of both the Lake Geneva Region and Gstaad Superski passes.

When the glacier is open there are some good, challenging runs round the back of the Oldenhorn, as well as down from Cabane to Oldenegg. The highest point on the glacier ski area is Scex-Rouge, 9,745 ft. (2,970 m.).

APRÈS-SKI

Après-ski in Les Diablerets is surprisingly impressive for a resort of this size. The best discos are La Pote, and Le Refuge in the Ermitage, which also boasts an English pub. Those seeking a more genuine Swiss atmosphere should head for the Auberge de la Poste, one of the resort's older buildings, where tra-

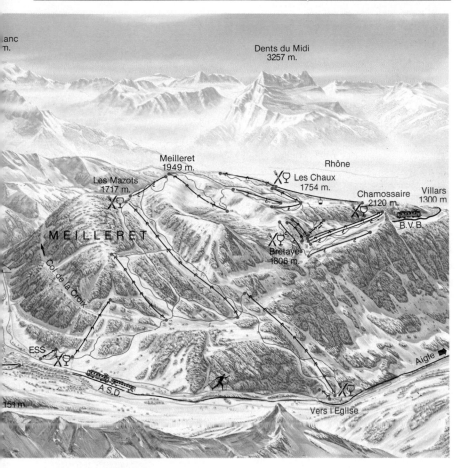

ditional Swiss dishes such as *raclette* and *fondue* are served. Les Lilas is a rustic-style restaurant, while the Locanda Livia is good for pizza.

OTHER ACTIVITIES

In the resort there are 15½ mi. (25 km.) of cross-country tracks, 12 mi. (20 km.) of prepared walks, skating, curling, swimming, horse-back riding and tobogganing. Excursions down to Lake Geneva (Lac Léman) and the towns on its banks like Montreux and Vevey are quite feasible even by train (with a change at Aigle).

261

ENGELBERG

Access: *Nearest airport*: Zurich
(1½ hrs.). *By road*: N2 Autobahn, exit
Stans-Süd. *By rail*: to Lucerne, then
Lucerne-Stans-Engelberg railway.

Tourist Office: Kur- und Verkehrsverein, 6390 Engelberg, Switzerland. Tel. (041) 94 11 61

Altitude: 3,445 ft. (1,050 m.).
Top: 9,909 ft. (3,020 m.)

Language: German

Runs: 32 mi. (52 km.)

Lifts: 24

Ski areas: Brunni, Titlis-Trübsee,
Jochpass/Engstlenalp, Jochstock

Ski schools: Schweizer Skischule
Engelberg-Titlis, Neue Skischule
Engelberg-Titlis

Linked resorts: None

Season: December to mid-April,
plus summer skiing

Kindergarten: *Non-ski*: 3–6 years.
With ski: 3–6 years

Prices: *Lift pass*: 6 days Sfr. 162 (children Sfr. 99). *Ski school*: Group
Sfr. 54 per day; private Sfr. 42 per
hour.

RATINGS

Skiing Conditions	5
Snow Conditions	6
For Beginners	5
For Intermediates	6
For Advanced Skiers	6
For Children	6
Après-Ski	7
Other Sports	7
Value for Money	7

THE RESORT

Engelberg, close to Lucerne in central Switzerland, possesses a real
sense of tradition. This is hardly surprising, since there has been a settlement on this site for centuries. A
Benedictine abbey was first founded
in 1120, but was burned down three
times. The present building dates
back to 1730. The resort is sizable
and features an assortment of architectural styles; the scene is dominated by the remarkable Titlis mountain, 10,627 ft. (3,239 m.). Although
the altitude of the village itself is
low, it has a good snow-holding record. Engelberg is the home of racing champion Erika Hess.

THE SKIING

Engelberg has two main ski areas
on opposite sides of the valley. The
lifts on the Brunni side, peaking at

Schonegg, 6,693 ft. (2,040 m.), rise from the village to sunny, intermediate slopes, which run through woodland toward the bottom.

The more challenging skiing is on the Trübsee/Titlis side, which has more extensive skiing, but none of it is really difficult and it is tiresome to reach. A bus or a long walk from the center of the village takes you to the start of the lift system. Either the combination of a funicular railway and a cable car, or a recently constructed two-stage gondola carries you up to Trübsee. The new gondola has largely alleviated what used to be a very major crowding problem, although lines are still to be expected in Engelberg at weekends and peak holiday periods simply because the resort is so accessible from some of Switzerland's major population centers.

From Trübsee, a plateau up at 5,906 ft. (1,800 m.), a two-stage cable

car runs up to Stand at 8,038 ft. (2,450 m.), and then on to Klein-Titlis, 9,909 ft. (3,020 m.). There is one surface lift and some summer skiing up here, but in winter the one run down from Klein-Titlis to Stand is difficult, so all but expert skiers tend to ride up only as far as Stand. The runs from there to Trübsee are all pleasant intermediate cruising *pistes*. A new four-seater chairlift links Trübsee with Jochpass.

APRÈS-SKI

The après-ski scene in Engelberg is moderate, but there is a good variety of restaurants, bars, cafés and discos, to cater to all tastes and pocketbooks, plus a movie theater. As in so many traditional Swiss resorts, much of the activity at night takes place inside hotels. The Ring-Hotel and the Bellevue-Terminus are among the larger establish-

ments. The restaurant of the Hotel Hess is the finest in town and serves excellent *rösti*.

OTHER ACTIVITIES

You can make use of 22 mi. (35 km.) of cross-country tracks, and the same number of paths for walking, and indulge in skating, curling, swimming, indoor tennis, tobogganing and sleigh rides. You can visit the abbey (Monday to Friday), the museum of local culture and history, or take an excursion down to the delightful town of Lucerne, tour its historic sights or cruise on its lake in an old-world paddlewheel steamer.

FLIMS/LAAX

⛷⛷⛷⛷

Access: *Nearest airport*: Zurich (2 hrs.). *By road*: N13 Autobahn, exit Chur, then direction Flims. *By rail*: to Chur, then by post bus.

Tourist Office: Kur- und Verkehrs-verein, 7031 Laax 1, Switzerland. Tel. (086) 3 43 43. Or 7018 Flims Wald-haus, Switzerland. Tel. (081) 39 10 22

Altitude: 3,347 ft. (1,020 m.). *Top:* 9,902 ft. (3,018 m.)

Languages: German, Romansch

Runs: 137 mi. (220 km.)

Lifts: 33

Ski areas: Crap Sogn Gion/Crap Ma-segn, Vorab Glacier, Cassonsgrat, Grauberg

Ski schools: Schweizer Skischule Laax, Schweizer Skischule Flims

Linked resort: Falera

Season: Mid-December to mid-April, plus summer skiing

Kindergarten: *Non-ski:* from 3 years. *With ski*: from 4 years

Prices: *Lift pass:* 6 days Sfr. 208 (chil-dren Sfr. 104). *Ski school:* Group Sfr. 160 for 5 days; private Sfr. 100 for half-day.

RATINGS

Skiing Conditions	8
Snow Conditions	7
For Beginners	6
For Intermediates	8
For Advanced Skiers	7
For Children	6
Après-Ski	7
Other Sports	8
Value for Money	7

THE RESORTS

These neighboring resorts share a huge, common ski area, but Flims is the older and more established town. Equally popular in summer and winter, it has been a tourist des-tination for a century. It is divided into Flims Dorf and Flims Waldhaus. Dorf is where the ski lifts begin, while Waldhaus, the smarter, resi-dential part, is where most of the hotels are located. It is quite a long walk from Waldhaus to and from the bottom of the lifts, but there is a pub-lic bus and most hotels run their own mini-bus shuttles in the mornings and afternoons.

Laax was developed as a ski re-sort much more recently, but here again the lifts are a long walk—or more realistically a bus ride—from the hotels. Murschetg, a newer sat-ellite of Laax, is closer to the lifts.

THE SKIING

The whole Flims/Laax ski area is known as the White Arena. It is one huge, interconnected complex with a tremendous vertical, outstanding skiing for intermediates and a hand-ful of challenging *pistes* and much off-*piste* skiing for experts. The ter-rain sprawls over half-a-dozen peaks (one topped by a glacier for year-round skiing), peppered with mountain restaurants. The lift sys-tem is being upgraded rapidly and now includes three high-speed quad chairs (the most recent added for the 1989/90 season). There are three access points into the vast are-na—from Flims, Laax and the sub-urb of Falera.

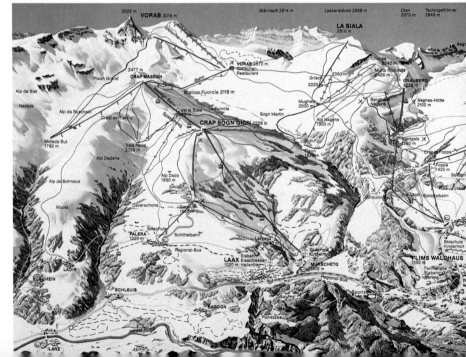

Flims Dorf has beginner slopes at the edge of the village and two main lifts to higher ground. In one direction is the connection from Naraus by stages to Cassonsgrat, 8,777 ft. (2,675 m.), with one ungroomed *piste* and lots of terrain for intermediate and advanced skiers on a steep snowfield. In the other direction, a two-stage gondola goes toward Startgels, from which lifts climb to the Grauberg, 7,310 ft. (2,228 m.), and access to the high snowfields and good novice to intermediate terrain of La Siala, 9,220 ft. (2,810 m.).

It is possible to ski down into a valley between La Siala and Crap Sogn Gion (a couple of lifts also link the two). Here is the densest network of lifts, plus access to other sectors. The more direct route to Crap Sogn Gion is from Laax, again offering two options—one a cable car and the other via Curnius chairlifts 1 and 2 (another chair from Falera feeds into the ski area where skiers transfer between them). The slopes below are very gentle.

Still another cable car climbs from Crap Sogn Gion to Crap Masegn, 8,127 ft. (2,477 m.), along a ridge, with steepish runs down the sides. Off the back is the Midada Sut chair, which serves just three mild *pistes* but also swings experts descending the Alp da Ruschein route from above into the circuit. The access to Vorab is via gondola from Crap Sogn Gion to the Glacier Restaurant, 8,432 ft. (2,570 m.), from which there are two more lifts on the glacier itself. Most of the terrain is flat enough for a beginner (there is even a small cross-country loop), but the expert run down to Midada Sut not only starts in a steep *couloir* but has a thigh-burning vertical of over 4,052 ft. (1,235 m.).

APRÈS-SKI

The clientele in Flims Waldhaus is relatively middle-aged and seems mostly satisfied with the entertainments laid on in hotel bars and nightclubs. Flims Waldhaus has several grand old hotels, the smartest being the much redeveloped Park Hotel Waldhaus. Down in Flims Dorf, young people congregate mainly in the Albana pub, next to the bottom of the lift station. Meiler's, a new club, is attracting a young crowd. Most of the English-speaking visitors in this area are American, and many of them stay in Laax at a hotel/entertainment complex called the Rancho Sporthotel.

OTHER ACTIVITIES

Laax and Flims have 37 mi. (60 km.) of cross-country tracks (nearly 2 mi. [3 km.] floodlit) and 31 mi. (50 km.) of paths for walking. There is also skating and curling, indoors or outdoors, tobogganing, swimming, tennis, squash, horseback riding, skibobbing and bowling.

GRINDELWALD

Access: *Nearest airport*: Zurich (3 hrs.). *By road*: N6 Autobahn, exit Spiez, then via Interlaken. *By rail*: to Interlaken, then narrow-gauge railway to Grindelwald.

Tourist Office: Verkehrsbüro, 3818 Grindelwald, Switzerland. Tel. (036) 53 12 12

Altitude: 3,445 ft. (1,050 m.). *Top:* 8,098 ft. (2,468 m.)

Language: German

Runs: 93 mi. (150 km.) in Jungfrau Region

Lifts: 41 in Jungfrau Region

Ski areas: First-Oberjoch, Kleine Scheidegg-Männlichen

Ski school: Schweizer Skischule Grindelwald

Linked resort: Wengen

Season: Mid-December to mid-April

Kindergarten: *Non-ski*: from 3 years. *With ski*: from 3 years

Prices: *Lift pass*: 6 days, Jungfrau Region Sfr. 198 (children Sfr. 132). *Ski school*: Group Sfr. 20 for half-day; private Sfr. 40 per hour.

RATINGS

Skiing Conditions	6
Snow Conditions	5
For Beginners	6
For Intermediates	8
For Advanced Skiers	7
For Children	6
Après-Ski	7
Other Sports	8
Value for Money	7

THE RESORT

The village of Grindelwald is dominated by the hulking grandeur of the Eiger, one of the most famous mountains in the Alps. Compared to Mürren and Wengen, its partners in the magnificent Jungfrau Region, Grindelwald is positively sophisticated. It also allows cars, although this is a mixed blessing, since easy road access means a lot of weekend visitors. It has a good range of grand hotels and smart shops.

THE SKIING

While Grindelwald gives the impression of being smack in the middle of massive mountains, it doesn't ski that way. The terrain, developed long before the concept of ski-in, ski-out lodgings was created, is not convenient for most accommodations, and the lifts are in need of upgrading, for many are old, slow and can't handle today's crowds. Most of the slopes in the heart of these staggeringly steep mountains are surprisingly mild.

East of Grindelwald is the Bodmi novice area, with lifts rising to First and then to Oberjoch, 8,098 ft. (2,468 m.). This small terrain is in need of faster lifts, but is mostly on wide, sunny snowfields (including one called Grindel, though the *Wald*, or woods, are farther down).

Grindelwald's main ski area is interconnected with the Männlichen/Kleine Scheidegg complex. From Grund, a picturesque cog railway climbs to Kleine Scheidegg, 6,762 ft. (2,061 m.), and a slow gondola serves Männlichen, 7,317 ft.

(2,230 m.). The terrain is wide, open intermediate skiing on top, taming into woods in the middle before opening up to beginner slopes at the bottom (one served by the Aspen T-bar).

Kleine Scheidegg is the linchpin of the Jungfrau network. Skiers go off the back via Wixi to Wengen or continue by cog railway to ski the Eiger Glacier, 7,612 ft. (2,320 m.), or visit the Jungfraujoch, 11,333 ft. (3,454 m.), one of the Alps' scenic high points. Some of the glacier runs rank among the steepest in the Jungfrau Region, including some commendable off-*piste* challenge on the Grindelwald side.

APRÈS-SKI

Grindelwald is reasonably lively after dark, with several small bars and cafés, although much of the nocturnal activity takes place in the main hotels. The Grand Hotel Regina is a fairly formal hotel, with a good restaurant. Popular nightspots include the Spider nightclub at the Hotel Spinne, and the Cava-Bar at Hotel Derby Bahnhof, with dancing.

OTHER ACTIVITIES

Grindelwald has a modern sports center with a large indoor ice rink for skating and curling, a swimming pool and fitness facilities. Several hotels have pools, gyms and saunas, too. Horseback riding, hang-gliding and skibobbing and 20 mi. (32 km.) of cross-country trails are also available, plus the longest toboggan run, 5 mi. (8 km.), in Switzerland.

There is a spectacular excursion by train (not included on the lift pass) from Kleine Scheidegg up through the inside of the Jungfrau mountain to the Jungfraujoch, the highest railway station in Europe.

GSTAAD

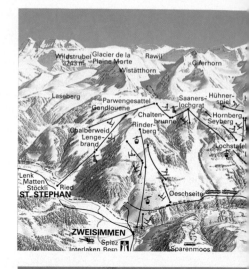

Access: *Nearest airport*: Geneva (2½ hrs.) *By road*: N12 Autoroute, exit Bulle. *By rail*: station in Gstaad, (MOB railway from Montreux).

Tourist Office: Verkehrsverein, 3780 Gstaad, Switzerland.
Tel. (030) 4 10 55

Altitude: 3,609 ft. (1,100 m.).
Top: 6,365 ft. (1,940 m.).

Language: German

Runs: 155 mi. (250 km.) in Gstaad Superski Region

Lifts: 14 (69 in Gstaad Superski Region)

Ski areas: Eggli, Wispile, Wasserngrat

Ski school: Skischule Gstaad

Linked resorts: Rougemont, Saanen, Schönried, Saanenmöser, Gsteig, St. Stephan, Lauenen, Zweisimmen

Season: December to April

Kindergarten: *Non-ski*: 4–8 years. *With ski*: ski school from 4 years

Prices: *Lift pass*: 6 days Sfr. 188 (children Sfr. 90–113). *Ski school*: Group Sfr. 19 for half-day; private Sfr. 45 per hour.

RATINGS

Skiing Conditions	6
Snow Conditions	5
For Beginners	6
For Intermediates	7
For Advanced Skiers	7
For Children	5
Après-Ski	7
Other Sports	7
Value for Money	6

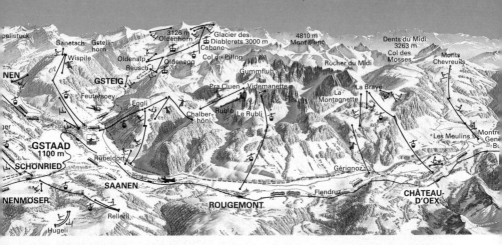

THE RESORT

Despite its jet-set clientele and reputation, Gstaad remains a pretty Alpine village. You are as likely to see a farmer driving a tractor pulling a cartload of manure through the main street as you are to see a fur-clad film star driving a Rolls Royce. The jet-set season, which is largely focused on the Palace Hotel, is short—January and February—and outside of these times Gstaad can really be very quiet. It is far smaller and less pretentious than one might expect, though prices remain high.

THE SKIING

Gstaad is the headliner in the Gstaad Superski Region—ten resorts on the same lift pass but as far as 18 mi. (30 km.) apart (better explored if you have a car at your disposal).

There are three main ski areas which begin in Gstaad itself, from different starting points. Eggli, 5,483 ft. (1,671 m.), has some good, long intermediate runs and connects with neighboring Rougemont. From here you can either take a gondola back up and ski down to Eggli or take a train (included in the lift pass) back to Gstaad.

The Wasserngrat, at 6,372 ft. (1,942 m.), is probably the most famous mountain in Gstaad. (Close to its peak is the Eagle Club—the most exclusive lunch club in the Alps. Those without membership must be content to dine in the nearby Wasserngrat restaurant, a more egalitarian place which does excellent *rösti.*) There is a wide range of runs down from here—something to please intermediates and experts alike. With a guide, you can find good off-*piste* routes through the trees, especially in powder-snow conditions.

Wispile, at 6,398 ft. (1,950 m.), is less challenging, but there are still quite a few runs that will interest the advanced intermediate.

With a low elevation and modest vertical, Gstaad's snow conditions can be iffy. Included in the lift pass is the nearby Diablerets Glacier, which has snow year-round.

APRÈS-SKI

For the fashionable, après-ski centers on the Palace Hotel—its Grill, Fromagerie, Sans Cravatte and GreenGo disco/nightclub are all popular.

More relaxed entertainment can be found in the charming Hotel Olden, in the center of town. This is a favored rendezvous spot immediately after skiing, and the hotel's La Cave restaurant has a good reputation.

For an inexpensive dinner, there is pizza at the Arc-en-Ciel. Spend slightly more and go to the Posthotel Rössli for Swiss specialties. A little out of town, the Chlösterli, a converted monastery, is fun, especially for groups. The movie theater shows films in various languages, including English.

OTHER ACTIVITIES

Many visitors come to Gstaad simply to relax, promenade and party. There are 31 mi. (50 km.) of walks and 18½ mi. (30 km.) of cross-country tracks in the vicinity. The sports center is particularly beautiful and well equipped. Non-ski sports include swimming, skating (artificial and natural rinks), curling, horseback riding, tennis, squash, toboganing and hot-air ballooning. Shopping (and window shopping) in elegant boutiques, jewelry stores and other purveyors of luxury goods is a popular pastime.

KLOSTERS

🎿🎿🎿🎿

Access: *Nearest airport*: Zurich (2 hrs.). *By road*: N3 Autobahn, exit Landquart. *By rail*: to Landquart, then Rhaetian Railway to Klosters.

Tourist Office: Kur- und Verkehrsverein, 7250 Klosters, Switzerland. Tel. (083) 4 18 77

Altitude: 3,937 ft. (1,200 m.).
Top: 9,331 ft. (2,844 m.)

Language: German

Runs: 171 mi. (276 km.) with Davos

Lifts: 55 with Davos

Ski areas: Madrisa, Gotschna/Parsenn

Ski school: Schweizer Skischule Klosters

Linked resort: Davos

Season: December to April

Kindergarten: *Non-ski*: 2–5 years. *With ski*: ski school from 4 years

Prices: *Lift pass*: 5 days Regional Sfr. 174 (children Sfr. 106). *Ski school*: Group Sfr. 25 for half-day (children Sfr. 22); private Sfr. 45 for 50 min.

RATINGS

Skiing Conditions	8
Snow Conditions	6
For Beginners	6
For Intermediates	8
For Advanced Skiers	8
For Children	6
Après-Ski	7
Other Sports	7
Value for Money	6

THE RESORT

In contrast to the neighboring town of Davos, with which it shares a skiing area, Klosters is a traditional but fashionable Alpine village which has been relatively unsullied by mass tourism. Socially, it is a very smart resort, patronized by aristocrats and royals, particularly British ones. Klosters comprises mainly chalets, whose owners tend to stay for months at a time enjoying their privacy and comfort, but there are also several elegant hotels and good apartment complexes.

THE SKIING

The capacity of the cable car to the Gotschna, 7,544 ft. (2,300 m.), Klosters' most popular skiing, was recently doubled. This ski area leads to Davos and connects with the Parsenn and in turn with the Weissfluhjoch and the Schatzalp/Strela areas. There are plenty of wide cruising *pistes* in the Parsenn sector, but skiers in search of more difficult terrain should proceed to the top of the Weissfluhgipfel, 9,328 ft. (2,844 m.). The runs down beside the Parsennbahn to Davos are demanding, as is the Gipfel Nord run to Kreuzweg. For a real challenge, skiers can try the Wang run, directly under the Gotschna cable car, which has a reputation for being one of the most difficult in Europe, but it is often closed due to lack of snow or avalanche danger.

There is some pleasant, picturesque skiing through forests down to valley villages like Conters and Serneus, from where you can catch a train back to Klosters. These forest trails also take you to the charming *Schwendi*—rustic mountain restaurants specializing in all kinds of Swiss fare.

The Madrisa sector on the other side of the Klosters valley is a pleasant, undemanding ski area. There are about half-a-dozen surface lifts up to 8,340 ft. (2,542 m.), but the area is really of more interest to early-intermediates and sun-worshippers.

APRÈS-SKI

The best après-ski in Klosters takes place behind closed doors in private chalets, but there is still plenty of stylish activity in the resort's hotels. The Chesa Grischuna's Cellar Bar is a popular rendezvous point. The greatest dinner in Klosters is to be had at the Hotel Wynegg, where the specialty is *fondue chinoise* (meat cooked in bouillon, with vari-

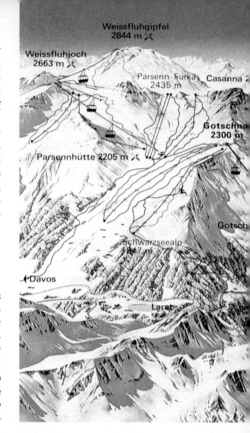

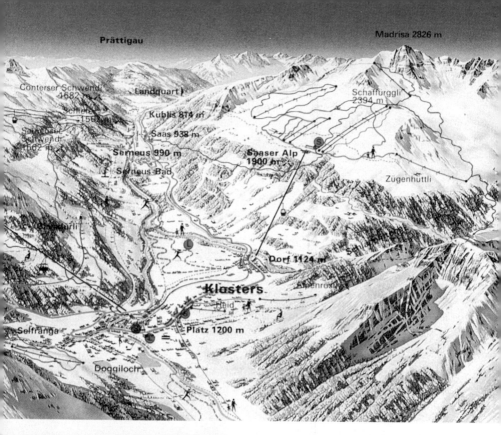

Prättigau

Madrisa 2826 m

Conterser Schwendi 1682 m

Landquart

Schaffürggli 2394 m

Kublis 814 m

Saas 938 m

Serneus 990 m

Spaser Alp 1900 m

Serneus Bad

Zügenhüttli

Dorf 1124 m

Klosters

Alpenrösli

Selfränga

Platz 1200 m

Doggiloch

ous sauces). This unpretentious hotel is where Prince Charles used to stay in his bachelor days.

The most inviting places to take tea are up in the mountains. For later at night, the Casa Antica is the best disco.

OTHER ACTIVITIES

There are 25 mi. (40 km.) of cross-country trails, plus skating (on a natural rink), curling, swimming (in hotels), squash, fitness center, 21 mi. (34 km.) of cleared walks, tobogganing and sleigh rides. There are three art galleries, and the local history museum opens three times a week. A wider range of activities is available in neighboring Davos. Visitors with a car enjoy making expeditions to St. Moritz or Lenzerheide.

LENZERHEIDE-VALBELLA

Access: *Nearest airport*: Zurich (2½ hrs.). *By road*: N13 Autobahn, exit Chur-Süd. *By rail*: to Chur, then by bus.

Tourist Office: Verkehrsbüro, 7078 Lenzerheide, Switzerland. Tel. (081) 34 34 34

Altitude: 4,922 ft. (1,500 m.). *Top*: 9,400 ft. (2,865 m.)

Language: German

Runs: 93 mi. (150 km.)

Lifts: 38

Ski areas: Rothorn-Scalottas, Danis, Stätzerhorn

Ski schools: Schweizer Skischule Lenzerheide, Schweizer Skischule Valbella, Caselva Skischule Valbella

Linked resorts: Parpan, Churwalden

Season: December to April

Kindergarten: *Non-ski*: no age limit. *With ski*: from 3 years

Prices: *Lift pass*: 6 days Sfr. 162 (children Sfr. 97). *Ski school*: Group Sfr. 20 for half-day; private Sfr. 45 per hour.

RATINGS

Skiing Conditions	6
Snow Conditions	5
For Beginners	6
For Intermediates	7
For Advanced Skiers	5
For Children	5
Après-Ski	5
Other Sports	7
Value for Money	6

THE RESORT

Lenzerheide is the larger "half" of a complex that is now called Lenzerheide-Valbella. These two villages were originally separated by the

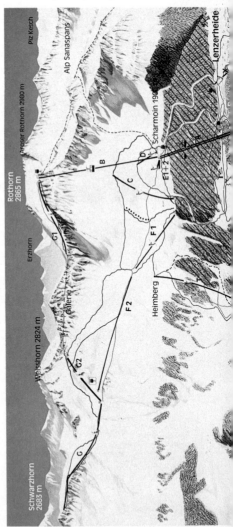

Heidsee lake, but expansion along the lakeside has meant that they now virtually sprawl into one another. Popular in summer as well as winter, both of these are long-established, traditional resorts. It is not an especially pretty place, with grand hotels in the traditional Swiss style, but the setting is beautiful and there are lovely views across the lake and through woodland to the mountains below.

Lying in the Grisons, on the road to the Julier Pass, Lenzerheide was a popular destination for English family holidays in the sixties and early seventies Britain's Thatcher family visited Lenzerheide regularly.

THE SKIING

The skiing is divided into two separate areas which do not interconnect. You have to return to the vil-

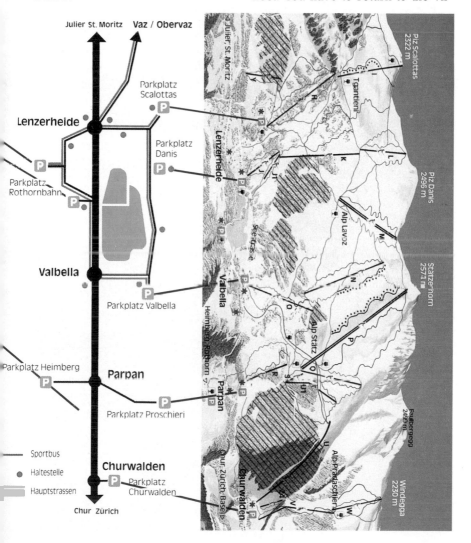

279

lage to get from one to the other—indeed you usually need to take a bus because the lifts on the Rothorn side lie an inconvenient walk from the village itself.

The Rothorn is where the best skiing is to be found. A two-stage cable car, which recently doubled its capacity, climbs from a bottom station between the Lenzerheide and Valbella centers to 9,401 ft. (2,865 m.). There are just two, fairly demanding, runs from this peak that offer more in the way of scenery than varied skiing. Beyond is the Schwarzhorn, 8,803 ft. (2,683 m.), which offers more scenery, another two *pistes* and an off-*piste* route to Arosa's Hörnli. Most of the Rothorn's terrain is played out in short runs close to the tree line.

Across the valley is a long ridge, with several skiable peaks, the highest being the Stätzerhorn, with lifts to 7,976 ft. (2,431 m.). Served by a slew of surface lifts, this is essentially one wide slope providing tremendous ego skiing for novices and low-intermediates. There is also a feeble connection to Alp Pradaschier, 5,253 ft. (1,601 m.), a minor ski area with just three lifts.

APRÈS-SKI

Lenzerheide's après-ski revolves, not surprisingly, around its numerous hotels. The grandest and most important is the Grand Hotel Kurhaus Alpina. Its Steivetta bar is a popular meeting-place and the Tic-Tac nightclub is the only noteworthy one in the resort. Otherwise there are some quiet but pleasant cafés/restaurants around the resort. In Valbella the Posthotel Valbella and the Valbella-Inn are the principal après-ski venues.

OTHER ACTIVITIES

Bowling at the Hotel Schweizerhof is a popular après-ski activity. In addition there are 31 mi. (50 km.) of cross-country tracks, 22 mi. (35 km.) of prepared walks, skating, curling, swimming, squash, indoor tennis and sleigh rides.

MÜRREN

Access: *Nearest airport*: Zurich (3 hrs.). *By road*: to Lauterbrunnen, then train, or to Stechelberg, then cable car. *By rail*: to Interlaken, then BOB/BLM railway.

Tourist Office: Verkehrsbüro, 3825 Mürren, Switzerland. Tel. (036) 55 16 16

Altitude: 5,414 ft. (1,650 m.).
Top: 9,745 ft. (2,970 m.)

Language: German

Runs: 93 mi. (150 km.) in Jungfrau Region

Lifts: 41 in Jungfrau Region

Ski areas: Schilthorn, Winteregg

Ski school: Schweizer Skischule Mürren

Linked resorts: None

Season: Mid-December to mid-April

Kindergarten: *Non-ski*: from 4 months. *With ski*: from 3 years

Prices: *Lift pass*: 6 days Sfr. 148 (children Sfr. 99). *Ski school*: Group Sfr. 20 for half-day; private Sfr. 90–100 for half-day.

RATINGS

Skiing Conditions	5
Snow Conditions	7
For Beginners	5
For Intermediates	6
For Advanced Skiers	7
For Children	6
Après-Ski	4
Other Sports	6
Value for Money	6

THE RESORT

Mürren, a tiny car-free village, is one of the cradles of skiing. Sir Arnold Lunn, one of the sport's pioneers, organized the first slalom race here in 1922, and the British have been flocking here ever since. It is the home of the famous Kandahar Ski Club, an Alpine institution. Its cable car starred in the James Bond film *On Her Majesty's Secret Service*.

THE SKIING

For such a small place, Mürren offers some remarkably good skiing. The most famous summit is the Schilthorn, 9,748 ft. (2,971 m.), whose Piz Gloria revolving panoramic restaurant was also used in the Bond film over 20 years ago; the restaurant still makes much of this association. The top section of the run down from the Schilthorn is very difficult, with large icy moguls covering a steep, narrow path before widening out for a few hundred yards leading to a long *Schuss*.

There are several unremarkable T-bars in Mürren, which access some fairly demanding runs. The Gimmeln lift offers two good short shots, the Kandahar and the Black Line. The Allmendhubel and Maulerhubel above Winteregg offer mild intermediate skiing, much of it through wooded areas.

Mürren comes alive at the end of January each year for the Inferno race, which was organized in 1928 by the Kandahar and Mürren ski clubs. The course is from the top of the Schilthorn right down to Lauter-

 For map see pp. 270–271.

brunnen, if snow conditions permit. The best racers do the 8½-mi. (14-km.) race in about 15 minutes.

Mürren is part of the Jungfrau Region, but to use the combined pass fully requires a daily commute down to Lauterbrunnen and back up the parallel but unconnected valley to Grindelwald or Wengen.

APRÈS-SKI

There is not much après-ski life here and what there is tends to revolve around hotels. The Eiger and the Jungfrau both have good bars and restaurants, and the Eiger has a nightclub, often with live music.

OTHER ACTIVITIES

Mürren has a large, modern sports center for a resort of its size. Facilities include swimming, skating (artificial outdoor ice rink), curling, squash and tennis. There is a tiny cross-country track in Mürren and a 7½-mi. (12-km.) track down in the Lauterbrunnen valley, 9 mi. (15 km.) of walks, sleigh rides and a toboggan run to Gimmelwald.

Day-trips to Wengen and perhaps on up to Kleine Scheidegg are included on the Jungfrau Region pass. The trip up from Kleine Scheidegg to the Jungfraujoch is extra but spectacular.

SAAS-FEE
⛷⛷⛷⛷

Access: *Nearest airport*: Geneva (3½ hrs.). *By road:* N9 Autoroute, exit Sion, then via Visp and Stalden. *By rail*: to Visp or Brig, then post bus.

Tourist Office: Verkehrsverein, 3906 Saas-Fee, Switzerland. Tel. (028) 57 14 57

Altitude: 5,906 ft. (1,800 m.). *Top:* 11,484 ft. (3,500 m.)

Language: German

Runs: 50 mi. (80 km.)

Lifts: 26

Ski areas: Felskinn/Mittelallalin, Längfluh/Spielboden, Plattjen, Hannig, Stafelwald

Ski school: Schweizer Skischule Saas-Fee

Linked resorts: None

Season: November to April, plus summer skiing

Kindergarten: *Non-ski*: 3–6 years. *With ski*: ski school from 5 years

Prices: *Lift pass*: 6 days Sfr. 190 (children Sfr. 115). *Ski school*: Group Sfr. 20 for half-day; private Sfr. 40 per hour.

RATINGS

Skiing Conditions	7
Snow Conditions	8
For Beginners	6
For Intermediates	8
For Advanced Skiers	7
For Children	7
Après-Ski	8
Other Sports	8
Value for Money	7

THE RESORT

Lying in its own valley at the eastern end of the Rhône Valley, Saas-Fee is often described as a miniature version of nearby Zermatt. Both are carfree villages steeped in mountain tradition. Unlike Zermatt, Saas-Fee is accessible by road, and cars can be left in the covered parking areas at the end of the village. Penned in by the mountains, the village itself can be rather dark, particularly early in the season. Because it sprawls over the hillsides, visitors must be prepared to do quite a bit of walking. There are plenty of good hotels, offering impeccable Swiss service and hospitality.

THE SKIING

Saas-Fee nestles at the head of the valley, with skiing on three sides. There are odd hitches to this seemingly convenient layout. The main ski area is Felskinn/Mittelallalin. To get to the bottom of the Felskinn cable car (for which there are often long lines—even in low season), you first have to take a surface lift from the edge of the village. At the top of the Felskinn cable car, you transfer to the Metro Alpin, Saas-Fee's celebrated underground express funicular, the world's highest. There are seldom bad lines here, and if you have to wait a bit you can always admire the murals on the tunnel walls. At the top of Mittelallalin, 11,484 ft. (3,500 m.), is a revolving restaurant (also "the world's highest"), with spectacular views and rather less spectacular food.

Before the creation of its present

slogan "Pearl of the Alps", Saas-Fee used to call itself the "Glacier Village". It is easy to see why when you ski down the beautiful, open *pistes* on the Feegletscher below the restaurant. You really have a sense of being on a boulevard of ice, and you can frequently hear it moving. The *pistes* here have to be redefined regularly to take account of the behavior of the glacier according to the time of year. This area offers the most exhilarating skiing. There are a couple of T-bars or you can either take another surface lift back to Felskinn and take the Metro Alpin again, ski all the way on back to the village or cruise across to Längfluh. (The connection in the opposite direction, from Längfluh to the Feegletscher is via Fee-Chatz, a kind of snow-cat bus service.)

The Längfluh section offers more challenge. On the way down to the village, make a stop at the Gletscher-Grotte café hidden away in the woods beside the *piste.* The slopes from Plattjen offer some steep, open *pistes* high up and some interesting trails lower down. The Hannig area is for novices and intermediates, and there are good beginner slopes close to the village.

APRÈS-SKI

There are plenty of cozy, atmospheric bars, including the Fee Pub, the Pic Pic and the Walliser Stübli. The Hotel Dom's restaurant specializes in all kinds of *rösti* and other Swiss dishes. The Schäferstube, a short uphill walk toward Hohnegg, is a charming rustic place whose specialty is a *fondue* in which the meat is cooked in wine. The Vieux Chalet concentrates on all the other varieties of *fondue*. The Fletschhorn, a longish walk out of town, has an excellent reputation for gourmet food which makes it worth the

hike—or taxi ride. Discos in Saas-Fee are not very sophisticated: the Sans Souci suits the younger crowd, while older people prefer the Walliserhof. The movie theater sometimes shows films in English.

OTHER ACTIVITIES

Saas-Fee has one of the most impressive and modern sports centers in the Alps, which includes a swimming pool, indoor tennis and fitness center. Outdoors, there is skating and curling on natural rinks, just 5 mi. (8 km.) of cross-country trails, 12½ mi. (20 km.) of hiking paths and, if conditions are right, tobogganing.

The Saaser Museum gives a fascinating glimpse into the lives of people in this area in years gone by.

ST. MORITZ

Access: *Nearest airport*: Zurich (4 hrs.). *By road*: N13 Autobahn, exit Chur, then via Julier-Pass. *By rail*: mainline station in St. Moritz.

Tourist Office: Kur- und Verkehrs-verein, 7500 St. Moritz, Switzerland. Tel. (082) 3 31 47

Altitude: 6,090 ft. (1,856 m.). *Top:* 11,263 ft. (3,433 m.)

Languages: German, Romansch

Runs: 50 mi. (80 km.); 250 mi. (400 km.) in Engadine Region

Lifts: 26 (59 in Engadine Region)

Ski areas: Corviglia/Piz Nair, Marguns, Corvatsch, Furtchellas

Ski schools: Schweizer Skischule St. Moritz, Schweizer Skischule Suvretta, Schweizer Skischule Palace

Linked resort: Celerina (Corviglia)

Season: November to mid-April, plus summer skiing

Kindergarten: *Non-ski*: 3–12 years. *With ski*: 4–12 years

Prices: *Lift pass*: 6 days Sfr. 204 (children Sfr. 150). *Ski school*: Group Sfr. 32 for half-day (children Sfr. 24); private Sfr. 70 per hour.

RATINGS

Skiing Conditions	7
Snow Conditions	7
For Beginners	5
For Intermediates	7
For Advanced Skiers	8
For Children	6
Après-Ski	9
Other Sports	10
Value for Money	7

THE RESORT

St. Moritz consists of two village centers—chic, expensive St. Moritz-Dorf and less prepossessing, less expensive St. Moritz-Bad down the road. Although it is not an attractive place to look at—it is a mishmash of countless architectural styles—St. Moritz is a beautiful place to look out from. There are spectacular views across the frozen lake, on which horse racing and polo take place, to the mountains beyond. The resort gets the sun for much of the day and the "champagne climate" claim

does not seem entirely bogus. With an abundance of smart hotels, including five that are in the unabashed luxury category, fine restaurants, fabulous nightspots and chic shops, the atmosphere in the resort is more that of a glamorous town than a mountain village.

THE SKIING

St. Moritz has been welcoming winter visitors for more than a century, and it was also one of the first to institute organized Alpine skiing. The fact that it is still the ski resort of choice for many of the richest, noblest Europeans who could afford to ski anywhere has as much to do with the quality of skiing as the glittering resort.

While the Engadine regional ski pass covers six complexes, the high rollers ski Corviglia/Piz Nair and nothing but. The traditional access is via the historic (and often crowded) funicular from Dorf to Corviglia, 8,163 ft. (2,488 m.). (At the top is La Marmite, which has been praised as the gastronomically finest restaurant in the Alps. Specialties include caviar, truffled dishes, exotic sea-

food and exquisite desserts—all at the price levels you'd expect of a culinary mecca.)

There is also access into the Corviglia system from St. Moritz-Bad and the outlying village of Celerina, the latter via Marguns, 7,477 ft. (2,279 m.). What little beginner facilities exist on this massif are found around Chantarella and Salastrains, but for the most part, the terrain is middling-difficult and the *pistes* are sometimes crowded, for this mountain is really the crossroads of St. Moritz skiing.

The best skiers don't float around Corviglia for more than a transit stop and perhaps a meal. They take the cable car to Piz Nair, 10,030 ft. (3,057 m.), where the snow is almost always good, the runs are long and steep and the off-*piste* splendid.

St. Moritz's most snow-sure area is the high bowl atop the Corvatsch, 11,263 ft. (3,433 m.), most conveniently reached by cable car from Surlej near Silvaplana, a small town a couple of lakes up the valley from St. Moritz. There is another cable car to the summit, where the most demanding terrain is found (including fabulous off-*piste* options), and below are a number of T-bars serving good intermediate runs. Summer skiing takes place here, too. It is possible to ski down to Furtschellas, a relatively small but rather challenging area on the Corvatsch's lower slopes. Furtschellas can also be accessed by lift directly from Sils/Maria at the bottom.

The Engadine pass is good also at Piz Lagalp, Diavolezza and Muottas Muragl, all closer to Pontresina.

APRÈS-SKI

Après-ski here is among the most sparkling (and expensive) in the Alps. Hanselmann, a landmark pastry shop, is the best-known tea-time rendezvous, and the back room of Glattfelder is popular for sampling their specialities of tea, coffee and caviar. All the top hotel bars are spectacular, particularly the Sunny Bar of the Kulm, headquarters of the predominantly British Cresta Club. All the smart hotels have good, expensive restaurants, but for a reasonably priced dinner in a pleasant atmosphere, try the pizzeria of the Chesa Veglia. The most famous and costly nightclub in town is the King's Club in Badrutt's Palace Hotel, but even this can seem quiet outside the jet-set's peak periods. The Steffani Hotel is a good venue for late-night drinking.

OTHER ACTIVITIES

There's a wealth of things to do in St. Moritz, including horse races and golf on the frozen lake, paragliding and Alpine flights, horseback riding, and sleigh excursions to the Roseg and Fex valleys, the famed Cresta Run, which is the world's only course for skeleton sledding. The more usual sports abound: nearly 100 mi. (160 km.) of great cross-country trails, 75 mi. (120 km.) of walks, plus skating, curling, swimming, tennis, squash and bowling.

The Engadine Museum displays typical furniture, tile stoves and historic weapons in a building based on regional architectural style, while the Segantini Museum exhibits works of the Italian landscape painter Giovanni Segantini (1858–99).

St. Moritz is a railroad buff's nirvana. The Glacier Express, a Rhaetian Railway, is the most fabulous narrow-gauge ride in Europe. Its 150 mi. (240-km.) journey, called the world's slowest express train, runs over 291 bridges and through 91 tunnels from St. Moritz to Zermatt. The Bernina Express goes to Tirano in Italy via Poschiavo and Alp Grüm.

VERBIER

🎿🎿🎿🎿🎿

Access: *Nearest airport*: Geneva
(2 hrs.). *By road*: N9 Autoroute, exit
Martigny, then via Sembrancher. *By
rail*: to Martigny or Le Châble, then
bus, or gondola from Le Châble.

Tourist Office: Office du Tourisme,
1936 Verbier, Switzerland.
Tel. (026) 31 62 22

Altitude: 4,922 ft. (1,500 m.).
Top: 10,926 ft. (3,330 m.)

Language: French

Runs: 200 mi. (320 km.) in 4 Vallées

Lifts: 38 (86 in 4 Vallées)

Ski areas: Les Ruinettes, Mont-Fort,
Savoleyres, Les Attelas.

Ski schools: Ecole Suisse de Ski Verbier, Ecole du Ski Fantastique

Linked resorts: Haute-Nendaz, Vey-
sonnaz, Thyon 2000, Les Collons

Season: December to April, plus
summer skiing

Kindergarten: *Non-ski*: 18 months–
8 years. *With ski*: 3–10 years

Prices: *Lift pass*: 6 days Sfr. 252 with
Mont-Fort (children Sfr. 126). *Ski
school*: Group Sfr. 92 for 6 half-days
(children Sfr. 80); private Sfr. 42 per
hour.

RATINGS

Skiing Conditions	9
Snow Conditions	8
For Beginners	6
For Intermediates	8
For Advanced Skiers	10
For Children	8
Après-Ski	8
Other Sports	5
Value for Money	7

THE RESORT

To look at this pretty resort, comprising mainly chalet-style buildings on a sunny hillside above the
Rhône Valley, you would be unlikely to guess that Verbier has only existed since the late 1940s. Fortunate-
ly, its architects had great regard
for tradition and aesthetics. The resort retains a village atmosphere
and life tends to center on chalets
and apartments rather than hotels.

Verbier is conveniently close to
Geneva—though transfer by road is
much easier than by train—and is
popular with weekend skiers.

THE SKIING

Verbier offers some of the best and
most interlinked skiing in Europe,
and the lift pass is priced according-
ly. (All good intermediate and better skiers will find it worthwhile to
pay the supplement for the pass that
includes Mont-Fort.) Getting up the
mountain from the village has often
been a problem, but the new 150-
passenger cable car (the largest in
Switzerland) from La Chaux to Mont-
Fort has helped relieve congestion
higher up.

The skiing around Les Attelas, Lac
des Vaux and Les Ruinettes, a trio of
interconnected peaks with lots of
lifts and runs, is best for good intermediates, and there are also some
steepish bump runs like Les Fonta-
nays. Tortin is a notorious mogul
run; the first three turns are the
hairiest—after that, it gets a little
easier. The fussiest skiers go for
Mont-Fort, 10,926 ft. (3,330 m.), the
jewel of the 4 Vallées. The steep

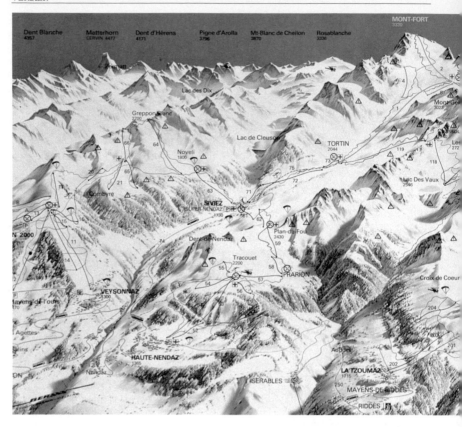

mogul run from the top of Mont-Fort to Col des Gentianes is heavenly for expert skiers. The runs down the Tortin side of Gentianes are quite challenging, too, but the one from Gentianes to La Chaux is a real cruiser with fantastic views. If the snow cover is very good, you can ski all the way down to Le Châble, 2,694 ft. (821 m.), below Verbier. For the last stretch, you have to pick your way through vineyards!

The Savoleyres sector, linked to town by a bus service, is ideal for intermediates, but on the far side of this area, there is a good deal of interesting off-*piste* skiing to La Tzoumaz. Much of this is through fairytale woodland and so provides good orientation in poor light.

The "4 Vallées" circuit, a day tour from Verbier which takes in neighboring resorts like Haute-Nendaz, is an adventure for intermediates, but is less interesting for better skiers.

Verbier is famous for the extent and variety of its off-*piste* skiing, but you need to take a guide to discover the best of it. The resort is less famous for its mountain restaurants, but try the upstairs (service) restaurant at Les Ruinettes, as well as Chez Dany, Au Mayen and, in the Savoleyres sector, La Marmotte.

APRÈS-SKI

After skiing, drinks in the Mont-Fort Pub and milkshakes in the Milk Bar are popular. Early evening drinking

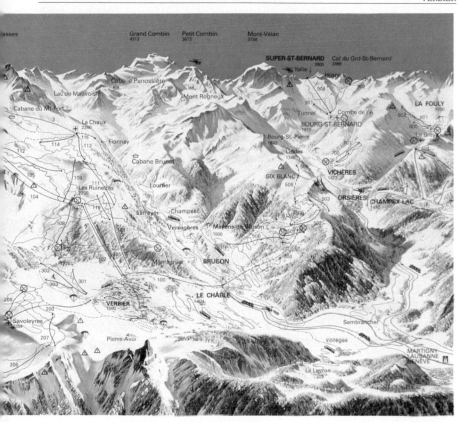

continues in the Nelson Pub and La Luge, which also has an excellent steak restaurant in its basement. The Au Fer à Cheval pizzeria is a key meeting point serving cheap food, while the Hotel Rosalp opposite has one of the best restaurants in Switzerland.

Late at night, the Farm-Club is the smartest place to go. The very young or impoverished may prefer the Scotch. The movie theater shows films in English.

OTHER ACTIVITIES

There is minimal cross-country skiing in Verbier itself, but 18½ mi. (30 km.) of trails down in Le Châble. The large, modern sports center offers indoor skating, curling, swimming, squash and a fitness center.

There are organized bus tours to Aosta in Italy and the Grand Saint Bernard. For trips down to the valley towns of Sion and Martigny, you have to go independently.

VILLARS

Access: *Nearest airport*: Geneva (1½ hrs.). *By road*: N9 Autoroute, exit Aigle. *By rail*: to Bex, then connection to Villars, or Aigle, then by bus.

Tourist Office: Office du Tourisme, 1884 Villars, Switzerland. Tel. (025) 35 32 32

Altitude: 4,265 ft. (1,300 m.). *Top:* 6,956 ft. (2,120 m.)

Language: French

Runs: 31 mi. (50 km.); 56 mi. (90 km.) with Les Diablerets

Lifts: 23 (39 with Les Diablerets)

Ski areas: Bretaye, Barboleusaz-Les Chaux, Roc d'Orsay

Ski schools: Ecole Suisse de Ski Villars, Ecole de Ski Moderne

Linked resort: Les Diablerets

Season: Mid-December to mid-April

Kindergarten: *Non-ski*: 3–10 years. *With ski*: 3–10 years

Prices: *Lift pass*: 6 days Sfr. 155 (children Sfr. 125). *Ski school*: Group Sfr. 18 for half-day; private Sfr. 40 per hour.

RATINGS

Skiing Conditions	7
Snow Conditions	5
For Beginners	7
For Intermediates	8
For Advanced Skiers	5
For Children	7
Après-Ski	8
Other Sports	7
Value for Money	7

THE RESORT

Villars is a mixture of architectural styles, but it enjoys a spectacular—and spectacularly sunny—south-west-facing position on the northern side of the Rhône Valley, above Aigle and Bex. The village affords superb panoramic views which take in Mont Blanc and many other famous peaks. The resort has recently regained popularity with the British, making for an increase in English-speaking guests.

Villars is a cosmopolitan resort that caters fairly well to all ages and nationalities. A number of international schools add to the United Nations feel. Villars is also a good place for non-skiers, with a fair number of chic shops and the potential for excursions up the mountain by train or down to towns on Lake Geneva, such as Montreux and Lausanne.

THE SKIING

Villars is a resort for novices and intermediates rather than experts. The ski area is not enormous, but there is a good variety of pleasant, sunny slopes. The resort now has a useful link with Les Diablerets and its glacier, which extends the range of the skiing, but it does not provide any significantly more difficult runs. The glacier means that some skiing is available at either end of the season when Villars' own south-facing slopes may not be well covered. Skiing off the glacier lifts, however, although included in the regional lift ticket, is not covered by the local pass.

The main skiing area centers on Bretaye, 5,906 ft. (1,800 m.), a plateau reached either by mountain railway from the middle of Villars—this line in fact runs all the way up from Bex in the valley—or by gondola from Chesières to Roc d'Orsay, 6,562 ft. (2,000 m.), and then a short run down. Chair and surface lifts fan out from here, offering lots of easy intermediate skiing, but also quite a few undemanding off-*piste* possibilities. There is a more challenging off-*piste* run down a *couloir* at the back of Chaux de Conches, but this is often closed.

The smaller, less interesting Villars ski area is Les Chaux, 5,742 ft. (1,750 m.), and Croix des Chaux, 6,628 ft. (2,020 m.). It links with Bretaye, but can also be reached by gondola from Barboleusaz, just above the village of Gryon. The slopes provide fun intermediate skiing, but get a lot of sun.

OTHER ACTIVITIES

These include 18½ mi. (30 km.) of cross-country tracks, 15½ mi. (25 km.) of prepared walks, skibobbing, swimming, skating, curling, tennis, squash, indoor golf, bowling, horseback riding and a fitness center. Villars is well placed for excursions down to Lake Geneva and the towns along its banks.

APRÈS-SKI

Villars does not exactly throb by night, but there is a good range of après-ski venues to please all but the most dedicated après-skiers. Restaurants include Le Peppino in the highly regarded Eurotel and Le Sporting which has a superb list of Swiss wines (many of them from vineyards around Villars). La Suisse is less expensive and is ideal for *fondues*. The Panorama incorporates the Kam Yu, a good but pricey Chinese restaurant, and the New Sam, one of the most lively and sophisticated discos in the Alps. For less affluent disco-goers, the alternative is El Gringo.

WENGEN

Access: *Nearest airport*: Zurich (2½ hrs.). *By road*: N6 Autobahn, exit Spiez, via Interlaken to Lauterbrunnen, then narrow-gauge railway (WAB). *By rail*: to Lauterbrunnen, then WAB to Wengen.

Tourist Office: Verkehrsbüro, 3823 Wengen, Switzerland. Tel. (036) 55 14 14

Altitude: 4,187 ft. (1,276 m.). *Top:* 8,111 ft. (2,472 m.)

Language: German

Runs: 93 mi. (150 km.) in Jungfrau Region

Lifts: 41 in Jungfrau Region

Ski areas: Kleine Scheidegg, Männlichen

Ski school: Schweizer Skischule Wengen

Linked resort: Grindelwald

Season: November to April

Kindergarten: *Non-ski*: 3–7 years. *With ski*: ski school from 3 years

Prices: *Lift pass*: 6 days Sfr. 168 (children Sfr. 112). *Ski school*: Group Sfr. 19 for half-day; private Sfr. 40 per hour.

RATINGS

Skiing Conditions	7
Snow Conditions	5
For Beginners	7
For Intermediates	8
For Advanced Skiers	7
For Children	8
Après-Ski	8
Other Sports	7
Value for Money	7

THE RESORT

Wengen is one of the prettiest, most atmospheric ski resorts in Switzerland, indeed in the world. It is an old village, still owned and run by mountain people, but because the British have been coming here ever since skiing was invented, English-speaking guests have a special place in the locals' hearts. There are some grand hotels in Wengen, but this car-free resort, dominated by the Eiger and the Jungfrau, still retains the feeling of being a small Alpine village, almost cut off from the rest of the world and reached only by a mountain railway.

THE SKIING

Wengen is the central resort in the vast Jungfrau ski area, which also includes Grindelwald and Mürren. The Jungfrau pass is only marginally more expensive than the standard Wengen (Kleine Scheidegg/Männlichen) pass and is worth the extra for skiers who want to explore the whole region. A day-trip to Mürren is a bit of an expedition, but quite fun all the same.

There is lots of good skiing for advanced intermediates in Wengen, as well as a few more challenging runs for experts. Since there are beginner slopes right in the middle of the village, this is an ideal place to learn. Much of the best skiing is reached by the mountain railway which runs from the center of town up to Kleine Scheidegg, 6,762 ft. (2,061 m.), with several stops en route. From here you can ski the famous Lauberhorn course, the

longest downhill on the men's World Cup circuit, and a lovely trail for recreational skiers. There are pretty runs through the trees to Innerwengen, 4,625 ft. (1,300 m.), as well as some short, demanding runs next to the Innerwengen chairlift and, farther up, beside the aptly named Bumps T-bar. There is also good skiing off the Wixi chairlift. The best restaurant for lunch in this sector is the Jungfrau Hotel at Wengernalp, but this stylish place by the railway tracks is so popular with the British and others that you need to reserve your table in advance.

The Grindelwald/Grund slopes can be reached either by skiing down the other side from Kleine Scheidegg or by taking the Männlichen cable car up from Wengen. (To return to the Wengen side, however, you need to take the Grindelwald train up to Kleine Scheidegg.) The skiing on this side consists mainly of broad, open *pistes*, but there are also some pretty trails through the woods, such as that down to the middle railway station at Brandegg. It is often better to use the lifts higher up in this area, since there can be bad lines for the long gondola from Grund to Männlichen.

APRÈS-SKI

Après-ski begins on the mountain. Mary's Café or the Café Oberland are good places to stop for a spiked coffee on the final run home. The Eiger Bar, the Pizzeria Bar of the Victoria Lauberhorn and the Tanne Bar are all popular places. Most eating out must be done in hotel restaurants. The Carrousel nightclub at the Regina Hotel is the smartest late-night meeting place. One wall is all glass, giving fantastic views over the village and the mountains. The movie theater shows a good variety of films, mainly in English.

OTHER ACTIVITIES

There's a 7½-mi. (12-km.) cross-country track in the Lauterbrunnen valley and 13 mi. (20 km.) of walks, as well as skating and curling on artificial and natural rinks, sleigh rides, skibobbing, tobogganing, hang-gliding, and swimming (in hotel pools not open to the public).

The railway excursion from Kleine Scheidegg through the Jungfrau mountain to the Jungfraujoch, 11,333 ft. (3,454 m.), is not included on the lift pass but should excite even the most jaded sightseers.

ZERMATT

🎿🎿🎿🎿🎿

Access: *Nearest airport*: Geneva (4½ hrs.). *By road*: N9 Autoroute and E2 to Visp. Then by road to Täsch and by train to Zermatt. *By rail*: to Visp, then connection to Zermatt.

Tourist Office: Kur- und Verkehrsverein, 3920 Zermatt, Switzerland. Tel. (028) 66 11 81

Altitude: 5,315 ft. (1,620 m.). *Top*: 12,533 ft. (3,820 m.)

Language: German

Runs: 93 mi. (150 km.)

Lifts: 37

Ski areas: Schwarzsee/Klein Matterhorn, Sunnegga/Rothorn, Gornergrat/Stockhorn

Ski school: Schweizer Skischule Zermatt

Linked resort: Cervinia (Italy)

Season: Late November to late April, year-round skiing on glacier

Kindergarten: *Non-ski*: 1 month–8 years. *With ski*: from 4 years

Prices: *Lift pass*: 6 days Sfr. 226 (children Sfr. 113). *Ski school*: Group Sfr. 165 for 6 days; private Sfr. 110 for half-day.

RATINGS

Skiing Conditions	9
Snow Conditions	8
For Beginners	5
For Intermediates	8
For Advanced Skiers	9
For Children	6
Après-Ski	9
Other Sports	8
Value for Money	7

THE RESORT

Dominated by Switzerland's most famous landmark, the Matterhorn, Zermatt is the country's best all-round ski resort. Moreover, there are many, many skiers who would have no hesitation in naming Zermatt as the best ski resort in the world. Partly because of the Matterhorn, but also due to the absence of cars and the resort's great sense of tradition, Zermatt has a special, alluring atmosphere that is superior to that of any other resort in Switzerland—and perhaps the Alps.

From the moment you arrive at the main station by mountain railway and catch your first glimpse of the

THE SKIING

ever-changing Matterhorn, it is clear that you are in one of the world's great mountain villages. Indeed, despite all the development in recent years, Zermatt has succeeded in retaining a village atmosphere—perhaps because this is a resort that is as busy in summer as in winter and has a substantial year-round population. In fact, the community is still essentially controlled by half-a-dozen local families. Many are hoteliers going back generations, and Zermatt has some of the finest luxury hotels in the Alps, including the Mont Cervin, the Zermatterhof and the Monte Rosa. But even hotels in the middle and lower brackets are excellently run.

There are three main ski areas in Zermatt. They do not interconnect perfectly and each system starts from a different point in the village. It is therefore impossible to find a hotel that is near all three bottom lift stations. A certain amount of walking in ski boots with your skis on your shoulder is necessary in Zermatt, but few visitors really mind, especially since everybody else is walking in ski boots with skis over their shoulders. The only real logistics problem is that you cannot ski from Klein Matterhorn into the Gornergrat sector; you *can* go from Riffelalp in the Gornergrat to Furri on the Klein Matterhorn side. Otherwise, interconnections between the ski areas are pretty good. In practice, each of the areas is large enough to keep even an expert skier busy for a whole day.

The Schwarzsee/Trockener Steg/ Klein Matterhorn system, 12,533 ft. (3,820 m.), offers the highest skiing in Europe and excellent summer skiing. The highest cable-car station, built into the rock of the Klein Matterhorn, is an amazing feat of engineering. It is nearly always very cold up there, even in spring, but the low temperatures also mean that the snow stays in excellent condition. The slopes at the top of the Klein Matterhorn are fairly gentle and well suited to early intermediates. However, below Trockener Steg, the slopes become steeper and more demanding. (From the top, it is also possible to ski down to Cervinia, Italy. The runs are not difficult, and good intermediates can manage them easily. You have to pay a supplement to use the lifts back up from the Italian side.)

There is some challenging skiing beside the Garten T-bar, but the most demanding skiing is over by the Hörnli lift, which gives access to steep narrow runs like Mamatt and Tiefbach. All the runs from Furgg or Schwarzsee to Furri involve at least some very tough sections, except for the easier Weisse Perle. Furgg– Furri and Schwarzsee–Furri are both long, challenging *pistes*. From Furri to the bottom there are easy trails past appealing restaurants like Zum See and Blatten.

The Riffelberg/Gornergrat/Stockhorn sector is generally reached by the slow and ancient Gornergrat mountain railway, which can take anything up to an hour to reach the summit of Gornergrat. All the runs leading directly down from Gornergrat are intermediate, giving plenty of opportunity for highway skiing. From Gornergrat there is a two-stage cable car to Stockhorn, 11,172 ft. (3,405 m.), via Hohtälli. There is a huge variety of tough skiing (often not open until early February) from Hohtälli, Rote Nase and Stockhorn, including the legendary Triftji mogul field. Good skiers could scarcely wish for more challenging terrain. These runs are too steep to be groomed, and most eventually lead to Gant, from which there is a gondola up to Blauherd.

The Sunnegga/Blauherd/Unterrothorn sector is easily reached by the miraculous Sunnegga express underground funicular which brings skiers up to Sunnegga in just five minutes. Lines for this lift are very, very rare. In fact the crowding problems that dogged Zermatt a decade ago have now largely been eliminated, except at peak holiday periods. From Sunnegga there is a gondola to Blauherd and then a cable car up to Unterrothorn. Over the back of Unterrothorn, the Kumme chairlift leads to terrain with good snow conditions all winter. From Unterrothorn, 9,886 ft. (3,013 m.), there are some fairly demanding runs like the Chamois and Marmotte, which eventually lead right down to resort level. There is also a good, broad run round the other side of Unterrothorn to Gant, passing by the Fluhalp mountain restaurant. This run provides a liaison with the Stockhorn/Gornergrat area. The runs directly from Blauherd to Sunnegga are easy, but Blauherd also provides access to the tricky National black run down to resort level.

Below Sunnegga lies the tiny hamlet of Findeln, which contains a cluster of mountain restaurants. There are some 40 in the whole Zermatt area. The best one is Enzo's Hitta, one of the finest mountain restaurants in the Alps.

APRÈS-SKI

Someone once said, "après-ski" in Zermatt begins at noon, and they were far from wrong. It is also very much the custom, particularly in spring, to linger up the mountain into the early evening. Mountain restaurants such as the Olympia Stubli, on the trail down from Sunnegga to the resort, are popular drinking places at the end of the day. In the resort itself, the Papperla Pub and—for the rich—Elsie's Bar are also favored meeting places.

The variety of Zermatt's nightlife is as great as the variety of its skiing. There are bars and restaurants to suit all tastes and budgets. Le Mazot, specializing in superb grilled lamb, is the best restaurant in town. The Stockhorn, the Alex Rotisserie Tenne and Chez Gaby are other restaurants with good reputations.

Most hotels of any size have their own bars, often with live entertainment, but the most remarkable is the Hotel de la Poste. It is a vast nighttime complex that includes two discos—the Village and the Broken Bar— pasta restaurants and a gourmet restaurant, the Zamoura, which specializes in seafood and has a chic adjacent cocktail bar. The Pink Elephant is an elegant bar where there is often live jazz or other music. Those who cannot find something to please them at night in the Poste can always try the Hotel Alex or the Hotel Pollux for entertainment.

OTHER ACTIVITIES

Because there are funiculars, this is a good resort for non-skiers to meet skiing friends for lunch on the mountain.

In addition, there is a whole range of other sporting activities available: 15½ mi. (25 km.) of cross-country tracks, 18½ mi. (30 km.) of cleared walking paths, skating on natural rinks, curling and swimming (14 pools in hotels and one salt-water pool open to the public), squash, tennis, and a fitness center in the Hotel Christiania.

There is also a fascinating Alpine museum and a cemetery dedicated to souls claimed by the mountains.

BEST OF THE REST

ANZÈRE

Nestled into a hillside high above the Rhône Valley, Anzère is one of the rare new ski resorts that looks as if it's been around for ever, thanks to a car-free center and chalet-style buildings placed to catch the sun and provide splendid views. The skiing is mostly for intermediates, who appreciate long sunny slopes above the tree line, but require neither a great vertical nor steep terrain. Après-ski is generally family-oriented, although three discos and 15 restaurants suit the family that might want to boogie or dine out.

CHAMPÉRY

Champéry is the main Swiss component of the grandiose Portes du Soleil, which straddles the Franco-Swiss border and includes hundreds of miles of *pistes*, untold acres of off-*piste* skiing and 220 lifts on a single lift pass. Champéry's closest neighbors are Avoriaz, France, and Les Crosets, Switzerland. The infamous Swiss Wall, which serves as the mogul-studded main way from Avoriaz into Champéry, has been called the best-known run in the entire Portes du Soleil. Champéry's remaining skiing tends more toward wide-open, easy slopes. The picturesque old resort is relatively quiet at night.

CHÂTEAU-D'OEX

Château-d'Oex still resembles the farming village it originally was, but has more recently become a worthy ski resort. The skiing on La Braye, the closest mountain, is limited in comparison with some of its neighbors. But it participates in the Gstaad Superski Pass, which also includes Gstaad, Rougemont, Saanenmöser, half a dozen other interlinked ski stations and even the Diablerets Glacier. It is almost the last French-speaking outpost of the Lake Geneva Region, though it is located across the cantonal line in the Bernese Oberland.

GRÄCHEN

Overshadowed by two famous nearby resorts—Zermatt and Saas-Fee—Grächen is an unheralded town with a low-key atmosphere and turbocharged terrain. For a fairly small place with just 14 lifts, it offers a high proportion of challenging skiing. Skiing is divided between two sectors, Seetalhorn/Plattja and Wannehorn/Hannigalp. The former is basically for advanced skiers; the latter has the easier terrain. The town caters to families, so nightlife is fairly tame.

LENK

Lenk is a quiet, restful town at the foot of the Wildstrubel, favored by German families and skiers in their middle years. Skiing is on two mountains. The Hahnenmoos, whose most challenging terrain is awkward to reach, is also the link to the skiing at nearby Adelboden. The Leiterli/Betelberg area has wide-open skiing for various ability levels and some runs through the trees. Lenk's cross-country skiing is on 33 mi. (53 km.) of trails. There are many good restaurants and hotels in Lenk, and nightlife is sedate.

LEYSIN

Skiing in this eclectic Vaudois town is mainly for novices and intermediates, though the Lake Geneva Region lift pass (good also at Les Diablerets, Les Mosses and Villars) accesses more extensive and demanding ski areas, too. Leysin's Mayen sector is a sunny, particularly pleasant place for new skiers. The Berneuse, which features a spectacular revolving restaurant at the top of the gondola, provides somewhat challenging terrain. The town is not especially pretty, but it wears an international mantle, thanks to several boarding schools with students from the world over.

PONTRESINA

Sometimes called the "poor man's St. Moritz", Pontresina actually stands as a quality resort in its own right, though far less glamorous than its Engadine neighbor. Surrounded by woodlands, and a bus ride from the best skiing in the Engadine, Pontresina is also good for cross-country skiers. The two closest Alpine ski areas of the Engadine quintet are Piz Lagalp and Diavolezza, small but quite challenging sectors located in the direction of the Bernina Pass (and Italy). Pontresina's après-ski is on the mild side, too, compared with its more famous neighbor.

ROUGEMONT

This pretty village between Gstaad and Château-d'Oex is part of the Gstaad Superski Pass program, which includes several large and small resorts, as well as the Diablerets Glacier. Rougemont's terrain, interlinked with Gstaad's Eggli, offers some of the most challenging skiing in the area. The Videmanette boasts some mogul slopes and good off-*piste* options. There is cross-country skiing and not-too-boisterous nightlife, but most other options are lacking in the village.

SWITZERLAND-INFO

ACCOMMODATIONS

The standards of accommodations in Switzerland are the highest in the world. The Swiss Hotel Association (SHA) annually rates accommodations in six categories designated with stars (five stars being the highest category, none the lowest) and one special classification for country inns. The SHA designates as "country inns" those establishments with good regional cuisine, plus comfortable lodging and sufficient parking space.

Hotels. A hotel, from palatial to rustic, has by definition a lobby, front desk, accommodations and food service. The leading luxury hotels of Switzerland are superlative, on a par with the finest on earth for accommodations, multi-lingual staff, dining and extra facilities and service, and are usually equipped with such contemporary conveniences as an indoor swimming pool, whirlpool, sauna and solarium. The lower end of the scale indicates simple family-run hotels with little public space, few amenities and perhaps some shared bathrooms. All, however, are clean, comfortable and indicate value in their category. Most resort hotels are in the two- to four-star category.

The majority of Swiss resort hotels offer *demi-pension* (half-board or MAP, Modified American Plan), which includes breakfast (usually a lavish buffet) and full dinner in the price of the room.

Hotel Garni. This is the Swiss equivalent of a Bed and Breakfast (B&B), a small, casual hotel with breakfast (but no other meals) included in the room rate.

Chalets. Especially popular with British groups who find them congenial and economical, staffed chalet-style residences are rented out to groups of six or more. Some can be as elaborate as a hotel with their own bar and disco. Meal plans vary with the chalet arrangement.

Apartments. What Americans call condos are known as *Ferienwohnungen* or *appartements* in Switzerland. They are available on a limited basis in some resorts, and the Swiss National Tourist Office can provide a list of rental agencies. The apartments can range from a small studio to luxury accommodations with en suite bathrooms and south-facing balconies.

Club Med. There are several of the French-based Club Med ski villages in Switzerland: in Engelberg, Leysin, Pontresina, St. Moritz (2 clubs), Villars, Wengen and several smaller resorts. In Switzerland, they tend to draw a particularly international, multi-lingual crowd. The organization is on the Club Med all-inclusive formula, including double-occupancy accommodations, all meals, ski pass, ski instruction and après-ski entertainment.

Room types. A single room will have one single bed; a double room will have two single beds (placed right next to each other, but with separate sets of bedclothes). The American double, known in German-speaking countries as a "French bed", and occasionally the queen are only beginning to gain favor; what Americans know as double-doubles and kings are not found in Switzerland.

If a room is described as having a bath it will have just that—a bathtub, usually with a hand shower. If the room is described as having a shower, it won't have a tub.

CUSTOMS/ENTRY REGULATIONS

Most visitors, including citizens of Britain, the United States and the majority of other English-speaking countries, need only a valid passport to enter Switzerland. British subjects can use the simplified British Visitor's Passport. Without further formality, you are generally allowed to stay for up to 90 days.

There is no restriction on the import or export of either Swiss or foreign currencies.

DRIVING

Rental cars are available at major airports and in large resorts. Some are affiliates of international chains. The minimum driving age in Switzerland is 18, but you must be at least 21 to rent a car (sometimes 25). A valid driver's license is sufficient for a stay of up to 90 days in Switzerland, but it should have been held for at least one year.

Insurance. Coverage requirements vary according to the car rental company, but unlimited liability and property damage is generally included. Collision damage insurance is also included, with an average deductible of Sfr. 1,000. Additional insurance, to cover the deductible, is approximately Sfr. 15 per day. Passenger accident and baggage insurance is not included but is also available at a small additional charge. There is no value added tax on car rentals in Switzerland.

If you are bringing your own car into Switzerland, a Green Card is a recommended but not obligatory extension to your regular insurance policy, validating it for foreign countries.

Speed limits. Where no specific speed limits are posted, these are 50 kph (31 mph) in town, 80 kph (50 mph) on main roads outside of built-up areas, and 120 kph (75 mph) on the *autoroute* and *Autobahn*.

Rules of the road. Drive on the right, overtake (pass) on the left. Traffic on main roads has the right of way over that coming out from secondary roads. Seatbelts are required for front seat passengers. Children from the age of 7 may sit in the front seat, provided they are properly attached. Drinking and driving is a serious offense. The permissible blood-alcohol level is 0.8 per mille.

Automobile associations. The *Touring Club der Schweiz/Touring Club Suisse* (TCS) offers 24-hour breakdown assistance. Dial 140. Emergency call boxes are posted at regular intervals on the motorways, and even on some mountain roads. Members of an affiliated automobile association will not be charged for service. Otherwise you'll have to pay the full bill for the help of a serviceman or patrolman.

Mountain driving. Snow tire and chain laws may be in effect on mountain pass roads. Practice putting on your chains *before* you get stuck in heavy snow. On difficult stretches of mountain roads, priority is given to post buses, otherwise to the ascending vehicle. Sounding your horn is recommended on blind corners of mountain roads; avoid it everywhere else.

There is a special art to driving on ice and in snowy conditions. The golden rule is always to drive more slowly than you think you should. Avoid sharp reactions or sudden braking; it's better to anticipate well in advance, keeping a good distance from the car in front (two or three times the normal braking distance). When starting off or going uphill, put the car in the highest possible gear to avoid wheel spin. Never drive in ski boots.

Road conditions. In general, road conditions are excellent. A well-developed *autoroute/Autobahn* system links all the big towns. Motorists who use the network must purchase a sticker (valid for the current year) to be displayed on the windscreen. Failure to do so carries a heavy fine. Rental cars will come already equipped with one.

For details on road conditions, itineraries and other tourist information, phone the TCS at (022) 35 80 00—24 hours a day. There is almost always someone there who speaks English. Or telephone 163 and 120 for recorded information in French, German or Italian, depending on the language of the area you are phoning from.

ELECTRIC CURRENT

Standard voltage throughout Switzerland is 220 volts, 50 cycles AC. American and British small appliances and electrical gadgets require an adapter/converter, though many electric clocks, record players and tape recorders will not work properly even with such devices. Bathrooms in Swiss hotels may be equipped with low-wattage outlets suitable only for razors; hairdryers and electric curlers, whether American models used with converters or European models, will not work from these outlets.

GETTING THERE

By air. Zurich is the most convenient international airport for all the resorts eastward from Interlaken, gateway to the Jungfrau Region (Grindelwald, Wengen, Mürren), and Geneva is best for all the French-speaking resorts, as well as for

Saas-Fee and Zermatt in southwestern Switzerland. There are non-stop or direct flights from Atlanta, Boston, Chicago, Los Angeles, New York, Montreal and Toronto.

From the UK, regular scheduled flights leave daily from London to Zurich and Geneva. Non-stop flights operate from Manchester to Zurich (daily) and from Birmingham to Zurich and Geneva (several times a week).

Fly/Rail Baggage Service. This splendid convenience, instituted in cooperation between Swissair and the Swiss Federal Railroads, is unique to Switzerland. There are railroad stations right in the terminals at Zurich and Geneva airports, which accept baggage for over 100 resorts in Switzerland, no matter how many train changes are involved. For a small charge per piece, you can check your baggage in at your departure airport for a Swissair flight and claim it at your resort destination. You must request special green tags, which also serve as Swiss Customs declarations, prior to departure. On return, you check your baggage at the resort railroad station and pick it up at baggage claim on arrival at your home airport.

By rail. From Britain, this is a good choice, especially if traveling to a resort either with, or close to, a railroad station, as it can cut transfer times considerably. On arrival there are buses that meet the train and transport you to the resort. There are daily direct services from Ostend (Belgium) to Chur for Arosa, or Landquart, giving connections to Klosters and Davos. For other destinations in Switzerland, you will need to change at Paris or Basle. The TGV has daily services from Paris to Geneva and Lausanne.

By coach. There is a regular coach service from London Victoria coach station to Geneva. Call (01) 730 0202 for details.

spot and submit your claim to your insurance company on your return home.

On-*piste* accident victims are taken from the mountain by the ski patrol, who are paid professionals. In some cases, this service is free. On arrival, ask your hotel, the local tourist office or the lift-ticket office whether there is a charge and, if not, how you can purchase short-term insurance for such services.

The Swiss Ski Association handles rescue operations when an avalanche comes down on controlled ski runs, and the Swiss Alpine Club performs rescue feats in off-*piste* areas with difficult access. The handlers of Switzerland's famed avalanche search dogs are volunteers who belong to the Swiss Alpine Club. When called upon, Swiss Air Rescue dispatches a helicopter to the nearest handler and dog team and flies the duo to the avalanche site. Subsequent flights will bring in a doctor if necessary. More than 600,000 Swiss and foreign donors support the SAR fleet of 12 helicopters and two ambulance jet planes, which provide search, rescue and transportation services free to supporters; a non-patron is charged the flight cost.

HOLIDAYS AND SPECIAL EVENTS

Legal holidays falling during the ski season are: Christmas Day, December 26, New Year's Day, Good Friday and Easter Monday.

The busiest times in Swiss resorts are New Year and Easter. Christmas itself is not too overcrowded, since many families do not head for the resorts until December 26 or later. Swiss schools have a week's break in February. Exact dates vary according to canton, but this is always a busy time on the slopes. French half-term holidays also affect Swiss resorts, especially those close to the border.

HEALTH

Comprehensive health insurance is recommended for all visitors to Switzerland. If you become ill or are injured, you will find that most resort doctors are multilingual and accustomed to arranging payment from patients who are visitors from abroad. If there is a problem, your hotel can help straighten it out. You must pay your doctor or medical bills on the

MAIL

Stamps can be bought at post offices, the hotel front desk and many shops that sell postcards, as well as from vending machines.

Post offices display a distinctive sign bearing the letters PTT. Most are open from 7.30 a.m. to noon and 1.45 to 6.30 p.m. on weekdays and 7.30 to 11 a.m. on Saturdays.

MONEY MATTERS

Currency. The unit of currency in Switzerland is the Swiss *franc* (abbreviated Sfr.), divided into 100 *centimes*. (The word for centimes among German-speaking Swiss is *rappen*, but you will not see that word stamped on any coin.)

Coins: 5, 10, 20 and 50 centimes and 1, 2 and 5 francs.

Bills: 10, 20, 50, 100, 500 and 1,000 francs.

Credit cards and traveler's checks. Most major hotels and restaurants accept credit cards, as do shops. Swiss service stations do not usually accept credit cards, although those also found in America, such as Mobil, Shell or Texaco, may take oil-company cards. Traveler's checks are always welcome.

Banks. Banks offer the best exchange rate on traveler's checks and foreign currency. Banking hours are 8.30 a.m. to 4.30 p.m. on weekdays. Branches at airports and major city railway terminals are open daily until 10 p.m.

SKI SCHOOL

The Swiss Ski School (*Ecole Suisse de Ski; Schweizer Skischule*) has an excellent reputation and its instructors are trained to a very high standard. In most resorts this will be the only ski school, but some do have other, smaller ski schools, usually specializing in a particular area, such as off-*piste*. Finding English-speaking instructors is not usually a problem in Switzerland.

You can either go into group lessons or take a private instructor. Individual instruction is charged by the hour, half-day or full day. It is very expensive on a one-to-one basis, but you learn extremely quickly. If on holiday with a few friends of similar standard, it can be worthwhile sharing private lessons (instructors will take up to six people).

More advanced skiers will benefit from occasionally joining Class 1 (or even the Competition class), where there is very little hanging about and plenty of fast skiing behind the instructor. Expert skiers take an instructor if they want to explore the area off-*piste* or perfect skiing in the bumps.

TELEPHONE

Hotels usually add high surcharges onto phone calls, so these are to be avoided—especially for overseas calls. The most economical calls are from phone booths, which are found at railway stations, airports, outside post offices and in outdoor public spaces.

The phone system is completely automated. Insert several coins (at least 40 centimes for a local call) and dial the number. When the other party answers, the phone will automatically consume the money as long as you stay on the line, and a counter and digital display indicate how much money you have left. When the money runs out, the call is disconnected without warning. Unused coins will be returned, but no change is made for time left when large-denomination coins are used.

For calls back to the U.S., the best deal is AT&T's USADIRECT program. Dial (046) 05-0011 in Switzerland. You may have to wait for up to 30 seconds before being connected directly to an AT&T operator, who will then place a credit card or collect call for you.

TIPPING

A gratuity is automatically included in all hotel and restaurant bills; an additional tip is neither necessary nor expected.

TOURIST INFORMATION OFFICES

The Swiss National Tourist Office can supply specific resort information, hotel price lists and other useful data. For further details on a resort, contact the local tourist office directly.

In the U.S. the main office is at 608 5th Ave., New York, N.Y. 10020; tel. (212) 757 5944. There are also branch offices in Chicago, San Francisco and Toronto. All are open during normal business hours. From early December through the end of March, 24-hour snow condition reports are available from the Swiss National Tourist Office in New York; call (212) 757 6336.

In Britain, the main office is in the Swiss Centre, New Coventry Street, London W1V 8EE; tel. (01) 734 1921.

SKI-INFO EUROPE

An A–Z Summary of Practical Information,
Facts and Advice

CONTENTS

Airports	Discos	Lift Lines
Altitude	Driving	Lift Passes
Booking	Equipment	Off-Piste Skiing
Britishisms	Grooming	Seasons
Children	Ground	Ski Schools
Climate	Transportation	Terrain Rating
Clothing and	Insurance	Tipping
Accessories	Lifts	Tour Operators

AIRPORTS

The major traditional Alpine gateways for the Alps from North America are Geneva, Milan, Munich and Zurich. There are also some limited non-stop services from North America to Lyon, Salzburg and Venice. Flights to Innsbruck or Turin require a change of plane. For specific details, see individual Info sections for each country.

ALTITUDE

Europeans make a big deal of resort altitude and mountain elevations with good reason. Far more than in the Rockies or the Sierra, where snow conditions tend to be consistent from base to summit, or in the East where snowmaking does it all, conditions in European resorts vary according to altitude. Low-lying resorts tend to have bare (or barely skiable) lower slopes early and late in the season or during a snow-poor winter. This means that skiers normally take a cable car to high snowfields, ski all day and ride down again in the afternoon. In higher resorts, not only will the snow be better overall, but it will be possible to ski back at the end of the day. When a resort offers glacier skiing, it is a virtual guarantee that something will be skiable, no matter what nature provides in the way of snow cover.

BOOKING

The best deal, and most convenient planning mechanism, for American skiers is the package, which normally includes accommodations, transfers by train and/or motorcoach between airport and resort, and local taxes and gratuities. The packages are booked in conjunction with air travel, which may be calculated separately. Lift passes (see p. 315) and airlines sell packages, which may also be booked through travel agents. Ski clubs and local ski shops may also offer trips to Europe for their members and customers respectively.

The overwhelming majority of hotels in Alpine ski resorts accept only Saturday-to-Saturday bookings, so most ski packages will feature a Friday departure from North America, Saturday arrival in Europe, Sunday through Friday skiing and Saturday return. During Christmas, bookings of a minimum of two weeks are normally accepted.

If currency fluctuations are expected, ask if the package price is guaranteed "in dollars", to ensure that you will not be hit with a surcharge in case the dollar drops between the time you book and the time you travel. If the dollar rises, some tour operators may issue a refund.

And always, read the fine print regarding advance purchase, cancellation and refund policies (see also INSURANCE).

BRITISHISMS

When English is spoken or appears in European resort literature, it is the British, not the American version. Here are some common British ski terms which you will read or hear:

Anorak: Parka
Button tow: Platterpull (Pomalift or similar)
Crèche: Infant-care nursery
Drag lift: Surface lift (usually T-bar)
Hire: Rental (as in "ski/car hire")
Kindergarten: Children's facility, whether a nursery for non-skiing pre-schoolers or a ski school for young children
Nursery slope: Beginner slope
Path: Trail (usually through the woods on the lower part of the mountain)
Piste: A marked, groomed run above the treeline
Pisted: Groomed (unpisted, therefore, is ungroomed)
Purpose-built resort: New, built-for-skiing resort (as opposed to old village)
Queue (pronounced cue): Line (as in "lift queue")
Salopettes: Insulated ski pants
Self-catering: Accommodations with kitchens and without meal service
Standard: Ability level
Stick: Pole
Tram: Streetcar; what Americans refer to as a "tram" is only a "cable car" to British
Tuition: Instruction (as in "ski tuition")

CHILDREN

European children all learn to ski in the Alps, and Europe can be an exciting and educational addition to an American youngster's ski experiences—especially for older children. If you have pre-schoolers, however, be aware that most Alpine resorts do not offer nursery care for infants or toddlers (France being the major exception), although larger hotels may include child care in their services. Also, European ski schools provide children's instruction only from age 4 or sometimes 5 (rather than 3, as most American resorts do). Finally, European ski schools usually have far larger classes for children than North American ski schools do (10 to 12 per instructor is not uncommon, while 6 to 8 is the rule in America). In North America, children are grouped by age and skiing ability; in Europe, they are usually grouped by

ability and language. The good news for Alps-bound families is that children's rates extend to youngsters as old as 15 or 16 in many resorts. Children's discounts for lifts and lodging are usually greater than in North American resorts.

CLIMATE

Temperatures in the Alps tend to be comparable to the Rockies—that is, warmer than New England and the Midwest. However, December, January and early February can be cold, but are usually not bitter.

The main problem is that when it snows, visibility can be minimal. So much Alpine skiing is above the timber line that you will find yourself literally skiing in a cloud, finding your way from *piste*-marker to *piste*-marker in a treeless snowfield. Some skiers find this extremely disorienting, and almost all find it exhausting skiing. Late February, March and April, by contrast, are normally mild and sunny. Skiers should protect themselves with sunscreen.

One feature of the weather that skiers dread in the Tyrol and Switzerland is the *Föhn*, a warm wind from northern Africa, which scoots across the Mediterranean, jeopardizes the snow cover, and may even leave a deposit of fine grains of sand on the slopes. The *Föhn* is usually endured once or twice a winter, and in normal years, snow recovery is swift.

CLOTHING AND ACCESSORIES

European skiers tend to dress in higher style than their American counterparts. One- and two-piece suits are popular. Jeans are not seen as skiwear. Dress in layers, as you would in the States, to prepare yourself for a variety of conditions, but you will probably want to leave your down parka at home. It just doesn't get that cold in the Alps.

For après-ski wear, informality is the rule—though what Europeans consider "informal" might be quite dressy in most American resorts. Also, five-star, deluxe hotels may include one or two black-tie evenings a week, though these are usually optional. In any case, men will want to bring a jacket and tie and women one dressy outfit. For less formal evenings, more casual attire is fine.

DISCOS

If there is anything short of an emergency or a major shopping spree that will knock a hole in a ski vacation budget, it is the European discotheque. A resort disco typically features a high cover charge and hefty bar bills. Hard liquor is especially pricey, and in some discos, wine and beer are served reluctantly or not at all.

EQUIPMENT

If you own your equipment, take it. Always bring your own boots, and, unless you are dismally unhappy with your own skis, you ought to take them as well. Most airlines now let you check a ski bag as part of your normal baggage allotment of two checked pieces. If you do not own skis with which you are happy, you *may* wish to rent from a top local shop at home. Rental equipment in the Alps tends to be very uneven. Some shops offer current models of excellent equipment; most do not. In the Alps, ski shops' rental stocks tend to consist of a hodgepodge of leftover skis, boots and poles of assorted vintages—and in various states of care.

The huge rental operations with efficient supermarket-style service do not exist in the Alps, and mechanical testing procedures for rental bindings, which are now mandated in the litigious U.S., are not required in Europe. If you plan to rent equipment, be prepared to visit several ski shops until you find a set that you are comfortable with (which may be difficult in high season).

Your European vacation may be the ideal time to purchase new ski gear. Since snowfall during the 1988/89 season was record low and record late, good deals on leftover equipment are anticipated for a year or two. Coupled with refunds on Value Added Tax, detailed in the individual Info sections for each country, this can amount to a real bargain on ski equipment.

GROOMING

Contrary to myth, ski mountains in Europe *are* groomed. The grooming is simply different and usually involves packing loose snow on top rather than using a powder-maker on hardpack or ice on the lower mountain. Because so much terrain is wide bowls above the tree line, a *piste* is normally cut between stakes which mark the run. The area outside of the *piste* is left ungroomed, giving skiers the choice of skiing packed snow with the throngs or sampling whatever snow conditions can be found off-trail.

GROUND TRANSPORTATION

European trains are excellent—especially in Austria and Switzerland, where they go directly to or very near most major resorts. Train transfers between arrival city and resort are included in many ski packages. (For skiers flying to Geneva or Zurich, and soon to Lyon, the railway station is right at the airport.) Baggage can be checked through to your final rail destination for a small charge, a considerable convenience when changing trains with tight connections. Other resorts, especially in France and Italy, are more easily reached by motorcoach. Transfers from the airport to the resort, or often to the specific hotel, are included in many packages. Some skiers like the freedom and independence of a rental car, available as an optional add-on in some ski packages.

INSURANCE

Short-term insurance, compensating such unforeseen occurrences as trip cancellation and interruption, lost baggage, medical expenses for unexpected illness or accident, personal liability and life insurance, is now available to travelers. (These programs cover the duration of travel; the accident and life insurance sold at airport booths provides coverage only while in transit.) Some policies include tracking of lost luggage, 24-hour hotlines staffed by English-speaking operators who will help with medical translations, primary collision damage coverage for car rentals, legal assistance, cash transfers and other services.

Policies can be obtained through the travel agent who books or the tour operator who packages your ski trip (look for a section on insurance in the tour folder or an application included in your travel documents), with use of certain credit cards or directly through the insurance carriers.

LIFTS

The daily pattern for skiing the Alps is: take a major transit or feeder lift from the resort each morning, ski the upper mountain all day (usually using a large network of chair- and surface lifts) and ski (or ride) back down only at the end of the day. Summit-to-base skiing is the exception rather than the rule in Europe.

Lifts available on one pass may number in the hundreds and spread over many resorts—and it also sometimes seems as if every lift is a different type. You will ride everything from antique T-bars to ultra-high-tech cable cars and funiculars. Here are the basic types:

Cable car. The most common feeder lift, especially in the German-speaking Alps, consists of two large cabins carried by a heavy cable suspended from a few high pylons. The newest cable cars carry up to 150 people per cabin. Everyone holds skis and poles and rides standing up.

Gondola. Traditionally, skiers ride seated (from two to eight per car) in a string of smaller cabins on a cable suspended from lower pylons. Skis are carried on outside racks. Particularly in France, new hybrid *télécabines* carry 10 to 20 skiers, standing as if in a cable car, but in a gondola-like string of cabins.

Funicular. A rack-and-pinion train, riding on a stable track, with one set of cars climbing as another descends, is both the oldest and the newest lift technology in the Alps. Old funiculars have been ferrying skiers for decades, while the newest—in Saas-Fee and Zermatt—are technological marvels. Their main advantage over other types of feeder lifts is that they are not wind-vulnerable and therefore rarely close due to bad weather conditions.

Chairlifts. The Alps are peppered with a mind-boggling array of chairlifts, ranging from slow-moving relics with single or double chairs (some with riders seated sideways) to the most modern high-speed detachable quads. Normally, even if there is a lift attendant, he will not hold the chair for you—and he won't brush the snow off the seat either.

Surface lifts. While surface lifts are rare in North America (and virtually non-existent in destination resorts), they still provide the bulk of the high-mountain lift capacity in the Alps. In Austria, Germany and Switzerland, T-bars are more common. In France and Italy, platterpulls (what Americans generically call Poma-lifts, regardless of the manufacturer) are more usual. Many are self-service, and most are far faster than old chairlifts.

LIFT LINES

If there is one overpowering unpleasantness to skiing the otherwise civilized Alps, it is lift lines. They can be awesomely long (especially for feeder lifts between 9.30 and 11 a.m.) and they are a case of survival of the fittest and meanest. Europeans, so formal and polite in other circumstances, use elbows, shoulders, poles planted between other people's skis, the centimeter-by-centimeter aggressive shuffle and even the tread-on-the-other-guy's-skis approach to wedge ahead of everybody else in line. Waiting one's turn is unknown. Organized lift mazes are non-existent. Skiers herd at the bottom of a lift and jam their way into a funnel to load. Only when the lift check station (usually a turnstile with a visual check or scanner into which one inserts the lift pass) is passed does the horde sort itself into a semblance of a line—sometimes.

LIFT PASSES

Multi-day lift passes are worn around the neck or in special holders. You may or may not need a picture, so take an extra passport photo if you have one—or come with coins the first day to get one from the photo machine which is found at or near all ticket offices.

OFF-PISTE SKIING

For good, strong skiers, the opportunity to ski what we would call out-of-bounds terrain is a grand reason to go to Europe. Untracked snowfields and powder pockets beckon, and normally, if you can see it, you can ski it. At its tamest, off-*piste* can be a brief foray into the unpacked snow just off a marked, groomed run. At its most challenging and thrilling, it is an excursion into the unmarked outback, away from *pistes*, lifts and crowds. It can even be extreme skiing for ultra-experts—the type normally seen just in ski films. Savvy skiers join a high-level class or hire a private instructor or guide, not only to find the best snow, but for safety and orientation. A good guide will offer an adventure that is akin to heli-skiing without a helicopter. Never go off-*piste* on a glacier except with a guide. Crevasses hidden by new snow are a genuine hazard.

SEASONS

The differences in prices and crowds during holiday, high, regular and low season vary more greatly in the Alps than in North America. Low season is before Christmas and sometimes after Easter. Early December can be iffy in the Alps. In higher resorts where the snow is likely to be better, December can also be bitterly cold. From just before Christmas until early January, sky-high holiday rates prevail, crowds are mammoth and reservations hard to obtain (and impossible to book for a period of less than two weeks). The weeks from early January through early February, and sometimes for a few weeks after Easter, are considered to be regular season. Conditions are likely to be among the season's best (though January can still be cold), prices are reasonable and crowds aren't too bad. Early February through Easter are high season. Somewhere in Europe, there seems always to be a school vacation during this period, which is (next to Christmas) the most popular time for family skiing.

SKI SCHOOLS

Ski school is ritual in the Alps. Classes meet once or twice a day for two hours and often lunch together. They provide an excellent opportunity to meet Europeans. Classes are normally divided by ability and languages and will be both larger and more highly structured than in North America. Even good skiers go into ski school—and, in fact, upper classes are more interesting and fun than regimented lower-level classes.

Each European country has a national ski school, which sets a standard skills progression and certifies instructors. France, Germany and, most recently, Austria also allow private ski schools to teach on their mountains. In France especially, these ski schools specialize in off-*piste* powder instruction, mono-skiing, snowboarding (which Europeans call surf) and other trendy snow sports.

TERRAIN RATING

Green-marked slopes, where they exist, are for real beginners; runs marked blue are for novices, red are for intermediates and black for experts. Dotted lines (which may be yellow or may be coded blue or black to indicate difficulty) designate marked but ungroomed ski routes, which are the safest off-*piste* runs to take without a guide, for they are patroled and commonly skied.

Blue/red/black color codes are found on *piste* maps and also on round signs affixed to poles which mark runs above the tree line. In a white-out, you ski your way from marker to marker, which sometimes will be coded with a *piste* number, sometimes with numerals in series from the highest at the top of the run to 1 at the bottom and sometimes both. More recently, globes in two fluorescent colors have been installed to mark some Alpine *pistes*. You ski on the green side of the globes; the red half denotes the off-*piste* side.

Europeans will refer to "skiing a red (or black) run", rather than an intermediate or expert one.

Avalanche danger is marked by a yellow and black checkered flag and must be taken seriously.

TIPPING

Most service charges are included in the price of your package trip, hotel or dinner. In Austria and Switzerland, additional gratuities are neither anticipated nor expected. The exceptions are 10 per cent of the fare to the taxi driver, the equivalent of a couple of dollars to the porter who carries your bags to the room, the same for the chambermaid and a gratuity to the concierge of a deluxe or first-class hotel for any special services. In France and Italy, it is customary to leave a small supplementary gratuity of no more than 5 per cent to a waiter or waitress.

TOUR OPERATORS

Scores of tour operators offer ski packages to the Alps. Here is a list of selected operators in the United States who have wide-ranging programs:

	Telephone out of-state	in-state	
The Adventurers Company	(713) 946-0946		
Adventures on Skis	(800) 628-9655		
Alphorn Ski Tours	(215) 794-5653		
Alpine Resources Intl.	(800) 543-5895	(508) 664-1456	
Alpine Skiing and Travel	(800) 343-9676	(800) 551-8822	in MA
American Airlines	(800) 433-7300		
American Express	(800) 241-1700	(404) 368-5200	
Austria Ski	(800) 333-5533	(713) 960-0900	
Avanti Tours	(800) 222-0440	(in western U.S.)	
Cavalcade Tours	(800) U-CAN-SKI	(212) 594-1911	in NY
Central Holiday Tours	(800) 526-6045	(800) 742-2836	in NJ
Club Med	(800) CLUB-MED		
DER Tours	(800) 421-4343	(800) 252-0606	in CA
Dial Austria	(800) 221-5980	(212) 661-4660	
Dial Switzerland	(800) 223-5105		
Expeditions, Inc.	(800) 888-9400	(203) 966-2691	
Holidaze (Pan Am)	(800) 626-2827	(800) 662-3055	in NJ
International Ski Espace	(800) 251-7171	(800) 634-8004	in CA
Joli Tours	(800) 333-JOLI	(212) 213-3396	
Jet Vacations (Air France)	(800) JET-0999	(212) 830-4123	
Lathrop Sports Vacations	(800) 222-LATH	(617) 497-7744	
Lufthansa	(800) 645-3880	(516) 794-9800	
Lynx Tours	(800) 422-LXNX	(203) 846-3910	in CT
Powder Ski Adventures	(800) 888-6262	(714) 859-7919	
Ski Jetaway	(800) 554-4756	(800) 932-0753	in GA
Ski Journeys	(800) 547-9557		
Sno Search Ski Tours	(800) 628-8884	(800) 453-2233	in CA
Steve Lohr's Ski Hoidays	(800) 223-1306	(201) 798-3900	
Sullour Tours	(800) 633-3365	(617) 837-1333	
Swisspak (Swissair)	(800) 221-6644	(718) 995-4400	in NY
Target Sports Tours	(800) 225-9116	(617) 332-1300	
The Travel Committee	(800) 638-6188	(301) 363-6663	
Value Holidays	(800) 558-6850	(414) 241-6373	
Wing-Aways	(800) 232-2-SKI	(609) 983-0838	

SOME USEFUL EXPRESSIONS
Equipment

I'd like to rent/buy...	J'aimerais louer/acheter...	Ich würde gerne... mieten/kaufen	Vorrei noleggiare/comprare
ski boots	des chaussures de ski	Skischuhe	degli scarponi da sci
ski poles	des bâtons de ski	Skistöcke	dei bastoncini da sci
skis	des skis	Ski	degli sci
What length poles/skis should I have?	Quelle longueur de bâtons/skis me faut-il?	Wie lang sollten meine Stöcke/Ski sein?	Per me di che lunghezza devono essere i bastoncini/gli sci?
Can you adjust the bindings?	Pouvez-vous régler mes fixations?	Könnten Sie bitte meine Bindungen einstellen?	Può regolare gli attacchi?
Can you wax my skis?	Pouvez-vous farter mes skis?	Könnten Sie bitte meine Ski wachsen?	Può dare la sciolina ai miei sci?
Can you sharpen the edges?	Pouvez-vous aiguiser les carres?	Könnten Sie bitte die Kanten schärfen?	Può affilare le lamine?
I am a ...	Je suis un(e) ...	Ich bin ein ...	Sono un/una ...
a beginner	débutant(e)	Anfänger	principiante
an intermediate skier	skieur (skieuse) de niveau moyen	mittelguter Fahrer sportlicher Fahrer	sciatore medio/sciatrice media
an advanced skier	skieur (skieuse) avancé(e)		buon sciatore/buona sciatrice

I weigh ... kilos.	Je pèse ... kilos.	Ich wiege ... Kilo.	Peso ... chili.
My shoe size is ...	Je chausse du ...	Meine Schuhgrösse ist ...	Il mio numero di scarpe è il ...
These boots are ... too big too small uncomfortable	Ces chaussures sont ... trop grandes trop petites inconfortables	Diese Schuhe sind ... zu gross zu klein unbequem	Questi scarponi sono ... troppo grandi troppo piccoli scomodi
Do you have any rear-entry boots?	Avez-vous des chaussures (de ski) qui s'ouvrent à l'arrière?	Haben Sie Schuhe mit Fersenverschluß?	Hai scarponi con apertura posteriore?

Problems

My skis are too long/too short.	Mes skis sont trop longs/ trop courts.	Meine Ski sind zu lang/ zu kurz.	I miei sci sono troppo lunghi/troppo corti.
My ski/pole has broken.	Mon ski/bâton s'est cassé.	Mein Ski/Stock ist kaputt.	Si è rotto uno sci/un bastoncino.
My bindings are too loose/too tight.	Mes fixations sont trop lâches/trop serrées.	Meine Bindungen sind zu locker/zu fest.	Gli attacchi sono troppo allentati/troppo stretti.
The buckle on my boot is broken.	La boucle de ma chaussure s'est cassée.	Die Schnalle an meinem Schuh ist kaputt.	Si è rotto il gancio del mio scarpone.
My boots hurt me.	Mes chaussures me font mal.	Meine Schuhe tun mir weh.	Gli scarponi mi fanno male ai piedi.

Clothing and accessories

fanny pack (bumbag)	banane	Hüfttasche	Il marsupio
gloves	gants	Handschuhe	i guanti
goggles	lunettes de ski/goggles	Schneebrille	gli occhiali da neve
hat	bonnet	Mütze	la cuffia
headband	bandeau	Stirnband	la fascia per capelli
jacket	veste	Jacke	la giacca
lip salve	stick protecteur (pour les lèvres)	Lippenpomade	la pomata per le labbra
mittens	moufles	Fäustlinge	le manopole
backpack	sac à dos	Rucksack	uno zaino
ski suit	combinaison (de ski)	Skianzug	un completo da sci
ski pants	fuseau(x)	Skihose	i pantaloni da sci
socks	chaussettes	Socken	le calze
sunglasses	lunettes de soleil	Sonnenbrille	gli occhiali da sole
sun cream	crème solaire	Sonnencreme	la crema solare

Lifts and lift passes

I'd like a ... lift pass. day season week	J'aimerais un abonnement ... journalier pour la saison hebdomadaire	Ich hätte gerne eine ... Tageskarte Saisonkarte Wochenkarte	Vorrei ... un abbonamento giornaliero stagionale settimanale
I'd like a book of ... lift coupons. ten/twenty/thirty	J'aimerais un carnet de ... coupons. dix/vingt/trente	Ich hätte gerne eine Punktkarte mit ... Punkten. zehn/zwanzig/ dreissig	Vorrei un blocchetto di ... abbonamenti a punti. dieci/venti/trenta
Do I need a photo?	Est-ce qu'il me faut une photo?	Ist ein Foto nötig?	Occorre una fotografia?

317

cable car	téléphérique	Luftseilbahn	funivia
chairlift	télésiège	Sessellift	seggiovia
surface lift	téléski	Schlepplift	sciovia
gondola	télécabine	Gondel	telecabina
Can I have a piste map, please?	Puis-je avoir un plan des pistes, s'il vous plaît?	Könnte ich bitte einen Plan der Pisten haben?	Potrei avere una carta delle piste?

On the slopes

Where are the beginner slopes?	Où sont les pistes pour débutants?	Wo sind die Anfängerhügel?	Dove sono le piste per principianti?
Which is the easiest way down?	Quelle est la descente la plus facile?	Welche Piste ist am einfachsten?	Qual è la pista più facile?

It's a(n) ... run.
  easy/difficult
  gentle/steep
	C'est une piste ...
	  facile/difficile
	  en pente douce/escarpée
		Es ist eine ... Piste.
		  leichte/schwere
		  flache/steile
			È una pista ...
			  facile/difficile
			  in leggera pendenza/ripida

The piste is closed.	La piste est fermée.	Die Piste ist gesperrt.	La pista è chiusa.
The piste is very icy.	La piste est très gelée.	Die Piste ist sehr vereist.	La pista è molto ghiacciata.

... snow
  powder
  sticky
	neige ...
	  poudreuse
	  lourde
		...Schnee
		  Pulverschnee
		  Pappschnee
			neve ...
			  farinosa
			  appiccicosa

mogul (bump)	bosse	Bodenwelle	la gobba
rock	rocher/caillou	Stein	la roccia
tree	arbre	Baum	l'albero
Watch out!	Attention!	Achtung/Vorsicht!	Attenzione!

Ski school

I'd like some ski lessons.	J'aimerais prendre des leçons de ski.	Ich möchte Skistunden nehmen.	Vorrei prendere lezioni di sci.
Is there an English-speaking instructor?	Y a-t-il un moniteur qui parle anglais?	Gibt es einen englisch-sprachigen Lehrer?	C'è un maestro che parli inglese?
snowplow	chasse-neige	Schneepflug	la spazzaneve
parallel turn	virage parallèle	Parallelschwung	la curva parallela
downhill ski	ski aval	Talski	sci a valle
uphill ski	ski amont	Bergski	sci a monte
herringbone	montée en ciseaux	Grätenschritt	a spina di pesce
side-stepping	montée en escalier	Treppenschritt	il passo a scala
side-slipping	dérapage	seitwärts abrutschen	lo slittamento

Emergencies

I can't move ...	Je ne peux pas bouger ...	Ich kann ... nicht bewegen.	Non posso muovere ...

My ... hurts.
  back
  knee
  neck
  wrist
	... me fait mal.
	  dos
	  genou
	  jambe
	  poignet
		Mein ... tut weh.
		  Rücken
		  Knie
		  Hals
		  Handgelenk
			Mi fa male ...
			  la schiena
			  il ginocchio
			  il collo
			  il polso

I've pulled a muscle.	Je me suis claqué un muscle.	Ich habe eine Muskelzerrung.	Ho uno strappo muscolare.
Please get help.	Allez chercher de l'aide, s'il vous plaît.	Bitte holen Sie Hilfe.	Per favore, cercate aiuto.
Don't move.	Ne bougez pas.	Bewegen Sie sich nicht.	Non muovetevi.
avalanche danger	danger d'avalanche	Lawinengefahr	pericolo di valanghe
rescue service	équipe de secours	Rettungsdienst	il servizio soccorso

INDEX

An asterisk "*" after a page number indicates a map reference. Where there is more than one set of page references, the one in bold type refers to the main entry. For index to Practical Information, see p. 311.

Adelboden 10–11*, **243–245**, 244–245*, 304
Albertville 10–11*, 98, 144, 149
Alpbach 10–11*, **90**
Alpe d'Huez 10–11*, 99, 100, **103–104**, 104–105*, 124
Altenmarkt/Radstadt 10–11*, 15, 19–21, 20–21*
Andermatt 10–11*, 240, 246–247*, **246–248**
Annecy 10–11*, 136
Anzère 10–11*, **304**
Arcs, Les 10–11*, 99, 100, 106–107*, **106–108**, 144, 145
Argentière 10–11*, 99, 115, 114–115*, 116, **158**
Arosa 10–11*, 240, **249–250**, 250–251*, 280
Avoriaz 10–11*, 99, 100, 110–111*, **109–112**, 159, 304
Axamer Lizum 27*, 27, 28, 49
Bad Hofgastein, see Badgastein/Bad Hofgastein
Bad Kleinkirchheim 10–11*, **90**
Badgastein/Bad Hofgastein 10–11*, 15, **22–25**, 24–25*
Bardonecchia 10–11*, 99, 100, 104, 124, 159, **230**
Belle Plagne 98, 144
Berchtesgaden 10–11*, 34, 82, 168, **169–170**, 170–171*
Bormio 10–11*, 188, **195–196**, 196–197*, 310
Cervinia 10–11*, 187, 198–199*, **198–200**, 208, 302
Chambéry 10–11*, 144
Chamonix 10–11*, 98, 99, 114–115*, **114–117**, 135, 136, 159, 208
Champagny 100, 144
Champéry 10–11*, 110–111*, **304**
Château-d'Œx 10–11*, 240, 273*, **304**, 305
Clavière 10–11*, 159, 188, 189, 218, **230**
Clusaz, La 10–11*, **158**
Cortina d'Ampezzo 10–11*, 47, 187, 188, 190–191*, 193, 202–203*, **202–204**
Corvara 189, 190–191*, 221
Courchevel 10–11*, 99, **118–121**, 137, 138–139*, 140, 141, 156
Courmayeur 10–11*, 99, 187, 188, 206–207*, **206–208**
Crans-Montana 10–11*, 240, 252–253*, **252–254**
Croix du Sud 99

Davos 10–11*, 71, 240, 256–257*, **255–258**, 275, 277
Deux Alpes, Les 10–11*, 99, 100, 122–123*, **122–125**, 159
Diablerets, Les 10–11*, 240, **259–261**, 260–261*, 295
Dolomiti Superski Region 188, 216, 222, 231
Ellmau 14, 80*
Engadine Region 287, 288–289*, 290
Engelberg 10–11*, 240, **262–264**, 262–263*
Espace Killy 99, 146–147*, 149
Europa Sport Region 15, 83, 84–85*, 85
Fieberbrunn 10–11*, **90**
Filzmoos 10–11*, 15, **90**
Flachauwinkl 19, 20
Flaine 10–11*, 100, **126–130**, 128–129*
Flims/Laax 10–11*, 240, **265–267**, 266–267*
Fulpmes 26–27*, 48, 50
Galtür 10–11*, 71, **90**
Gargellen 10–11*, 69, 70, 71
Garmisch-Partenkirchen 10–11*, 74, 165, 172–173*, **172–175**
Gaschurn 69, 70, 71
Gastein Superski Region 22, 24–25*
Gets, Les 10–11*, 110–111*, 112, **158**
Grächen **304**
Grand-Bornand, Le 10–11*, **158**
Grand Massif 100, 127
Grande Galaxie Region 99, 100, 124, 159
Graz 67
Grindelwald 10–11*, 240, **268–269**, 270–271*, 282, 298, 299
Gstaad 10–11*, 240, 241, 272–273*, **272–274**, 304, 305
Gstaad Superski Region 260, 272 273*, 274, 304, 305
Haus 15
Hintertux 10–11*, 14, 44
Hochgurgl 51, 52*, 52, 53
Hochsölden 77, 78–79*
Hungerburg 27
Igls, see Innsbruck/Igls
Innsbruck/Igls 10–11*, 14, 26–27*, **26–29**, 34, 36, 46, 50, 54, 59, 71, 72, 74, 82
Ischgl 10–11*, 14, 29, 30–31*, **30–32**
Isola 2000 10–11*, 100, 132–133*, **131–133**
Jenbach 14
Jochberg 36*, 37, 38
Jungfrau Region 269, 270–271*, 282, 298
Kaprun, see Zell am See/Kaprun
Kirchberg 10–11*, 14, **33–34**, 37*, 37
Kitzbühel 10–11*, 13, 14, 29, 33, **35–40**, 36–37*, 47, 80, 90
Kleinarl 19, 20
Klosters 10–11*, 70, 71, 256–257*, **275–277**, 276–277*
Laax, see Flims/Laax
Lake Geneva Region 260, 304, 305
Lech 10–11*, 13, 14, **41–43**, 61, 64, 71, 86, 86–87*, 87, 88, 89

Lenk   10–11*, **304**
Lenzerheide/Valbella   10–11*, 71, 240,
    277, 278–279*, **278–280**
Leysin   10–11*, **305**
Livigno   10–11*, 188, 196, **209–211**,
    210–211*
Madonna di Campiglio   10–11*, 188,
    212–213*, **212–214**
Marilleva   10–11*, **230**
Mayrhofen   10–11*, 14, 44–45*, **44–47**
Megève   10–11*, 99, 134–135*, **134–136**,
    159
Menuires, Les   10–11*, 99, **137–139**,
    138–139*, 156, 157
Méribel   10–11*, 99, 137, 138–139*,
    140–141, 156
Mieders   26–27*, 48, 50
Milky Way   99, 100, 104, 124, 159, 188, 189,
    217, 218, 218–219*, 224, 225, 230, 231
Mont Blanc Region   99, 100, 114–115*, 117,
    134–135*, 135, 159
Montafon, see Schruns/Montafon
Montgenèvre   10–11*, 99, 100, **159**, 189,
    218, 224, 231
Morzine   10–11*, 99, 100, 109, 110–111*,
    112, 158, **159**
Mürren   10–11*, 268, 271*, **281–282**, 298
Mutters   27

Neustift/Stubai Valley   10–11*, 26–27*,
    48–50, 49*

Obergurgl   10–11*, 14, **51–54**, 52–53*, 78,
    79
Oberstdorf   10–11*, 165, 176–177*,
    176–179
Obertauern   10–11*, 15, 20–21*, **55–56**
Ortisei (St. Ulrich)   10–11*, 188, 189,
    190–191*, **215–216**, 220–221*, 222, 231

Piancavallo   **230**
Plagne, La   10–11*, 99, 100, 142–143*,
    142–144, 145
Pontresina   10–11*, 290, **305**
Portes du Soleil, Les   99, 100, 109,
    110–111*, 112, 158, 159, 304

Radstadt, see Altenmarkt/Radstadt
Reit im Winkl   10–11*, 165, 180–181*,
    180–183
Reiteralm   15
Rohrmoos   15
Rosière, La   226, 227
Rougemont   10–11*, 273*, 274, 304, **305**
Saalbach-Hinterglemm   10–11*, 15, **57–59**,
    59*
Saas-Fee   10–11*, 246, **283–284**, 284–285*,
    304
St. Anton/St. Christoph   10–11*, 13, 14, 29,
    42, **60–64**, 62–63*, 71, 86, 89, 91
St. Christoph, see St. Anton/St. Christoph
St. Gallenkirch   69, 70, 71
St-Gervais   **159**
St. Johann im Pongau   10–11*, **90**
St. Johann im Tirol   15, 90
St. Moritz   10–11*, 193, 196, 211, 237, 239,
    240, 241, 277, **286–290**, 288–289*, 305

St. Ulrich, see Ortisei (St. Ulrich)
Samnaun   14, 30, 32
Samoëns   127, 128–129*
Sansicario   10–11*, 159, 188, **217–219**,
    218–219*, 225
Santa Caterina   188, 196, 210
Santa Cristina   10–11*, 189, 190–191*, 215,
    220–221*, 221, 222, **231**
Sauze d'Oulx   10–11*, 188, 189, 217, 218*,
    210, 224, 225, **231**
Schladming   10–11*, 15, 21, **65–67**, 66–67*
Schruns/Montafon   10–11*, 13, **68–71**,
    70–71*
Seefeld   10–11*, 14, 29, 72–73*, **72–74**
Sella Ronda   189, 216, 220–221*, 221, 222,
    231
Selva (Wolkenstein)   10–11*, 188, 189,
    190–191*, 215, 216, 220–221*, **220–222**,
    231
Serre Chevalier   10–11*, 100, 104, 124, **159**
Sestrière   10–11*, 159, 188, 189, 217, 218,
    218–219*, **224–225**, 231
Ski Ohne Grenzen   170
Ski-Grossraum Wilder Kaiser–
    Brixental   14, 80, 80–81*
Sölden   10–11*, 14, 51, **76–79**, 78–79*
Söll   10–11*, 80–81*, **80–82**
Stubai Valley, see Neustift/Stubai Valley
Stuben   10–11*, 14, 42, 61, 64, 86, 86–87*,
    91

Telfes   48, 50
Three Valleys   90, 100, 118, 137, 138–139*,
    140, 156
Thuile, La   10–11*, 145, 188, 208, **226–227**,
    228–229*
Tignes   10–11*, 99, 100, **145–148**, 146–147*
Top-Tauern-Skischeck   15, 19, 20–21*, 67
Tschagguns   69, 70, 70–71*, 71
Tulfes   27

Val d'Isère   10–11*, 99, 100, 145, 146–147*,
    150–151*, **149–152**
Val di Fassa   **231**
Val Thorens   10–11*, 99, 137, 138–139*,
    140, **156–157**
Valbella, see Lenzerheide/Valbella
Valmorel   10–11*, 97, 100, **153–154**,
    154–155*
Verbier   10–11*, 238, 240, 241, 292–293*,
    291–294
Villars   10–11*, 240, **295–297**, 296–297*
Wengen   10–11*, 35, 238, 268, 269,
    270–271*, 282, **298–299**
Westendorf   14
Wolkenstein, see Selva (Wolkenstein)

Zauchensee   15, 19, 20, 21*
Zell am See/Kaprun   10–11*, 15, 57, 59,
    83–85, 84–85*
Zell am Ziller   10–11*, 14, 44
Zermatt   10–11*, 198, 199, 200, 238, 240,
    241, 246, 283, 290, 300–301*, **300–303**,
    304
Zürs   10–11*, 13, 14, 41, 42, 61, 63, 64,
    86–87*, **86–89**